WRITINGS ON CIVIL DISOBEDIENCE
AND NONVIOLENCE

LEO TOLSTOY

WRITINGS ON CIVIL DISOBEDIENCE AND NONVIOLENCE

new society publishers

Philadelphia, PA   Santa Cruz, CA

Translation by Aylmer Maude, except "The Inevitable Revolution" translated and copyright 1975 by Ronald Sampson.

New Society Publishers gratefully acknowledges the library of the Philadelphia Yearly Meeting and Swarthmore College Peace Collection for their assistance in this project.

Inquiries regarding requests to republish all or part of *Writings on Civil Disobedience and Nonviolence* should be addressed to:
New Society Publishers
4527 Springfield Avenue
Philadelphia, PA 19143

ISBN:
Hardcover 0-86571-109-7
Paperback 0-86571-110-0

Cover design by Brian Prendergast.

To order directly from the publisher, add $1.50 to the price for the first copy, 50¢ each additional. Send check or money order to:
New Society Publishers
P.O. Box 582
Santa Cruz, CA 95061-0582

New Society Publishers is a project of the New Society Educational Foundation, a nonprofit, tax-exempt, public foundation. Opinions expressed in this book do not necessarily represent positions of the New Society Educational Foundation.

PUBLISHER'S NOTE

 once took what many would call a very fine, modern European history course. We used an excellent text and supplemented it with a wide range of readings, including commentary by participants in the events we studied. Our subject was, of course, the glorious saga of the rise of the nation-state and the changing role of the institutional Christian church. Looking back, it is entirely predictable and somewhat sad that, while we all knew about Tolstoy the novelist, we never read his critiques of the nation-state or institutional church.

It is predictable because Tolstoy's witness mars the glorious saga. Tolstoy consistently exposes and ridicules the ploys and propaganda, including the invocation of divine authority, used to justify the nation-state. He painstakingly describes the actual structure of the nation-state and its supporting institution, the church. And he returns again and again to the lives of the common citizens, the ones who are flattered and cajoled and driven to become soldiers—to fight their "foreign" neighbor five miles away or to suppress their colleague back home.

It is sad because reading about what seems like the distant past can sometimes help us to see the present—and our present work—that much better. Tolstoy's commentary is relevant today, and his insistence on action, even more pressing. While the historical details are very different, we are still being flattered and cajoled and driven to fight ever-changing "enemies" abroad and at home—all for our "way of life" and the continuing power of officers, priests, bureaucrats, and businessmen. And whatever other strategies we may embrace, one of the most effective and empowering things we can do—at any time—is to refuse to play at least some part of our role in the farce.

We here at New Society Publishers are proud to publish this collection of Tolstoy's *Writings on Civil Disobedience and Nonviolence*. It is a piece of our history; it is an inspiration to act. Imagine if this book were part of our official education.

T.L. Hill
for New Society Publishers

CONTENTS

FOREWORD

HO will ever be able to count the thousands, the hundreds of thousands who have been influenced by Count Leo Tolstoy's courageous stand for Christianity's clear, simple truth: "Love your enemies, love one another as brothers and sisters, stop slaughtering them, do not return evil with evil but return evil with good." Yes, this is the simple, clear truth taught by Jesus Christ, who died forgiving those who were crucifying Him. Yet how few are those who, like Tolstoy, stand tall, teaching and living His way to peace.

Tolstoy's writings were a great influence in my own life and in my conversion to peacemaking. His book *The Kingdom of God Is Within You* came almost like a shock, a welcome shock, at a time when I was beginning to see the absurdity of war and violence. I do not know how long it took Tolstoy to form his conscience on this issue, but I do know he too was in the military and that he saw the contrast between battle casualties and victory balls. I know he freed his own slaves before their general emancipation in Russia. But how long it took for him to reach his totally pacifist position I do not know. Was it a sudden illumination or did it take years of struggle?

For me it took many years to accept something so simple and clear as Christ's message for peace—nonviolent love, to love one another as He loved us. I too was in the military, as a chaplain in World War II. Like Tolstoy, perhaps, I believed sincerely that this was what God wanted, that this was His way of obtaining peace through killing and slaughter. On the island of Tinian in the western Pacific, I watched flights of hundreds of B-29s carrying their frightful cargoes of napalm bombs to burn out whole cities like Tokyo. I talked to crew members who described the horrors of the firestorms caused by the bombs, who described the tens of thousands of people burned to death in the deadly fire circles that had been carefully plotted out ahead of time. As a priest, I should have known that even under the just-war theory this was unlawful and sinful. It is murder to kill and torture innocent noncombatants, women, children, the elderly, in their straw houses. But the hypnotic grip of agelong propaganda on the legality of war kept me still sincerely convinced that, although war was hell, it was still necessary to gain peace. On August 6, 1945, I watched as the *Enola Gay* took off on its mission to Hiroshima. Oh, sure, we didn't know that it carried an atomic bomb. We were told that it was a much more powerful bomb, much stronger than any that had ever been dropped before. We called it the "gimmick" bomb. But then after 8:16 A.M. the word came back of the unbelievable devastation and slaughter that this one bomb had caused. But I guess we even rejoiced that now only one bomb could do what it had once taken hundreds of planes to do. Three days later came Nagasaki, which in a way should have jarred my conscience. This was a Catholic city, where Francis Xavier first taught the faith four hundred years before, where the faith grew and prospered, and where many martyrs died under persecution for almost two hundred years. I also knew that after the persecutions the missionaries came back, even finding some of the old Catholics who had kept the faith.

Then again the faith grew in numbers. What an irony that it was a Catholic pilot who flew the *Boks Car* on this mission, killing forty or fifty thousand instantly and leaving thousands horribly burned and irradiated. However, I was still in the military mindset, still convinced it was necessary. On August 15, I remember celebrating a Holy Day and Victory Mass at the 509th chapel. We were happy the war was over, sad that the price was so high, nearly two hundred thousand dead, thousands mutilated. Actually, however, it was not until I visited both cities three months later during the occupation that my conscience began to twitch. Walking through the devastation of both Hiroshima and Nagasaki, I saw the horrible suffering caused by those two bombs—little children with agonizing skin burns all over their bodies, lying quietly on their pallets. Yes, these were innocent; what could justify this crime, this torture of three- and four-year-old kids? Yes, that was a beginning, a pain in my gut that wouldn't go away. But coming back home, the pictures faded. Yes, it was hell—but, but, but, always those "buts." Something just wasn't right in the whole picture.

Tolstoy tells us in his writings that the government has a hypnotic influence on people, convincing them that war and killing is justified. He also includes schools, teachers, journalists, writers of patriotic songs, the clergy, all cooperating in a myth; making the slaughter of war something not only acceptable but glorious, glamorous. I call it brainwashing. We are fed from childhood, from our parents, our schools, our churches, that war and killing are acceptable and even glorious. We become brainwashed into thinking this is true, that it is in accordance with Christ's teaching, terrible but somehow necessary to maintain peace or obtain justice, despite what is written in the Sermon on the Mount and the example of Jesus.

Tolstoy recognizes that we are deceived by our government into this mode of thinking. "The fact is that they are deceitful with no wish to deceive but because they cannot be otherwise. They deceive with no consciousness of their deceit and usually with the naive assurance that they are doing something excellent and elevated, a view in which they are persistently encouraged by the sympathy and approval of all who surround them." He goes on:

> In the same way emperors, kings and their ministers, diplomatists and functionaries dressed up in uniforms with all sorts of ribbons and crosses, writing and docketing with great care upon the best paper, their hazy, involved, altogether needless communications, advices, projects, are quite assured that, without their activities the entire existence of nations would halt or become deranged. In the same manner military men, got up in ridiculous costumes, arguing seriously with what rifle or cannon men can be most expeditiously destroyed, are quite certain that their field days and reviews are most important and essential to the people. So likewise the priests, journalists, writers of patriotic songs and class books who preach patriotism and receive liberal remuneration are equally satisfied. Moreover, being all linked together they approve and justify one another's acts, kings, soldiers, functionaries, clergymen and teachers.

This is the sad fact—that we are deceived into thinking that war is good and necessary. But those deceiving us are very sincere and convinced themselves from their leaders on down. As I say, it is brainwashing that has come down through the centuries. It is not easy to break through it. It took me twenty-five years.

This is why we can learn from all of Tolstoy's writings. He knows the power, the hypnotic force of public opinion. We must learn to not only love our enemies but to be very understanding and repectful of those whose convictions differ from our own. This is the Christian way. As St. Francis said, "Grant that I may not so much seek to be understood as to understand."

We can learn from Tolstoy's courage in openly and clearly expounding the nonviolent way to peace in hostile circumstances. He was persecuted by both government and church for his radical views. He openly taught that God must be obeyed before men. Civil disobedience was one of his oft-repeated themes, especially when it came to military service. He states clearly that military service is participating and cooperating in murder or preparation for murder. One must be willing to suffer any pain, even death, rather than cooperate in this evil. This is a hard thing to grasp even today, although it should be clear that in whatever branch of the military a person may serve, he or she is cooperating, helping in some way to make possible the firing of thousands of nuclear warheads that would murder millions, perhaps billions, of people and could destroy our world. So civil disobedience in the military, certainly after Vietnam and now seeing the capabilities of nuclear and biochemical weapons, must be a definite, clear option. Henry David Thoreau, whom Tolstoy quotes, tells us that it is surprising that it happens so rarely.

Another great teaching that Tolstoy stresses is of course nonviolence. The peacemaker, pacifist, must not be passive, which many people confuse with pacifism. He or she must struggle, fight against evil wherever it is found, but the struggle must be with the weapon Jesus gave us— nonviolent, loving resistance, even unto death. Gandhi was a devoted student of Tolstoy and quotes him in his writings.

I hope this edition of Tolstoy's writings on civil disobedience and nonviolence will help many people to form their consciences on how we must sometimes disobey legal authority so that we may obey our God. For the Christian this is especially crucial, as Tolstoy himself said: "A Christian nation which engages in war ought, in order to be logical, not only take down the cross from its church steeples, turn the churches to some other use, give the clergy other duties, having first prohibited the preaching of the Gospel, but also ought to abandon all the requirements of morality which flow from Christian law." And again, "Until Christianity is abolished it is only possible to attract mankind toward war by cunning and fraud, as now practised. We who see this fraud and cunning cannot give way to it."

Father George B. Zabelka

INTRODUCTION

I

We must take the Sermon on the Mount to be
as much a law as the theorem of Pythagoras.[1]

EO Tolstoy's formula for the abolition of war
is simple. Wars will cease when people
individually and collectively refuse to fight
or to remain in complicity with the
institutions which make war possible.

The formula may not be very complex,
but it is by no means easy to follow. Tolstoy's formula should
be a thorn in the side, not so much of those who believe in
war and in the social, political, and economic institutions
upon which it is based, but of those who claim they are
engaged in a genuine search for peace, of those who believe
they are involved in the reform of government, and
especially of activists and peacemakers who profess belief in
Christianity. Stripped of its references to nineteenth century
persons, events, and concerns, Tolstoy's message is
surprisingly contemporary, even more salient today than
when it was first preached.

According to Tolstoy, war is not, as the nineteenth-century
military strategist Clausewitz argued, the health of the State,
but rather the only way the State can justify its continued

existence. He calls patriotism "the cruel tradition of an outlived period, which exists not merely by its inertia, but because the governments and ruling classes, aware that not their power only, but their very existence, depends upon it, persistently excite and maintain it among the people, both by cunning and violence" (p. 100).* He argues that the governments of nation-states cannot leave each other in peace, because "the chief, if not the sole, justification of governments is the pacification of nations, and the settlement of their hostile relationships. Hence governments evoke hostile relationships in order to exhibit their powers of pacification" (p. 101). While this analysis of the nation-state may seem radical today, it certainly was even more so in the context of a time when war and the institution of war were often extolled as moral forces through which men could exhibit the noble virtues of courage and fortitude.

This moral critique, however, is accompanied by a historical one. Tolstoy notes the importance of people's attachments to the land they work to gain their sustenance and to the customs, language, traditions, and ways of life that flow from their agrarian existence. He accepts as conceivable that in some former time patriotism in the form of "the desire of protection from barbarian assault" (p. 98) might have been a natural feeling. But Tolstoy notes that while it may prey upon these memories of an earlier time, modern patriotism can have virtually no significance in an age when "very often people of one country are nearer and more needful to their neighbors than are those latter to one another, as in the case of laborers in the service of foreign employers of labor, of commercial houses, scientists, and the followers of art"

* All citations in parenthesis refer to this edition
   of Tolstoy's work.

(p. 99). The conditions of modern life are such that "patriotism today is like a scaffolding which was needful once to raise the walls of the building but which, though it presents the only obstacle to the house being inhabited, is nonetheless retained, because its existence is of profit to certain persons" (p. 100). The modern nation-state, which our leaders would have us forget is as an institution barely two centuries old, is at best an anachronism. According to Tolstoy, modern patriotism arises precisely at such a time as it becomes necessary to enforce in the population a delusion, namely, that adherence to the abstract concept of the State, and allegiance to a particular state and to the persons embodying the concept, is a suitable and necessary replacement for the older traditions of allegiance to the land, customs, and traditions—in short, for the social and moral character of the community. But at the same time, the nation-state, the "scaffolding erected" to protect "us" from "them," is the very force that prevents us from living in "houses," the communities we long to protect. In this context, Tolstoy's seemingly reactionary critique becomes distinctly contemporary.

As is the case today, the liberals and progressives of Tolstoy's time attempted to argue that "peace is patriotic," that by finding ways to positively identify with the nation-state, peace-loving people could reclaim their national identity for peaceful purposes. Tolstoy identifies this as nothing but an illusion. "Patriotism in its simplest, clearest and most indubitable signification is nothing else but a means of obtaining for the rulers their ambitions and covetous desires, and for the ruled the abdication of human dignity, reason, and conscience, and a slavish enthralment to those in power. And as such it is recommended wherever it is preached. Patriotism is slavery" (p. 103).

"Yes," they [referring to the liberal and/or peace-loving apologists for the state] will say "wrong patriotism is an evil; but there is another kind, the kind we hold." But just what this good patriotism is, no one explains. If good patriotism consists in inaggressiveness, as many say, still all patriotism, even if not aggressive, is necessarily retentive; that is, people wish to keep what they have previously conquered. The nation does not exist which was founded without conquest; and conquest can only be retained by the means which achieved it—namely, violence, murder. But if patriotism is not even retentive, it is then the restoring patriotism of conquered and oppressed nations.... And this patriotism is about the very worst; for it is the most embittered and most provocative of violence. (p. 141)

But if patriotism is a historically based delusion inextricably bound up with the logic of maintaining the power of the nation-state, surely, one might argue, the "pacification of nations" is a sufficient justification for government. Some of Tolstoy's best descriptive prose in this volume is devoted to describing the 1894 Franco-Russian festivities—complete with descriptions of parades, gun-salutes, religious services, and the menus of the dinners—commemorating "friendship" between the two nations. "The speeches made were also published," notes Tolstoy, "but the menus were more varied than the speeches. The latter, without exception, always consisted of the same words in different combinations. The meaning of these words was always the same—We love each other tenderly, and are enraptured to be so tenderly in love. Our aim is not war, not a *revanche*, not the recovery of the lost provinces, our aim is only *peace*, the furtherance of *peace*, the security of *peace*, the tranquility and *peace* of Europe" (pp. 57–58).

Tolstoy goes so far as to describe these "outbreaks of peace" as a "well-defined psychopathic epidemic," based as they are not on any new condition of peace existing among people, but rather representing "the cry of a sick population for deliverance from inebriety and from pernicious social conditions" (p. 65). He further emphasizes that those who succumb "to this psychopathic epidemic are the masters of the most terrible weapons of slaughter and destruction" (p. 67).

Tolstoy is not surprised that "parties of war" and "parties of peace" forever vie for control of the state. The parties of peace may seem to have better intentions from time to time and may fashion themselves as more "liberal" and "progressive," but in Tolstoy's view they are part of a single political apparatus necessary to maintain both the institution of the State and State-initiated and organized violence.

Tolstoy does not oppose knowledge of and efforts to increase contact and friendship between peoples. But he insists that these efforts are neither panaceas nor even useful starting places for the prevention of war. Neighbors have fought against neighbors for centuries. Close and even intimate knowledge of "the enemy" in, to use Tolstoy's examples, the provinces on the Franco-German border has been no bar or hindrance to neighbors slaughtering each other for generations.

Tolstoy reserves his greatest scorn for those who believe that the problems of war can be dealt with effectively through international tribunals, arbitration, world government, and other institutional mechanisms. According to Tolstoy, those who preach peace through arbitration, world government, and the like point to reasonable people who settle their differences through argument, persuasion, and the intervention of disinterested third parties. There is no doubt that nations should act that way, and occasionally do. "But this argument applies only so far as it has reference to the people, and only to people who are not under the control of a government. But the people that subordinate themselves to a government cannot be reasonable, because the subordination is in itself a sign of want of reason" (pp. 103–104). "How can we speak of the reasonableness of men who promise in advance to accomplish everything, including murder, that the government may command?" Tolstoy inquires (pp. 103–104). "Men who can accept such obligations, and resignedly subordinate themselves to anything that may be prescribed by persons unknown to them...cannot be considered reasonable." Those who come into possession of the violent instruments of State power can "still less be considered reasonable, and cannot but misuse it, and become dazed by such insane and dreadful power" (p. 104).

Tolstoy's reasoning can be applied to those who analyze the dynamics of arms races and "peace" negotiations today as if the actors were individual "reasonable men," or through "game theory" developed on that premise. Arguments can and are advanced that "deterrence," "peace through strength," "unilateral governmental peace initiatives," or the establishment of "mutual trust relationships" are likely to prevent war, given our knowledge or opinions about individual human psychology. Again, here rather than being a reactionary thinker, Tolstoy is a profoundly modern one, maintaining that the contemporary nation-state, by the very fact of its existence, takes on a logic and rationality all its own that cannot be understood effectively by appeal to our commonsensical and somewhat primitive understanding of individual psychology. The wholly internal dynamics of the nation-state, according to Tolstoy, require that it maintain and occasionally escalate hostilities to justify its existence.

But Tolstoy was a writer and propagandist, not an expert in mass or cult psychology. As such, his censure of peace-seeking colleagues is trenchant:

> If a man is given to drink, and I tell him that he himself can leave off drinking and that he must do so, there is a hope that he will listen to me; but if I tell him that his drunkenness is a complicated and difficult problem which we learned men are trying to solve at our meetings, then in all probability he will, while awaiting the solution of this problem, continue to drink.
>
> Thus also with these false and refined external, scientific means of abolishing war, such as international tribunals, arbitration, and similar absurdities with which we occupy ourselves, while all the time carefully omitting to mention the most simple, essential, self-evident method of causing war to cease—a method plain for all to see....
>
> In order that people who do not want war should not fight, it is not necessary to have either international law, arbitration, international tribunals, or solutions of problems; but it is merely necessary that those who are subjected to the deceit should away and free themselves from the spell or enchantment under which they find themselves. The way to do away with war is for those who do not want war, who regard participation in it as a sin, to refrain from fighting. (pp. 128–129)

II

As a moralist, Tolstoy can seem overbearing, which is unfortunate, as it has for many obscured the existence, no less the validity, of his specifically historical critique of the modern nation-state. As a political thinker, Tolstoy is often viewed as sentimental, basing his faith in "individual"

solutions rather than social or political ones. But Tolstoy
provides a method for testing his hypothesis concerning the
abolition of war. Tolstoy argues that the reactions of
governments themselves reveal which strategies are most
threatening to the war system:

> Liberals entangled in their much talking, socialists, and other
> so-called advanced people may think that their speeches in
> Parliament and at meetings, their unions, strikes, and
> pamphlets are of great importance; while the refusals of
> military service by private individuals are unimportant
> occurrences not worthy of attention. The governments,
> however, know very well what is important to them and what
> is not. And the governments readily allow all sorts of liberal
> and radical speeches in Reichstags, as well as workmen's
> associations and socialist demonstrations, and they even
> pretend themselves to sympathize with those things,
> knowing that they are of great use to them in diverting
> people's attention from the great and only means of
> emancipation. But governments never openly tolerate
> refusals of military service, or refusals of war taxes, which
> are the same thing, because they know that such refusals
> expose the fraud of governments and strike at the root of their
> power. (p. 154)

Tolstoy's understanding of the power of individual
noncooperation places him as a successor to the early
American theorists of nonviolence Henry David Thoreau
and Adin Ballou. Tolstoy's chief theoretical advance upon
Thoreau's thinking lies in his acute understanding both that
the power of the nation-state is maintained not only by force,
but by public opinion, and that governments recognize that
this is so. Once they have recognized this, Tolstoy concludes
that in an age of expanding mass communication and contact
among peoples, governments *must* increasingly attempt to

intrude into if not monopolize all spheres of public life. Although not usually recognized as such, Tolstoy is thus one of the first critical theorists of totalitarianism. Tolstoy's thought helped form the basis of Mohandas Gandhi's philosophy of action, which harnessed individual non-cooperation on a mass scale to seize control of public opinion and so effect change in social and political institutions.

The arguments against what has been called Tolstoyan anarchism, the idea that individuals should abandon their allegiance to the nation-state and follow the dictates of their conscience, are obvious enough, and, on the surface at least, reasonable. It is certain that the conscience of different individuals might dictate different courses of action. Conflicts would then seem to be inevitable. Those with superior force might well attempt to use it for their own gain. If unchecked, disorder and chaos would increase. In the worst scenario, mob rule would become law.

From our vantage point late in the twentieth century, however, it is difficult to maintain that the devolution of society into a world without nation-states would have had worse consequences than what has actually occurred. As Tolstoy notes, before the end of the last century, it would have been unthinkable that military forces should be trained to kill innocent civilians. Since the Italian war in Ethiopia in the 1930s, and especially since World War II, military forces are prepared to do little else. The nation-states of the twentieth century, or rather, as Tolstoy would have it, the organization of violence and mass murder made possible solely through the perpetuation of the nation-state and the starvation and enslavement of entire populations resulting from the activities of the machinery of the nation-state, make the worst excesses imaginable under mob rule seem tame by comparison. Even in democracies such as the United

States, the average person involuntarily labors as much as ten years out of his or her working life to maintain the military machinery of the state. Some ten percent of the land mass of the United States has been expropriated for military purposes. And while some democracy still exists within the borders of the United States, through foreign intervention and the arms trade the United States and other nations support a worldwide network of unrelieved thuggery and brutality. The Tolstoyan critique is that in the contemporary world one has less to fear from any external nation-state enemy, real or imagined, than one does from the practices and excesses of the nation-state government under which one lives. And chief among these dangers is not physical harm—as great a threat as that might be from time to time— but individual moral culpability and complicity in political murder.

For Tolstoy, even if it could be demonstrated that the nation-state were a substantive good and could only be maintained through military readiness, a willingness to participate in state-organized murder would still be entirely unacceptable. In his "Notes for Officers," Tolstoy compares this possibility to one where establishments of the most useful kind—hospitals, schools, homes—depend for their support on profits from houses of prostitution. In such a situation, no consideration of the good produced by those philanthropic institutions should be weighed by the woman who wishes to free herself from an oppressive trade (p. 36).

Nor, according to Tolstoy, can considerations of this kind be left up to the nation-state in order that it might reform itself. Tolstoy compares this idea to attempting to free people from the miseries of gambling. "Instead of pointing out to them the temptations to which they are subjected, the fact that they are sure to lose, and the immorality of gambling, which is based on the expectation of other people's misfortunes—[we] assemble with grave faces at meetings and discuss how to arrange that the keepers of gambling-houses should of their own accord shut up their establishments; we should write books about it, and we put questions to ourselves as to whether history, law, and progress require the existence of gambling-houses, and as to what are the economical, intellectual, moral, and other consequences of roulette" (p. 128).

Implicit in Tolstoy's commitment to convincing individuals to find it in their consciences to resist the nation-state's dictates to kill is the faith that once the commands of such conscience are obeyed, individuals can and will be able to organize themselves to build a higher moral order. For this faith, Tolstoy points to the examples of the early Christians, Mennonites, Quakers, Molokans, and Dukhobors—all small sects to be sure—which, despite extreme pressures from the state, were able to build small versions of a "cooperative commonwealth" or "beloved community." Tolstoy accepts as an article of faith that this change could and would be accomplished, if only because it is in keeping with his understanding of humankind's true character:

> No feats of heroism are needed to achieve the greatest and most important changes in the existence of humanity;...and to accomplish this change no exertions of the mind are needed, nor the refutation of anything in existence, nor the invention of any extraordinary novelty....
> If only the hearts of individuals would not be troubled by the seductions with which they are hourly seduced, nor afraid of those imaginary terrors by which they are intimidated; if people only knew wherein their chiefest, all-conquering power consists—a peace which men have always desired,

not the peace attainable by diplomatic negotiations, imperial
or kingly progresses, dinners, speeches, fortresses, cannon,
dynamite, and melinite, by the exhaustion of people under
taxes, and the abduction from labor of the flower of the
population, but peace attainable by a voluntary profession of
the truth by every man, would long ago have been
established in our midst. (pp. 115, 123)

While Tolstoy insists the path to peace is simple, he is
neither sanguine about the ease of following it nor surprised
by the way other advocates of peace evade recognizing its
validity. The complicated choices faced by individuals and
the conflicting rationales by which human beings obscure
the choices and realities of their lives lie at the heart of the
characters of Tolstoy's fiction and serve as the foundation of
Tolstoyan tragedy, as seen in "The Death of Ivan Illich,"
"Master and Man," "The Kreutzer Sonata," and
Resurrection. Tolstoy understands only too well that both
cooperation and noncooperation, remaining in complicity or
resisting with all of one's being the demands of the state,
always involve a choice. This is true even when one of the
choices is likely to lead to hardship, suffering, or even death.
But for those who cooperate with the oppression of others
to admit to themselves that they have chosen to do so would
damage their self-respect and self-esteem.

In his fiction, especially in the late novel *Resurrection*,
Tolstoy embodies in virtually every character the rationales
individuals use to reassure themselves even as they
participate in a culture of violence. In the essays presented
here, the characters are stripped away, leaving a compelling,
even harrowing vision of self-deception:

One man does not assert the truth which he knows because
he feels himself bound to the people with whom he is
engaged; another, because the truth might deprive him of

the profitable position by which he maintains his family; a third because he desires to attain reputation and authority, and then use them in the service of humanity; a fourth, because he does not wish to destroy old sacred traditions; a fifth, because he has no desire to offend people; a sixth because the expression of truth would arouse persecution, and disturb the excellent social activity to which he has devoted himself.

One serves as emperor, king, minister, government functionary, or soldier, and assures himself and others that the deviation from truth indispensable to his condition is redeemed by the good he does. Another, who fulfills the duties of a spiritual pastor, does not in the depths of his soul believe all he teaches, but permits the deviation from truth in view of the good he does. A third instructs men by means of literature, and notwithstanding the silence he must observe with regard to the whole truth, in order not to stir up the government and society against himself, has no doubt as to the good he does. A fourth struggles resolutely with the existing order as revolutionist or anarchist, and is quite assured that the aims he pursues are so beneficial that the neglect of the truth, or even of the falsehood, by silence, indispensable to the success of his activity, does not destroy the utility of his work. (pp. 119–120)

Tolstoy urges that only by stripping away the veneer of self-rationalization will individuals be able to grasp the truth which is at the center of their existence.

III

I had intended to go to God, and I found my way into a stinking bog, which evokes in me only those feelings of which I am most afraid: disgust, malice, and indignation.[2]

Tolstoy's faith is often called "Christian anarchism," and it is no doubt true that his teachings about war and peace are intimately joined to his beliefs in Christ's teachings, specifically Jesus' injunctions of kindness, meekness, forgiveness of injuries, and love of one's enemies. Tolstoy believes that these teachings are universally applicable expressions of God's will and that as they receive greater circulation among the general populace better prepared to receive their message, universal peace will come to reign.

But those who would lay claim to Tolstoy as part of the Christian religious tradition in any larger sense, even as a harbinger of such contemporary movements as the Catholic Worker, are mistaken. Tolstoy rejects as intellectually and morally perverted virtually every Christian doctrine he was exposed to through the Orthodox tradition and the dominant Christian beliefs with which he came into contact. He calls the doctrine of the Trinity, the immaculate conception and the virginity of Mary, the existence of saints and the stories of miracles and relics, original sin and the fall of Adam and the redemption of humankind through the coming of the Son of God "nothing but a gross hash of Jewish superstitions and priestly frauds" (p. 166). In hundreds of pages of religious writings, Tolstoy is totally silent concerning the question of Christ's divinity. He traces the deviation of Christianity's teachings from those of Jesus to the Apostles, and specifically to the Apostle Paul's lust for power. He dismisses Christian sacraments as "savage customs." And he charges, "Of all the godless ideas and words there is none more godless than that of a Church. There is no idea which has produced more evil, none more inimical to Christ's teaching, than the idea of a Church" (p. 272).

Tolstoy views institutionalized Christianity as the single most important ideological pillar behind state-sanctioned violence. He argues that people who are trained from childhood to believe the "stupid and senseless" nonsense (p.

163) of Christianity are prepared to accept the ideological frauds perpetrated by the nation-state, frauds which, more likely than not, are supported by appeal to the Gospel's purported teachings. "So that the fraud played off on soldiers, when it is instilled into them that they may without sin kill people at the wish of those in command, is not an isolated fraud, but is bound up with a whole system of fraud, without which this one fraud would not deceive them" (p. 164).

Though he was a distant admirer of pacifist sects inspired by the life and teachings of Jesus, such as the Quakers, it would be a mistake to view Tolstoy as some kind of Christian reformer. Only the complete and utter destruction of institutionalized Christianity in all its manifestations would, according to Tolstoy, open the way for a full appreciation and acceptance of Jesus' universal teachings.

IV

Those familiar with the life of Tolstoy would be quick to note the difficulties Tolstoy the man had in adhering to his own teachings. The contradictions between Tolstoy the writer—the heir of fame, fortune, and the adulation of the rich and the intelligentsia—and Tolstoy the prophet—pursuing the virtues of poverty, anonymity, and identification with the poor—were contradictions he was never able to resolve. Tolstoy painfully and personally understood the shackles of history, of class, of culture in which we are all born and bred. But Tolstoy also looked upon history as at best containing only relative truths, at worst representing "a temple of false science," "a heap of myths and useless, trivial details, sprinkled with dates and names."[3] It is only in attempting to escape from the grasps of church and state; from identification with the concerns of the great and powerful; from middle-class focus on narrow creature comforts; and from complicity in acts and systems of violence, oppression, and human degradation that the individual can come to develop a moral syntax and to wrestle with the immortal truths at the center of his or her own being.

In the final analysis, the heart of Tolstoy's challenge is to have us all strive to strip away pretensions: the liberal pretension that the public good can be built on the foundations of a murderous nation-state; the Christian pretension of the exclusivity of belief and revelation and of the embodiment of that belief in mystifying language and in corrupt and corrupting institutions; the peace advocate's pretentious search for an end to war through the creation of still more social and political institutions rather than through simply advocating the refusal to fight. But Tolstoy's doctrine is not essentially negative or renunciatory. From his childhood, Tolstoy marvelled at the profound mystery which lay at the periphery of human interaction, and it is here that we find the core of his abundant faith. Reflecting back on his boyhood, Tolstoy wrote, "I used to believe that there was a green stick on which words were carved that would destroy all the evil in the hearts of men and bring them everything good, and I still believe today that there is such a truth, it will be revealed to men, and will fulfill its promise."[4] It is this truth that Tolstoy would have us continue to pursue.

   David H. Albert

1. Tolstoy; in Martin Green, *Tolstoy and Gandhi: Men of Peace* (New York, 1983), p.87.
2. Green, p. 194.
3. In Henri Troyat, *Tolstoy* (New York, 1980), p. 52.
4. Troyat, p. 16.

THE BEGINNING OF THE END

URING last year, in Holland, a young man named Van der Veer was called on to enter the National Guard. To the summons of the commander, Van der Veer answered in the following letter:—

"Thou Shalt do no Murder."

To M. Herman Sneiders, *Commandant of the National Guard of the Midelburg district.*

Dear Sir—Last week I received a document ordering me to appear at the municipal office, to be, according to law, enlisted in the National Guards. As you probably noticed, I did not appear, and this letter is to inform you, plainly and without equivocation, that I do not intend to appear before the commission. I know well that I am taking a heavy responsibility, that you have the right to punish me, and that you will not fail to use this right. But that does not frighten me. The reasons which lead me to this passive resistance seem to me strong enough to outweigh the responsibility I take.

I, who, if you please, am not a Christian, understand better than most Christians the commandment which is put at the head of this letter, the commandment which is rooted in human nature, in the mind of man. When but a boy, I allowed myself to be taught the trade of soldier, the art of killing; but now I renounce it. I would not kill at the command of others, and thus have murder on my conscience without any personal cause or reason whatever.

Can you mention anything more degrading to a human being than carrying out such murder, such massacre? I am unable to kill, even to see an animal killed; therefore I became a vegetarian. And now I am to be ordered to shoot men who have done me no harm; for I take it that it is not to shoot at leaves and branches of trees that soldiers are taught to use guns.

But you will reply, perhaps, that the National Guard is besides, and especially, to keep civic order.

M. Commandant, if order really reigned in our society, if the social organism were really healthy—in other words, if there were in our social relations no crying abuses, if it were not established that one man shall die of hunger while another gratifies his every whim of luxury, then you would see me in the front ranks of the defenders of this orderly state. But I flatly decline to help in preserving the present so-called "social order." Why, M. Commandant, should we throw dust in each other's eyes? We both know quite well what the "preservation of order" means: upholding the rich against the poor toilers, who begin to perceive their rights. Do we not know the rôle which the National Guard played in the last strike at Rotterdam? For no reason, the Guard had to be on duty hours and hours to watch over the property of the commercial houses which were affected. Can you for a moment suppose that I should shoot down working-people who are acting quite within their rights? You cannot be so blind. Why then complicate the question? Certainly, it is impossible for me to allow myself to be molded into an obedient National Guardsman such as you want and must have.

For all these reasons, but especially because I hate murder by order, I refuse to serve as a National Guardsman, and ask you not to send me either uniform or arms, because I have a fixed resolve not to use them.—I greet you, M. Commandant,

J. K. VAN DER VEER.

This letter, in my opinion, has great importance. Refusals of military service in Christian states began when in Christian states military service appeared. Or rather when the states, the power of which rests upon violence, laid claim to Christianity without giving up violence. In truth, it cannot be otherwise. A Christian, whose doctrine enjoins upon him humility, non-resistance to evil, love to all (even to the most malicious), cannot be a soldier; that is, he cannot join a class of men whose business is to kill their fellow-men. Therefore it is that these Christians have always refused and now refuse military service.

But of true Christians there have always been but few. Most people in Christian countries count as Christians only those who profess the doctrines of some Church, which doctrines have nothing in common, except the name, with true Christianity. That occasionally one in tens of thousands of recruits should refuse to serve did not trouble the hundreds of thousands, the millions, of men who every year accepted military service.

Impossible that the whole enormous majority of Christians who enter upon military service are wrong, and only the exceptions, sometimes uneducated people, are right; while every archbishop and man of learning thinks the service compatible with Christianity. So think the majority, and, untroubled regarding themselves as Christians, they enter the rank of murderers. But now appears a man who, as he himself says, is not a Christian, and who refuses military service, not from religious motives, but from motives of the simplest kind, motives intelligible and common to all men, of whatever religion or nation, whether Catholic, Mohammedan, Buddhist, Confucian, whether Spaniards or Japanese.

Van de Veer refuses military service, not because he follows the commandment, "Thou shalt do no murder," not because he is a Christian, but because he holds murder to be opposed to human nature. He writes that he simply abhors all killing, and abhors it to such a degree that he becomes a vegetarian just to avoid participation in the killing of animals; and, above all, he says, he refuses military service because he thinks "murder by order," that is, the obligation to kill those whom one is ordered to kill (which is the real nature of military service), is incompatible with man's uprightness.

Alluding to the usual objection that if he refuses others will follow his example, and the present social order will be destroyed, he answers that he does not wish to preserve the present social order, because it is bad, because in it the rich dominate the poor, which ought not to be. So that, even if he had any other doubts as to the propriety of serving or not serving, the one consideration that in serving as a soldier he must, by carrying arms and threatening to kill, support the oppressing rich against the oppressed poor, would compel him to refuse military service.

If Van der Veer were to give as the reason for his refusal his adherence to the Christian religion, those who now join the military service could say, "We are no sectarians, and do not acknowledge Christianity; therefore we do not see the need to act as you do."

But the reasons given by Van der Veer are so simple, clear, and universal that it is impossible not to apply them each to his own case. As things are, to deny the force of these reasons in one's own case, one must say:—

"I like killing, and am ready to kill, not only evil-disposed people, but my own oppressed and unfortunate fellow-countrymen, and I perceive nothing wrong in the promise to kill, at the order of the first officer who comes across me, whomever he bids me kill."

Here is a young man. In whatever surroundings, family, creed, he has been brought up, he has been taught that he must be good, that it is bad to strike and kill, not only men, but even animals; he has been taught that a man must value his uprightness, which uprightness consists in acting according to conscience. This is equally taught to the Confucian in China, the Shintoist in Japan, the Buddhist, and the Mohammedan. Suddenly, after being taught all this, he enters the military service, where he is required to do the precise opposite of what he has been taught. He is told to fit himself for wounding and killing, not animals, but men; he is told to renounce his independence as a man, and obey, in the business of murder, men whom he does not know, utter strangers to him.

To such a command, what right answer can a man of our day make? Surely, only this, "I do not wish to, and I will not."

Exactly this answer Van der Veer gives. And it is hard to invent any reply to him and to those who, in a similar position, do as he does.

One may not see this point, through attention not having been called to it; one may not understand the import of an action, as long as it remains unexplained. But once pointed out and explained, one can no longer fail to see, or feign blindness to what is quite obvious.

There may still be found men who do not reflect upon their action in entering military service, and men who want war with. foreign people, and men who would continue the oppression of the laboring class, and even men who like murder for murder's sake. Such men can continue as soldiers; but even they cannot now fail to know that there are others, the best men in the world—not only among Christians, but among Mohammedans, Brahmanists, Buddhists, Confucians—who look upon war and soldiers with aversion and contempt, and whose number grows hourly. No arguments can talk away this plain fact, that a man with any sense of his own dignity cannot enslave himself to an unknown, or even a known, master whose business is killing. Now just in this consists military service, with all its compulsion of discipline.

"But consider the consequences to him who refuses," I am told. "It is all very well for you, an old man exempted from this exaction, and safe by your position. to preach martyrdom; but what about those to whom you preach, and who, believing in you, refuse to serve, and ruin their young lives?"

"But what can I do?"—I answer those who speak thus.— "Because I am old, must I therefore not point out the evil which I clearly, unquestionably see, seeing it precisely because I am old and have lived and thought for long?

Must a man who stands on the far side of the river, beyond the reach of that ruffian whom he sees compelling one man to murder another, not cry out to the slayer, bidding him to refrain, for the reason that such interference will still more enrage the ruffian? Moreover, I by no means see why the government, persecuting those who refuse military service, does not turn its punishment upon me, recognizing in me an instigator. I am not too old for persecution, for any and all sorts of punishments, and my position is a defenseless one. At all events, whether blamed and persecuted or not, whether those who refuse military service are persecuted or not, I, whilst I live, will not cease from saying what I now say; for I cannot refrain from acting according to my conscience." Just in this very thing is Christian truth powerful, irresistible; namely, that, being the teaching of truth, in affecting men it is not to be governed by outside considerations. Whether young or old, whether persecuted or not, he who adopts the Christian, the true, conception of life, cannot shrink from the claims of his conscience. In this is the essence and peculiarity of Christianity, distinguishing it from all other religious teachings; and in this is its unconquerable power.

Van der Veer says he is not a Christian. But the motives of his refusal and action are Christian. He refuses because he does not wish to kill a brother man; he does not obey, because the commands of his conscience are more binding upon him than the commands of men. Precisely on this account is Van der Veer's refusal so important. Thereby he shows that Christianity is not a sect or creed which some may profess and others reject; but that it is naught else than a life's following of that light of reason which illumines all men. The merit of Christianity is not that it prescribes to men such and such acts, but that it foresees and points out the way by which all mankind must go and does go.

Those men who now behave rightly and reasonably do so, not because they follow prescriptions of Christ, but because that line of action which was pointed out eighteen hundred years ago has now become identified with human conscience.

This is why I think the action and letter of Van der Veer are of great import.

As a fire lit on a prairie or in a forest will not die out until it has burned all that is dry and dead, and therefore combustible, so the truth, once articulated in human utterance, will not cease its work until all falsehood, appointed for destruction, surrounding and hiding the truth on all sides as it does, is destroyed. The fire smolders long; but as soon as it flashes into flame, all that can burn burns quickly.

So with the truth, which takes long to reach a right expression, but once that clear expression in word is given, falsehood and wrong are soon to be destroyed. One of the partial manifestations of Christianity—the idea that men can live without the institution of slavery—although it had been included in the Christian concept, was clearly expressed, so it seems to me, only by writers at the end of the eighteenth century. Up to that time, not only the ancient pagans, as Plato and Aristotle, but even men near to us in time, and Christians, could not imagine a human society without slavery. Thomas More could not imagine even a Utopia without slavery. So also men of the beginning of this century could not imagine the life of man without war. Only after the Napoleonic wars was the idea clearly expressed that man can live without war. And now a hundred years have gone since the first clear expression of the idea that mankind can live without slavery; and there is no longer slavery in Christian nations. And there shall not pass away another hundred years after the clear utterance of the idea that mankind can live without war, before war shall cease to be. Very likely some form of armed violence will remain, just as wage-labor remains after the abolition of slavery; but, at least, wars and armies will be abolished in the outrageous form, so repugnant to reason and moral sense, in which they now exist.

Signs that this time is near are many. These signs are such as the helpless position of governments, which more and more increase their armaments; the multiplication of taxation and the discontent of the nations; the extreme degree of efficiency with which deadly weapons are constructed; the activity of congresses and societies of peace; but above all, the refusals of individuals to take military service. In these refusals is the key to the solution of the question. You say that military service is necessary; that, without soldiers, disasters will happen to us. That may be; but, holding the idea of right and wrong which is universal among men today, yourselves included, I cannot kill men to order. So that if, as you say, military service is essential—then arrange it in some way not so contradictory to my, and your, conscience. But, until you have so arranged it, do not claim from me what is against my conscience, which I can by no means disobey.

Thus, inevitably, and very soon, must answer all honest and reasonable men; not only the men of Christendom, but even Mohammedans and the so-called heathen, the Brahmanists, Buddhists, and Confucians. Maybe, by the power of inertia, the soldiering trade will go on for some time to come; but even now the question stands solved in the human conscience, and with every day, every hour, more and more men come to the same solution; and to stay the movement is, at this juncture, not possible. Every recognition of a truth by man, or rather, every deliverance from an error, as in the case of slavery before our eyes, is always attained through a conflict between the awakening conscience and the inertia of the old condition.

At first the inertia is so powerful, the conscience so weak, that the first attempt to escape from error is met only with astonishment. The new truth seems madness. Is it proposed to live without slavery? Then who will work? Is it proposed to live without fighting? Then everybody will come and conquer us.

But the power of conscience grows, inertia weakens, and astonishment is changing to sneers and contempt. "The Holy Scriptures acknowledge masters and slaves. These relations have always been, and now come these wiseacres who want to change the whole world;" so men spoke concerning slavery. "All the scientists and philosophers recognize the lawfulness, and even sacredness, of war; and are we immediately to believe that there is no need of war?"

So men speak concerning war. But conscience continues to grow and to become clear; the number increases of those who recognize the new truth, and sneer and contempt give place to subterfuge and trickery. Those who support the error make slow to understand and admit the incongruity and cruelty of the practice they defend, but think its abolition impossible just now, so delaying its abolition indefinitely. "Who does not know that slavery is an evil? But men are not yet ripe for freedom, and liberation will produce horrible disasters"—men used to say concerning slavery, forty years ago. "Who does not know that war is an evil? But while mankind is still so bestial, abolition of armies will do more harm than good," men say concerning war today.

Nevertheless, the idea is doing its work; it grows, it burns the falsehood; and the time has come when the madness, the uselessness, the harmfulness, and wickedness or the error are so clear (as it happened in the sixties with slavery in Russia and America) that even now it is impossible to justify it. Such is the present position as to war. Just as, in the sixties, no attempts were made to justify slavery, but only to maintain it; so today no man attempts any longer to justify war and armies, but only tries, in silence, to use the inertia which still supports them, knowing very well that this cruel and immoral organization for murder, which seems so powerful, may at any moment crumble down, never more to be raised.

Once a drop of water oozes through the dam, once a brick falls out from a great building, once a mesh comes loose in the strongest net—the dam bursts, the building falls, the net unweaves. Such a drop, such a brick, such a loosed mesh, it seems to me, is the refusal of Van der Veer, explained by reasons universal to all mankind.

Upon this refusal of Van der Veer like refusals must follow more and more often. As soon as these become numerous, the very men (their name is legion) who the day before said, "It is impossible to live without war," will say at once that they have this long time declared the madness and immorality of war, and they will advise everybody to follow Van de Veer's example. Then, of wars and armies, as these are now, there will remain only the recollection.

And this time is coming.

TWO WARS

HRISTENDOM has recently been the scene of two wars. One is now concluded, whereas the other still continues; but they were for a time being carried on simultaneously, and the contrast they present is very striking. The first—the Spanish-American war—was an old, vain, foolish, and cruel war, inopportune, out-of-date, barbarous, which sought by killing one set of people to solve the question as to how and by whom another set of people ought to be governed.

The other, which is still going on, and will end only when there is an end of all war, is a new, self-sacrificing, holy war, which was long ago proclaimed (as Victor Hugo expressed it at one of the congresses) by the best and most advanced—Christian—section of mankind against the other, the coarse and savage section. This war has recently been carried on with especial vigor and success by a handful of Christian people—the Dukhobors of the Caucasus—against the powerful Russian government.

The other day I received a letter from a gentleman in Colorado—Jesse Goldwin—who asks me to send him

"... a few words or thoughts expressive of my feelings
with regard to the noble work of the American nation,
and the heroism of its soldiers and sailors." This gentleman, together with an overwhelming majority of the
American people, feels perfectly confident that the work
of the Americans—the killing of several thousands of
almost unarmed men (for, in comparison with the equip-
ment of the Americans, the Spaniards were almost without
arms)—was beyond doubt a "noble work;" and he regards
the majority of those who, after killing great numbers of
their fellow-creatures, have remained safe and sound,
and have secured for themselves an advantageous position, as heroes.

The Spanish-American War—leaving out of account the
atrocities committed by the Spaniards in Cuba, which
served as a pretext for it—is very like this: An old man,
infirm and childish, brought up in the traditions of a
false honor, challenges, for the settlement of some misunderstanding, a young man, in full possession of his powers,
to a boxing-match. And the young man, who, from his
antecedents and professed sentiments, ought to be
immeasurably above such a settlement of the question,
accepts the challenge. Armed with a club, he then throws
himself upon this infirm and childish old man, knocks
out his teeth, breaks his ribs, and afterward enthusiastically relates his great deeds to a large audience of young
men like himself, who rejoice and praise the hero who has
thus maimed the old man.

Such is the nature of the first war, which is occupying
the attention of the whole Christian world. Of the other
no one speaks; hardly any one knows about it.

This second war may be described as follows: The
people of every nation are being deluded by their rulers,

who say to them, "You, who are governed by us, are all in danger of being conquered by other nations; we are watching over your welfare and safety, and consequently we demand of you annually some millions of rubles—the fruit of your labor—to be used by us in the acquisition of arms, cannon, powder, and ships for your defence; we also demand that you yourselves shall enter institutions, organized by us, where you will become senseless particles of a huge machine—the army—which will be under our absolute control. On entering this army you will cease to be men with wills of your own; you will simply do what we require of you. But what we wish, above all else, is to exercise dominion; the means by which we dominate is killing, therefore we will instruct you to kill."

Notwithstanding the obvious absurdity of the assertion that people are in danger of being attacked by the governments of other states, who, in their turn, affirm that they —in spite of all their desire for peace—find themselves in precisely the same danger; notwithstanding the humiliation of that slavery to which men subject themselves by entering the army; notwithstanding the cruelty of the work to which they are summoned—men nevertheless submit to this fraud, give their money to be used for their own subjugation, and themselves help to enslave others.

But now there come people who say: ."What you tell us about the danger threatening us, and about your anxiety to guard us against it, is a fraud. All the states are assuring us that they desire peace, and yet at the same time all are arming themselves against the others. Moreover, according to that law, which you yourselves recognize, all men are brothers, and it makes no difference whether one belongs to this state or to that; therefore the idea of our being attacked by other nations, with which you try to frighten us, has no terrors for us; we regard it as a matter of no importance. The essential thing, however, is that the law given to us by God and recognized even by you who are requiring us to participate in killing, distinctly forbids, not killing only, but also every kind of violence. Therefore we cannot, and will not, take part in your preparations for murder, we will give no money for the purpose, and we will not attend the meetings arranged by you with the object of perverting men's minds and consciences, and transforming them into instruments of violence, obedient to any bad man who may choose to make use of them."

This constitutes the second war. It has long been carried on by the best men of the world against the representatives of brute force, and has of late flamed up with special intensity between the Dukhobors and the Russian government. The Russian government has made use of all the weapons it had at command—police measures for making arrests, for prohibiting people moving from place to place, for forbidding all intercourse with one another, the interception of letters, espionage, the prohibition to publish in the newspapers information about anything concerning the Dukhobors, calumnies of them printed in the papers, bribery, flogging, imprisonment, and the ruin of families.

The Dukhobors have, on their part, employed their one religious weapon, viz., gentle intelligence and patient firmness; and they say: "One must not obey man rather than God. Therefore, whatever you may do to us, we cannot and will not obey you."

Men praise the heroes of the savage Spanish-American war, who, in their desire to distinguish themselves before the world, and to gain reward and fame, have slain great numbers of men, or have died while engaged in killing their fellow-creatures. But no one speaks or even knows about the heroes of the war against war, who—unseen and unheard—have died and are now dying under the rod, in foul prison cells or in painful exile, and who, nevertheless, to their last breath, stand firm by goodness and truth.

I knew dozens of these martyrs who have already died, and hundreds more who, scattered all over the world, are still suffering martyrdom for the truth.

I knew Drozhin, a peasant teacher, who was tortured to death in a penal battalion; I knew another, Izum-tchenko (a fried of Drozhin), who, after being kept for some time in a penal battalion, was banished to the other end of the world. I knew Olkhovikof, a peasant who re-fused military service, and was consequently sent to a penal battalion, and then, while on board a steamer which was transporting him into exile, converted Sereda, the soldier who had him in charge. Sereda, understanding what Olkhovikof said to him as to the sinfulness of mili-tary service, went to his superiors and said, like the ancient martyrs; "I do not wish to be among the torturers; let me join the martyrs." And forthwith they began to torture him, sent him to a penal battalion, and afterwards exiled him to the province of Yakutsk. I knew dozens of Dukhobors, of whom many have died or become blind, and yet they would not yield to demands which are contrary to the divine law.

The other day I read a letter from a young Dukhobor, who has been sent alone to a regiment stationed in Samarkand. Again, those same demands on the part of the officers, the same persuasion from the chaplain, the same threats and entreaties, and always the same simple and irresistible replies: "I cannot do what is opposed to my belief in God."

"Then we will torture you to death."

"That is your business. You do your work and I will do mine."

And this youth of twenty, forsaken of all, in a strange place, surrounded by men who are hostile to him, amid the rich, the powerful, and the educated, who are concentrating all their energies on the task of bringing him to subjection, does not submit, but still perseveres in his heroic deed.

But men say: "These are useless victims; these people perish, but the order of life will remain the same." This, I believe, is just what was said with regard to the sacrifice of Christ, as well as of all the other martyrs to truth. The men of our time, especially the learned, have grown so coarse that they, owing to their coarseness, are even unable to understand the significance and effect of spiritual force. A shell with 250 puds of dynamite, fired at a crowd of living men—this they understand and recognize as a force; but thought, truth, which has been realized and practised in the life, even to martyrdom, which has now become accessible to millions—this, according to their conception, is not a force, because it makes no noise, and.one cannot see broken bones and pools of blood. Learned men (true, it is those whose learning is misdirected) are using all the power of erudition to prove that mankind lives like a herd of cattle, that man is guided by economic considerations alone, and that his intellect is given him merely for amusement. But governments well know what it is that rules the world, consequently—guided by the instinct of self-preservation—they

are undoubtedly chiefly concerned about the manifestation of spiritual forces, upon which forces depend their
existence or their ruin.

And this is precisely the reason why all the energies
of the Russian government were, and still continue to
be, exerted to render the Dukhobors harmless, to isolate
them, to banish them beyond the frontier.

Notwithstanding all these efforts, however, the struggle
of the Dukhobors has opened the eyes of millions.

I know hundreds of military men, old and young, who,
owing to the persecution of the gentle, industrious Dukhobors, have begun to have doubts as to the legality of
their occupation. I know people who have, for the first
time, begun to meditate on life and the meaning of Christianity only after seeing or hearing about the life of these
people, and the persecutions to which they have been
subjected.

And the government that is tyrannizing over millions
of people knows this, and feels that it has been struck
to the very heart.

Such is the nature of the second war which is being
waged in our times, and such are its consequences. And
not to the Russian government alone are these consequences of importance; every government founded upon
violence and upheld by armies is wounded in the same
way by this weapon. Christ said, "*I have conquered the
world.*" And, indeed. He has conquered the world, if
men would but learn to believe in the strength of the
weapon given by Him.

And this weapon is the obedience of every man to his
own reason and conscience. This, indeed, is so simple,
so indubitable, and binding upon every man. "You wish
to make me a participator in murder; you demand of me

money for the preparation of weapons; and want me to take part in the organized assembly of murderers," says the reasonable man—he who has neither sold nor obscured his conscience. "But I profess that law—the same that is also professed by you—which long ago forbade not murder only, but all hostility also, and therefore I cannot obey you."

And it is just by this simple means, and by it alone, that the world is being conquered.

"NOTES FOR OFFICERS"

"It is impossible but that offenses
will come, but woe unto him
through whom they come."
LUKE xvii. 1, 2.

N all Russian barracks there hang, nailed
to the wall, the so-called "Notes for Sol-
diers" composed by General Dragomiroff.
These notes are a collection of stupidly
braggart sentences intermixed with blasphemous citations from the Gospels, and
written in an artificial barrack slang, which is, in reality,
quite strange to every soldier. The Gospel citations are
quoted in order to corroborate the statements that soldiers should kill and tear with their teeth the enemy: "If
your bayonet breaks, strike with your fists; if your fists
give way, bite with your teeth." The notes conclude with
the statement that God is the soldiers' General: "God is
your General."

Nothing illustrates more convincingly than these notes
that terrible degree of unenlightenment, servile submissiveness, and brutality which Russian men have
attained to at present. Since this most horrible blasphemy appeared and was first hung up in all the barracks
(a considerable time ago), not one commander, nor
priest—whom this distortion of the meaning of the Gospel
texts would seem to concern directly—has expressed any

condemnation of this obnoxious work and it continues to be published in millions of copies and to be read by millions of soldiers who accept this dreadful production as a guide to their conduct.

These notes revolted me long ago, and now, being afraid I may otherwise miss the opportunity of doing so before my death, I have now written an appeal to soldiers, in which I have endeavored to remind them that as men and Christians they have quite other duties toward God than those put forward in the notes. And a similar reminder is required, I think, not only by soldiers, but still more so by officers (by "officers" I mean all military authorities, from Subalterns to Generals), who enter the military service or continue in it, not by compulsion as privates do, but by their own free will. It was pardonable a hundred or fifty years ago, when war was regarded as an inevitable condition of the life of nations, when the men of the country with whom one was at war were regarded as barbarians, without religion, and evil-doers, and when it did not enter the mind of military men that they were required for the suppression and "pacification" of one's own people—it was pardonable then to put on a multi-colored uniform trimmed with gold braid and to saunter about with a clashing sword and jingling spurs, or to caracole in front of one's regiment, imagining oneself a hero, who, if he has not yet sacrificed his life for the defense of his fatherland, is nevertheless ready to do so. But at the present time, when frequent international communications, commercial, social, scientific, artistic, have so brought nations in touch with one another that any contemporary international war is like a dispute in a family, and breaks the most sacred human ties—when hundreds of peace societies and thousands of articles, not only in special but also in the ordinary newspapers, unceasingly demonstrate from every side the senselessness of militarism, and the possibility, even necessity, of abolishing war—at the present time, when, above all, the military are more and more often called out, not against foreign foes to repel invasions, or for the aggrandizement of the glory and power of their country, but against unarmed factory workmen or peasants—at the present time to caracole on one's little horse in one's little embroidered uniform and to advance dashingly at the head of one's company, is no longer a silly, pardonable piece of vanity as it was before, but something quite different.

In past times, in the days say of Nicholas I, (1825-1855), it entered into no one's head that troops are necessary chiefly to shoot at unarmed populaces. But at present troops are permanently stationed in every large town and manufacturing centre for the purpose of being ready to disperse gatherings of workmen; and seldom a month passes without soldiers being called out of their barracks with ball cartridges and hidden in secret places in readiness to shoot the populace down at any moment.

The use of troops against the people has become indeed not only customary—they are mobilized in advance to be in readiness for this very purpose; and the Governments do not conceal the fact that the distribution of recruits in the various regiments is intentionally conducted in such a way that the men are never drafted into a regiment stationed in the place from which they are drawn. This is done for the purpose of avoiding the possibility of soldiers having to shoot at their own relations.

The German Emperor, at every fresh call for recruits, has openly declared and still declares that soldiers who have been sworn in belong to him, body and soul; that they have only one foe—his foe; and that this foe are the Socialists (that is, workmen), whom the soldiers must, if he bids them, shoot down (*niederschiessen*), even if they should be their own brothers or even parents.

In past times, moreover, if the troops were used against the people, those against whom they were used were, or at all events were supposed to be, evil-doers, ready to kill and ruin the peaceful inhabitants, and whom therefore it might be supposed to be necessary to destroy for the general good. But at present every one knows that those against whom troops are called out are for the most part peaceful, industrious men, who merely desire to profit unhindered by the fruits of their labors. So that the principal permanent function of the troops in our time no longer consists in an imaginary defense against irreligious and in general external foes, and not against internal foes in the persons of riotous evil-doers, but in killing one's own unarmed brothers, who are by no means evil-doers, but peaceful, industrious men whose only desire is that they shall not be deprived of their earnings. So that military service at the present time, when its chief object is, by murder and the threat of murder, to keep enslaved men in those unjust conditions in which they are placed, is not only not a noble but a positively dastardly undertaking. And therefore it is indispensable that officers who serve at the present time should consider whom they serve, and ask themselves whether what they are doing is good or evil.

I know that there are many officers, especially of the higher grades, who by various arguments on the themes of orthodoxy, autocracy, integrity of the State, eternal inevitableness of war, necessity of order, inconsistency of socialistic ravings, and so on, try to prove to themselves that their activity is rational and useful, and contains nothing immoral. But in the depths of their soul they themselves do not believe in what they say, and the more intelligent and the older they become the less they believe.

I remember how joyously I was struck by a friend and old comrade of mine, a very ambitious man, who had dedicated his whole life to military service, and had attained the highest honors and grades (General Aide-de-Camp and Major-General), when he told me that he had burnt his "Memoirs" of the wars in which he had participated because he had changed his view of the military activity, and now regarded every war as an evil deed, which should not be encouraged by participation, but, on the contrary, should be discredited in every way. Many officers think the same, although they do not say so while they serve. And indeed no thoughtful officer can think otherwise. Why, one has only to recall to mind what forms the occupation of all officers, from the lowest to the highest—to the Commandant of an Army Corps. From the beginning to the end of their service—I am alluding to officers in the active service—their activity, with the exception of the few and short periods when they go to war and are occupied with actual murder, consists in the attainment of two aims: in teaching soldiers the best methods of killing men, and in accustoming them to an obedience which enables them to do mechanically, without argument, everything their commander orders. In olden times it used to be said, "Flog two to death, and train one," and so they did. If at present the proportion of flogged to death is smaller, the principle nevertheless is the same. One cannot reduce men into that state, not of animals but of machines, in which they will commit the deed most repulsive to the nature of man and to the faith he professes, namely, murder, at the bidding of any commander—unless not only artful frauds but also the most cruel violence have been perpetrated on them. And so it is in practice.

Not long ago a great sensation was created in the French press by the disclosure by a journalist of those awful tortures to which soldiers in the Disciplinary Battalions are submitted on the Island of Obrou, six hours' distance from Paris. The men punished have their hands and feet tied together behind their back and are then thrown to the ground; instruments are fixed on their thumbs while their hands are twisted behind their backs, and screwed up so that every movement produces a dreadful pain; they are hung with their legs upward; and so forth.

When we see trained animals accomplishing things contrary to nature: dogs walking on their forelegs, elephants rolling barrels, tigers playing with lions, and so on, we know that all this has been attained by the torments of hunger, whip, and red-hot iron. And when we see men in uniforms with rifles standing motionless, or performing all together the same movement—running, jumping, shooting, shouting, and so on—in general, producing those fine reviews and manœuvers which emperors and kings so admire and show off one before the other, we know the same. One cannot cauterize out of a man all that is human and reduce him to the state of a machine without torturing him, and torturing not in a simple way but in the most refined, cruel way—at one and the same time torturing and deceiving him.

And all this is done by you officers. In this all your service consists, from the highest grade to the lowest, with the exception of those rare occasions when you participate in real war.

A youth transported from his family to the other end of the world comes to you, after having been taught that that deceptive oath forbidden by the Gospel which he has taken irretrievably binds him—as a cock when laid on the floor with a line drawn over its nose and along the floor thinks that it is bound by that line—he comes to you with complete submissiveness and the hope that you his elders, men more intelligent and learned than he, will teach him all that is good. And you, instead of freeing him from those superstitions which he has brought with him, inoculate him with new, most senseless, coarse, and pernicious superstitions: about the sanctity of the banner, the almost divine position of the Tsar, the duty of absolute obedience to the authorities. And when with the help of the methods for stultifying men which are elaborated in your organization you reduce him to a position worse than animal, to a position where he is ready to kill every one he is ordered to kill, even his unarmed brothers, you exhibit him with pride to your superiors, and receive in return their thanks and rewards. It is terrible to be a murderer oneself, but by cunning and cruel methods to reduce one's confiding brothers to this state is the most terrible crime of all. And this you accomplish, and in this consists the whole of your service.

It is therefore not astonishing that amongst you more than amongst any other class everything which will stifle conscience flourishes: smoking, cards, drunkenness, depravity; and that suicides occur amongst you more frequently than anywhere else.

"It is impossible but that offenses will come, but woe unto him through whom they come."

You often say that you serve because if you did not the existing order would be destroyed and disturbances and every kind of calamities would occur.

But firstly, it is not true that you are concerned with the maintenance of the existing order: you are concerned only with your own advantages.

Secondly, even if your abstinence from military service did destroy the existing order, this would in no way prove that you should continue to do what is wrong, but only that the order which is being destroyed by your abstinence should be destroyed. Were establishments of the most useful kind—hospitals, schools, homes, to depend for their support on the profits from houses of ill-fame, no consideration of the good produced by these philanthropic establishments would retain in her position the woman who desired to free herself from her shameful trade.

"It is not my fault," the woman would say, "that you have founded your philanthropic institutions on vice. I no longer wish to live in vice. As to your institutions, they do not concern me." And so should every soldier say if the necessity of maintaining the existing order founded on his readiness to murder were put before him. "Organize the general order in a way that will not require murder," the soldier should say. "And then I shall not destroy it. I only do not wish to and cannot be a murderer."

Many of you say also: "I was educated thus. I am tied by my position, and cannot escape." But this also is not true.

You can always escape from your position. If, however, you do not, it is only because you prefer to live and act against your conscience rather than lose certain worldly advantages which your dishonest service affords. Only forget that you are an officer and recall to mind that you are a man, and the way of escape from your position will immediately disclose itself to you. This way of escape in its best and most honest form would consist in your calling together the men of whom you are in command, stepping in front, and asking their pardon for all the evil you have done them by deception—and then cease to serve in the army. Such an action seems very bold, demanding great courage, whereas in reality much less courage is required for such an action than to storm a fortification or to challenge a man to a duel for an insult to the uniform—which you as a soldier are always ready to do, and do.

But even without being capable of acting thus you can always, if you have understood the criminality of military service, leave it and give preference to any other activity though less advantageous.

But if you cannot do even this, then the solution for you of the question whether you will continue to serve or not will be postponed to that time—and this will soon appear for each one of you—when you will stand face to face with an unarmed crowd of peasants or factory workers, and be ordered to shoot at them. And then, if anything human remains in you, you will have to refuse to obey, and, as a result, to leave the service.

I know that there are still many officers, from the highest to the lowest ranks, who are so unenlightened or hypnotized that they do not see the necessity of either the one, the other, or the third solution, and quietly continue to serve even in the present conditions, ready to shoot at their brothers and even priding themselves upon this; but happily public opinion punishes such people with more and more repulsion and disapproval, and their number continually becomes smaller and smaller.

So that in our time, when the fratricidal function of

the army has become evident, officers not only can no longer continue in the ancient traditions of military self-complacent bravado—they cannot continue the criminal work of teaching murder to simple men confiding in them, and themselves to prepare for participation in murdering unarmed populaces, without the consciousness of their human degradation and shame.

It is this which should be understood and remembered by every thinking and conscientious officer of our time.

"NOTES FOR SOLDIERS"

> "Be not afraid of them which kill the body, but are not able to kill the soul: but rather fear him which is able to destroy both soul and body."—MATT. x. 28.
> "We must obey God rather than men."—ACTS v. 29.

OU are a soldier. You have been taught to shoot, to stab, to march, to do gymnastics. You have been taught to read and write, led to exercises and reviews; perhaps have been in a campaign and have fought with the Turks or Chinese, obeying all your orders. It has not even entered your head to ask yourself whether what you were ordered to do was good or bad.

But suddenly an order is received that your company or squadron shall march out, taking ball cartridges. You go without asking where you are being led.

You are brought to a village or factory, and you see before you gathered in an open space a crowd of villagers or factory hands—men, women with children, aged folk. The governor and public prosecutor approach the crowd with policemen and say something. The crowd is at first silent, then begins to shout louder and louder; and the authorities retreat. And you guess that the peasants or factory hands are rioting, and that you have been brought to "pacify" them. The authorities several times retreat from the crowd and again approach it, but the shouts become louder and louder, and the authorities consult each other and at last give you the order to load your rifles with the ball cartridges. You see before you men such as those from amongst whom you have been taken—men in peasants' coats, sheepskin overcoats, and bark shoes, and women in kerchiefs and jackets—women like your wife and mother..

The first shot is ordered to be fired above the heads of the crowd. But the crowd does not disperse, and shouts even louder; and you are then ordered to shoot in earnest, not over the heads, but straight into the middle, of the crowd.

It has been instilled into you that you are not responsible for the consequences of your shots. But you know that the man who falls bleeding from your shot is killed by you and by no one else, and you know that you could have refrained from shooting and that then the man would not have been killed.

What are you to do?

It would not be enough to lay down your rifle and refuse in this instance to shoot your brothers; for tomorrow the same thing could reoccur. And therefore, whether you wish it or not, you have to recollect yourselves and ask, "What is this soldier's calling which has brought me to the necessity of shooting my unarmed brothers?"

You are told in the Gospel that one should not only refrain from killing his brothers, but should not do that which leads to murder: one should not be angry with one's brothers, nor hate one's enemies, but love them.

In the law of Moses you are distinctly told, "Thou shalt not kill," without any reservations as to whom you can and whom you cannot kill. Whereas in the regulations which you have been taught you are told that a soldier must fulfil any order whatsoever of his superior, except an order against the Tsar; and in explanation of the Sixth Commandment you are told that although by this commandment killing is forbidden, yet he who kills an enemy during war does not sin against, this commandment.* And in the "Notes for Soldiers" which hang in your barracks, and which you have many times read and listened to, it is explained how a soldier should kill men: "If three fall on you, shoot one, stab another, and finish the third with the bayonet. . . . If your bayonet breaks, strike with the stock; if the stock gives way, hit with your fists; if your fists are hurt, bite with your teeth."

You are told that you must kill, because you have taken the oath, and that not you but your commanders will be responsible for your actions.

But before you took the oath, that is, before you promised men to obey their will, it was your duty, without need of oaths, to obey in everything the will of God, of Him who gave you life; and God forbids killing.

So that you could by no means swear that you would obey everything men might command. This is why it is distinctly stated in the Gospel, Matt. v. 34-37: "Swear not

---

* In your regulations you are told: "By the Sixth Commandment God forbids the taking of man's life by violence or cunning, and the disturbance in any way of one's neighbor's peace and safety; and therefore this commandment also forbids quarrels, anger, hatred, jealousy, cruelty. But he who kills the enemy in war does not sin against the Sixth Commandment, because in war we defend our faith, sovereign, and country."

at all. . . . But let your speech be, Yea, yea; nay, nay: and whatsoever is more than these is of the evil one."

And in the Epistle of James, chap. v. 12, the same thing is said, "But above all things, my brethren, swear not, neither by the heaven, nor by the earth." So that to take the oath is a sin. As to what they say about your commanders, not yourselves, being responsible for your deeds, this is obviously a falsehood. Is your conscience not in you, but in your sergeant, captain, colonel, or some one else? No one can decide for you what you can and must, and what you cannot and should not do. And a man is always responsible for what he does. Is not the sin of adultery much easier than that of murder? and yet can one man say to another: "Go and commit adultery. I shall bear your sin, because I am your commander"?

According to the Biblical narrative Adam sinned against God, and then said that his wife told him to eat the apple, while his wife said she was tempted by the devil. God exonerated neither Adam nor Eve, but told them that because Adam listened to the voice of his wife he would be punished, and that his wife would be punished for listening to the serpent. And neither were excused, but both were punished. Will not God say the same to you also when you kill a man and say that your captain ordered you to do it?

The deceit is apparent already, because in the regulation obliging a soldier to obey all his commander's orders, these words are added, *"Except such as tend toward the injury of the Tsar."*

If a soldier before obeying the orders of his commander must first decide whether it is not against the Tsar, how then can he fail to consider before obeying his commander's order whether it is not against his supreme

King, God? And no action is more opposed to the will of God than that of killing men. And therefore you *cannot* obey men if they order you to kill. If you obey, and kill, you do so only for the sake of your own advantage—to escape punishment. So that in killing by order of your commander you are a murderer as much as the thief who kills a rich man to rob him. He is tempted by money, and you by the desire not to be punished, or to receive a reward. Man is always responsible before God for his actions. And no power, whatever the authorities desire, can turn a live man into a dead thing which one can move about as one likes. Christ taught men that they are all sons of God, and therefore a Christian cannot surrender his conscience into the power of another man, no matter by what title he may be called: King, Tsar, Emperor. As to those men who have assumed power over you, demanding of you the murder of your brothers, this only shows that they are deceivers, and that therefore one should not obey them. Shameful is the position of the prostitute who is always ready to give her body to be defiled by any one her master indicates; but yet more shameful is the position of a soldier always ready for the greatest of crimes— the murder of any man whom his commander indicates.

And therefore if you do indeed desire to act according to God's will you have only to do one thing—to throw off the shameful and ungodly calling of a soldier, and be ready to bear any sufferings which may be inflicted upon you for so doing.

So that the true "Notes" for a Christian Soldier are not those in which it is said that "God is the Soldier's General" and other blasphemies, and that the soldier must obey his commanders in everything, and be ready to kill foreigners and even his own unarmed brothers—but those which remind one of the words of the Gospel that one *should obey God rather than men* and fear not those who can kill the body but cannot kill the soul.

In this alone consists the true, unfraudulent "Notes for Soldiers."

In Dragomiroff's "Notes for Soldiers" three passages are quoted from the Gospels: John xv. 10–13 and Matthew x. 22, 39. From John the words of the 13th verse are quoted: "Greater love hath no man than this, that a man lay down his life for his friends;" evidently for the purpose of implying that soldiers fighting in battle should defend their comrades to the utmost of their strength.

These words however cannot possibly refer to military action, but mean exactly the reverse. In verses 10–13 it is said: "If ye keep my commandments, ye shall abide in my love; even as I have kept my Father's commandments, and abide in his love. These things have I spoken unto you, that my joy may be in you, and that your joy may be fulfilled. This is my commandment, that ye love one another, even as I have loved you. Greater love hath no man than this, that a man lay down his life for his friends."

So that the words, "Greater love hath no man than this, that a man lay down his life for his friends," do not at all mean that a soldier should defend his comrades, but that a Christian should be ready to surrender his life for the fulfilment of Christ's commandment that men should love one another. And therefore he should be ready to sacrifice his life rather than consent to kill men.

From Matthew the end of the 22d verse of the 10th chapter is quoted, "He that endureth to the end, the same shall be saved," evidently in the sense that a soldier who fights bravely will be saved from the enemy. But again the meaning of this passage is not at all what the compiler wishes to attribute to it, but a contrary one.

The complete verse is: "And ye shall be hated of all men for my name's sake: but he that endureth to the end, the same shall be saved."

So that obviously this verse cannot relate to soldiers, soldiers not being hated by any one for Christ's name: and it is clear therefore that only those people can be hated for Christ's name who refuse in his name to do what the world demands of them, and, in the case in point, soldiers who disobey when murder is demanded of them.

Again, the end of the 39th verse of the 10th chapter of Matthew is quoted: "He that loseth his life shall find it," also in the sense that he who is killed in war will be rewarded in Heaven. But the sense is obviously not this. In the 38th verse it is said, "He that doth not take his cross and follow after me, is not worthy of me," and after this is added, "He that findeth his life shall lose it; and he that loseth his life for my sake shall find it;" that is, that he who desires to safeguard his corporal life rather than fulfil the teaching of love will lose his true life, but he who does not safeguard his corporal life, but fulfils the teaching of love, will gain the true, spiritual, eternal life.

Thus all the three passages assert, not, as the compiler desired, that in obedience to the Authorities one should fight, and crush, and rend men with one's teeth, but, on the contrary, they all, like the whole Gospel, express one and the same thing—that a Christian cannot be a murderer and therefore cannot be a soldier. And therefore the words, "A soldier is Christ's warrior," placed in the "Notes" after the Gospel verses, do not at all mean what the compiler imagines. It is true that a soldier, if he be a

Christian, can and should be Christ's warrior, but he will be Christ's warrior, not when, obeying the will of those commanders who have prepared him for murder, he kills foreigners who have done him no harm, or even his own unarmed fellow-countrymen, but only when he renounces the ungodly and shameful calling of a soldier, in the name of Christ—and fights not with external foes but with his own commanders who deceive him and his brothers, and fights them, not with a bayonet, nor with his fists or teeth, but with humble reasonableness and readiness to bear all suffering and even death rather than remain a soldier—that is, a man ready to kill any one whom his commanders indicate.

[The following are the "Notes for Soldiers" by General Dragomiroff to which Tolstoï alludes.—Eds.]

"Notes for Soldiers" (Soldatskaya Pamiatka), by General Dragomiroff

"Greater love hath no man than this, that a man lay down his life for his friend."—John xv. 13.

"He that endureth to the end, the same shall be saved."—Matt. x. 22.

"He that loseth his life shall find it."—Matt. x. 39.

A soldier is Christ's warrior. As such he should regard himself, and so he should behave.

Consider your corps as your family; your commander as your father; your comrade as your brother; your inferior as a young relative. Then all will be happy and friendly and easy.

Don't think of yourself, think of your comrades; they will think of you. Perish yourself, but save your comrade.

Under fire advance in open order; attack together.

Strike with your fist, not with your open hand.

One leg helps the other, one hand strengthens the other. Stick together. One evil is not an evil; two evils are half an evil; separation is the evil.

Don't expect relief. It won't come. Support will come. When you've thrashed them well, then you'll rest.

Only he is beaten who is afraid.

Always attack, never defend.

If your bayonet breaks, strike with the stock; if the stock gives way, hit with your fists; if your fists are hurt, bite with your teeth. Only he wins who fights desperately, to the death.

In action a soldier is like a sentinel; even dying he should not let his rifle go.

Keep your bullet for three days, even for a whole campaign, when you can't get more. Shoot seldom, but well. With the bayonet strike hard. The bullet may miss the mark, but the bayonet will not. The bullet is stupid, the bayonet is the plucky one.

Aim every bullet; to shoot without care only amuses the devil. Only the careful not the chance bullet finds the culprit. Hold your cartridges. If you spend them a long way off, when you get near, just when you want them, you'll have none. For a good soldier, thirty cartridges are enough for the hottest engagement.

From the dead and wounded take their cartridges.

If you knock up against the enemy unexpectedly or he against you, hit without hesitation. Don't let him collect himself. The plucky one is he who first cries "Hurrah." If three fall on you, shoot one, stab another, and finish the third with your bayonet. God defends the brave.

Where a bold one will get through, God will trip up the timid one.

For a good soldier there are neither flanks nor rear, but all is front, where the foe is.

Always keep your face toward the cavalry. Let it come to

two hundred yards, give it a volley, put the bayonet into position, and freeze there.

In war a soldier must expect short commons, short sleep, and sore feet. Because it is war. Even an old soldier finds it difficult, and for a green one it is hard. But if it's hard for you it isn't easier for the enemy; maybe harder still. Only you see your own hardships, but don't see the enemy's. Yet they are always there. So don't grow stale, but the harder it is, the more doggedly and desperately fight; when you've won you'll feel better at once, and the enemy worse. "He that endureth to the end, the same shall be saved."

Don't think that victory can be won straight off. The enemy can also be firm. Sometimes one can't succeed even the second and third times. Go at it a fourth, a fifth, a sixth time, till you win.

When fighting help the sound men. Only think of the wounded when you have won. The man who bothers about the wounded during the fight and leaves the ranks is a bad soldier and not a kind-hearted man. It is not his comrades who are dear to him but his own skin. If you win it will be well for all, both sound and wounded.

Don't leave your place on the march. If you stop for a minute and fall behind, hurry up and don't lag.

When you reach the bivouac all can't rest. Some must sleep, others guard. He who sleeps, let him sleep in peace till he is wakened; comrades are on guard. He who is on guard, let him watch alertly, though he has marched seventy miles.

When you are an officer, keep your men well in hand. Give your orders intelligently; don't merely cry "Forward, March." First explain what is to be done, so that every man can know where and why he has to go. Then "Forward, March" is all right. Every soldier should understand his actions.

"The chief gets the drink first, and the stick first."

Die for the Orthodox faith, for our father the Tsar, for Holy

Russia. The Church prays to God. "He who loses his life will find it." He who survives, to him honor and glory.

Do not offend the native; he feeds and supports. A soldier is not a thief.

Keep yourself clean, your clothes and ammunition in order. Guard your rifle, your biscuits, and your feet as the apple of your eye. Look after your socks (leg bands) and keep them greased. It's better for the foot.

A soldier should be healthy, brave, hardy, determined, just, pious! Pray to God! From Him is the victory! Noble heroes, God leads you, He is your General!

Obedience, education, discipline, cleanliness, health, tidiness, vigor, courage, dash, victory! Glory, glory, glory!

Lord of Hosts, be with us! We have no other helper than Thee in the day of our trouble! Lord of Hosts have mercy on us!

ON PATRIOTISM

HE Franco-Russian festivities which took place in October, 1894, in France made me, and others, no doubt, as well, first amused, then astonished, then indignant —feelings which I wished to express in a short article.

But while studying further the chief causes of this strange phenomenon, I arrived at the reflections which I here offer to the reader.

I

THE Russian and French peoples have been living for many centuries with a knowledge of each other—entering sometimes into friendly, more often, unfortunately, into very unfriendly, relations at the instigation of their respective governments—when suddenly, because two years ago a French squadron came to Kronstadt, and its officers, having landed, eaten much, and drunk a variety of wine in various places, heard and made many false and foolish speeches; and because last year a

Russian squadron arrived at Toulon, and its officers, having gone to Paris and there eaten and drunk copiously, heard and made a still greater number of silly and untruthful speeches—it came to pass that not only those who ate, drank, and spoke, but every one who was present, and even those who merely heard or read in the papers of these proceedings—all these millions of French and Russians—imagined suddenly that in some especial fashion they were enamored of each other; that is, that all the French love all the Russians, and all the Russians all the French.

These sentiments were expressed in France last October in the most unheard-of ways.

The following description of these proceedings appeared in the *Village Review*, a paper which collects its information from the daily press:—

"When the French and Russian squadrons met they greeted each other with salvos of artillery, and with ardent and enthusiastic cries of 'Hurrah!' 'Long live Russia!' 'Long live France!'

"To all this uproar the naval bands (there were orchestras also on most of the hired steamboats) contributed, the Russian playing 'God save the Tsar,' and the French the 'Marseillaise,' the public upon the steamboats waving their hats, flags, handkerchiefs, and nosegays. Many barges were loaded entirely with men and women of the working-class with their children, waving nosegays and shouting 'Long live Russia!' with all their might. Our sailors, in view of such national enthusiasm, could not restrain their tears.

"In the harbor all the French men-of-war present were ranged in two divisions, and our fleet passed between them, the admiral's vessel leading. A splendid moment was approaching.

"A salute of fifteen guns was fired from the Russian flagship in honor of the French fleet, and the French flagship replied with thirty. The Russian National Hymn pealed from the French lines; French sailors mounted their masts and rigging; vociferations of welcome poured uninterruptedly from both fleets, and from the surrounding vessels. The sailors waved their caps, the spectators their hats and handkerchiefs, in honor of the beloved guests. From all sides, sea and shore, thundered the universal shout, 'Long live Russia!' 'Long live France!'

"According to the custom in naval visits, Admiral Avellan and the officers of his staff came on shore in order to pay their respects to the local authorities.

"At the landing-stage they were met by the French naval staff and the senior officials of the port of Toulon.

"Friendly greetings followed, accompanied by the thunder of artillery and the pealing of bells. The naval band played the Russian National Hymn, 'God save the Tsar,' which was received with a roar from the spectators of 'Long live the Tsar!' 'Long live Russia!'

"The shouting swelled into one mighty din, which drowned the music and even the cannonade. Those present declare that the enthusiasm of the huge crowd of people attained at that moment its utmost height, and that it would be impossible to express in words the feelings which overflowed the hearts of all upon the scene.

"Admiral Avellan, with uncovered head, and accompanied by the French and Russian officers, then drove to the naval administration buildings, where he was received by the French Minister of Marine.

"In welcoming the admiral, the minister said, 'Kronstadt and Toulon have severally witnessed the sympathy which exists between the French and the Russian peoples. Everywhere you will be received as the most welcome of friends.'

"'Our government and all France greet you and your comrades on your arrival as the representatives of a great and honorable nation.

"The admiral replied that he was unable to find language to express his feelings. 'The Russian fleet, and all Russia,' he said, 'will be grateful to you for this reception.

"After some further speeches, the admiral again, in taking leave of the minister, thanked him for his reception, and added, 'I cannot leave you without pronouncing the words which are written in the hearts of every Russian: 'Long live France!'" (*Siel'sky Vyestnik*, 1893, No. 41.)

Such was the reception at Toulon. In Paris the welcome and the festivities were still more extraordinary.

The following is a description, taken from the papers, of the reception in Paris:—

"All eyes are directed toward the Boulevard des Italiens, whence the Russian sailors are expected to emerge. At length, far away, the roar of a whole hurricane of shouts and cheers is heard. The roar grows louder, more distinct. The hurricane is evidently approaching. The crowd surges in the Place. The police press forward to clear the route to the Cercle Militaire, but the task is not easy. Among the spectators the pushing and scrambling baffles description. . . . At last the head of the cortège appears in the Place. At once arises a deafening shout of 'Vive la Russie! Vivent les Russes!'

"All heads are uncovered; spectators fill the windows

and balconies, they even cover the housetops, waving handkerchiefs, flags, hats, cheering enthusiastically, and flinging clouds of tricolor cockades from the upper windows. A sea of handkerchiefs, hats, and flags waves over the heads of the crowd below; a hundred thousand voices shout frantically, 'Vive la Russie! Vivent les Russes;' the throng make wild efforts to catch a glimpse of the dear guests, and try in every possible way to express their enthusiasm."

Another correspondent writes that the rapture of the crowd was like a delirium. A Russian journalist who was in Paris at the time thus describes the entry of the Russian marines:—

"It may truthfully be said that this event is of universal importance, astounding, sufficiently touching to produce tears, an elevating influence on the soul, making it throb with *that love which sees in men brothers, which hates blood, and violence, and the snatching of children from a beloved mother.* I have been in a kind of torpor for the last few hours. It seemed almost overpoweringly strange to stand in the terminus of the Lyons Railway, amid the representatives of the French government, in their uniforms embroidered with gold, amongst the municipal authorities in full dress, and to hear cries of 'Vive la Russie!' 'Vive le Tsar!' and our national anthem played again and again.

"Where am I? I reflected. What has happened? What magic current has united all these feelings, these aspirations, into one stream? Is not this the sensible presence of the God of love and of fraternity, the presence of the loftiest ideal descending in His supremest moments upon man?

"My soul is so full of something beautiful, pure, and

elevated that my pen is unable to express it. Words are
weak in comparison with what I saw and felt. It was not
rapture, the word is too commonplace; it was better than
rapture. More picturesque, deeper, happier, more various.
It is impossible to describe what took place at the Cercle
Militaire when Admiral Avellan appeared on the balcony
of the second story. Words here are of no avail. During
the 'Te Deum,' while the choir in the church was singing,
'O Lord, save Thy people,' through the open door were
blown the triumphal strains of the 'Marseillaise,' played
by the brass bands in the street.

"It produced an astounding, an inexpressible impression." (*Novoye Vremya* (New Time), Oct. 1893.)

II

ON ARRIVING in France the Russian sailors passed, during a fortnight, from one festivity to another, and during
or after each they ate, drank, and made speeches. Information as to where and what they ate and drank on
Wednesday, and where and what on Friday, and what
they said on these occasions, was purveyed by telegraph
to the whole of Russia.

The moment one of the Russian commanders had drunk
to the health of France, it became known to the whole
world; and the instant the Russian admiral had said, "I
drink to beautiful France," his effusion was transmitted
round the globe. Moreover, for such was the solicitude
of the papers that they commemorated not merely the
toasts, but the dishes, not even omitting the hors-
d'œuvres, or *zakouskas*, which were consumed.

For instance, the following menu was published, with

the comment that the dinner it represented was a work of art:—

Consommé de volailles; petits pâtés.
Mousse de homard parisienne.
Noisette de bœuf à la béarnaise.
Faisans à la Périgueux.
Casseroles de truffes au champagne.
Chaudfroid de volailles à la Toulouse.
Salade russe.
Croûte de fruits toulonnaise.
Parfaits à l'ananas.
Dessert.

In a second number it said: "From a culinary standpoint nothing better could have been desired. The menu was the following:—

Potage livonien et Saint-Germaïn.
Zéphyrs Nontua.
Esturgeon braisé moldave.
Selle de daguet grand veneur. ... etc.

And a following issue gave still another menu. With each was a minute description of the wines which the feasters imbibed—such vodka, such old Burgundy, Grand Moet, etc.

In an English journal a list of all the intoxicating liquor drunk during the festivities was given. The quantity mentioned was so enormous that one hardly believes it would have been possible that all the drunkards in France and Russia could account for so much in so short a time.

The speeches made were also published, but the menus were more varied than the speeches. The latter, without exception, always consisted of the same words in different combinations. The meaning of these words was always the same—We love each other tenderly, and are enraptured to be so tenderly in love. Our aim is not war, not a *revanche,* not the recovery of the lost provinces; our aim is only *peace,* the furtherance of *peace,* the security of *peace,* the tranquility and *peace* of Europe.

Long live the Russian emperor and empress! We love them, and we love *peace.* Long live the President of the Republic and his wife! We love them and we love *peace.* Long live France, Russia, their fleets and their armies! We love the army, and *peace,* and the commander of the Russian fleet.

The speeches concluded for the most part, like some popular ditty, with a refrain, "Toulon-Kronstadt," or "Kronstadt-Toulon." And the reiteration of the names of these places, where so many different dishes had been eaten and so many kinds of wine drunk, were pronounced as words which should stimulate the representatives of either nation to the noblest deeds—as words which require no commentary, being full of deep meaning in themselves.

"We love each other; we love peace. Kronstadt-Toulon!" What more can be said, especially to the sound of glorious music, performing at one and the same time two national anthems—one glorifying the Tsar and praying for him all possible good fortune, the other cursing all tsars and promising them destruction?

Those that expressed their sentiments of love especially well on these occasions received orders and rewards. Others, either for the same reason or from the exuberance of the feelings of the givers, were presented with articles of the strangest and most unexpected kind. The French fleet presented the Tsar with a sort of golden book in which, it seems, nothing was written— or, at least, nothing of any concern; and the Russian admiral received an aluminium plow covered with flowers, and many other trifles equally astonishing.

Moreover, all these strange acts were accompanied by still stranger religious ceremonies and public services such as one might suppose Frenchmen had long since become unaccustomed to.

Since the time of the Concordat scarcely so many prayers can have been offered as during this short period. All the French suddenly became extraordinarily religious, and carefully deposited in the rooms of the Russian mariners the very images which a short time previously they had as carefully removed from their schools as harmful tools of superstition; and they said prayers incessantly. The cardinals and bishops everywhere enjoined devotions, and themselves offered some of the strangest of prayers. Thus a bishop at Toulon, at the launch of a certain ironclad, addressed the God of Peace, letting it, however, at the same time be felt that he could communicate as readily, if the necessity arose, with the God of War.

"What its destination may be," said the bishop, alluding to the vessel, "God only knows. Will it vomit death from its dreadful maw? We do not know. But if, having to-day pleaded with the God of Peace, we may hereafter have to call upon the God of War, we may be sure that it will advance against the foe in rank with the powerful men-of-war whose crews have to-day entered into so near and fraternal union with ours. But let this contingency be forgotten, and let the present festival leave none but peaceful memories, like those of the Grand Duke Constantine, who was here at the launch of the "Quirinal," and may the friendship of France and Russia constitute these two nations the guardians of peace!"

At the same time tens of thousands of telegrams flew from Russia to France and from France to Russia.

French women greeted Russian women, and Russian women tendered their thanks to the French. A troupe of Russian actors greeted the French actors; the French actors replied that they had laid deep in their hearts the greetings of their Russian colleagues.

The Russian law students of some Russian town or other expressed their rapture to the French nation. General So-and-so thanked Madame This-and-that; Madame This-and-that assured General So-and-so of the ardor of her sentiments toward the Russian nation. Russian children wrote greetings in verse to French children; and French children replied in verse and prose. The Russian Minister of Education assured the French Minister of Education of the sudden amity toward France of all the children, clerks, and scientists in his department. The members of the Society for the Prevention of Cruelty to Animals expressed their warm attachment toward the French. The municipality of Kazan did the same.

The canon of Arrare conveyed to the most reverend protopresbyter of the court clergy the assurance that a deep affection toward Russia, his imperial majesty the Emperor Alexander III, and all the imperial family, exists in the hearts of all the French cardinals and bishops, and that the French and Russian clergy profess almost a similar faith, and alike worship the Holy Virgin. To this the most reverend protopresbyter replied that the prayers of the French clergy for the imperial family were joyously echoed by the hearts of all the Russian people, lovingly attached to the Tsar, and that as the Russian nation also worships the Holy Virgin, France may count upon it in life and death. The same kind of messages were sent by various generals, telegraph clerks, and dealers in groceries.

Every one sent congratulations to every one else, and thanked some one for something.

The excitement was so great that some extraordinary things were done; and yet no one remarked their strangeness, but on the contrary every one approved of them, was charmed with them, and as if afraid of being left behind, made haste to accomplish something of a similar kind in order not to be outdone by the rest.

If at times protests, pronounced or even written and printed, against this madness made their appearance, proving its unreasonableness, they were either hushed up or concealed.*

* Thus I am aware of the following protest which was made by Russian students and sent to Paris, but not accepted by any of the papers:—

"AN OPEN LETTER TO FRENCH STUDENTS

"A short time back a small body of Moscow law students, headed by its inspector, was bold enough to speak in the person of the university concerning the Toulon festivities.

"We, the representatives of the united students of various provinces, protest most emphatically against the pretensions of this body, and in substance against the interchange of greetings which has taken place between it and the French students. We likewise regard France with warm affection and deep respect, but we do so because we see in her a great nation which has always been in the past the introducer and announcer of the high ideals of freedom, equality, and brotherhood for all the world; and first also in the bold attempts to incorporate these high ideals into life. The better part of Russian youth has always been prepared to acclaim

Not to mention the millions of working-days spent in these festivities; the widespread drunkenness of all who took part in them, involving even those in command; not to speak of the senselessness of the speeches which were made, — the most insane and ruthless deeds were committed, and no one paid them any attention.

For instance, several score of people were crushed to

France as the foremost champion of a loftier future for mankind. But we do not regard such festivities as those of Kronstadt and Toulon as appropriate occasions for such greetings.

"On the contrary, these receptions represent a sad, but, we hope, a temporary condition—the treason of France to its former great historical rôle. The country which at one time invited all the world to break the chains of despotism, and offered its fraternal aid to any nation which might revolt in order to obtain its freedom, now burns incense before the Russian government, which systematically impedes the normal organic growth of a people's life, and relentlessly crushes without consideration every aspiration of Russian society toward light, freedom, and independence. The Toulon manifestations are one act of a drama in the antagonism between France and Germany created by Bismarck and Napoleon III.

"This antagonism keeps all Europe under arms, and gives the deciding vote in European affairs to Russian despotism, which has ever been the support of all that is arbitrary and absolute against freedom, and of tyrants against the tyrannized.

"A sense of pain for our country, of regret at the blindness of so great a portion of French society, these are the feelings called forth in us by these festivities.

"We are persuaded that the younger generation in France is not allured by national Chauvinism, and that, ready to struggle for that better social condition toward which humanity is advancing, it will know how to interpret present events, and what attitude to adopt toward them. We hope that our determined protest will find an echo in the hearts of the French youth.

(Signed) "The United Council of Twenty-four Federate Societies of Moscow Students."

death, and no one found it necessary to record the fact.

One correspondent wrote that he had been informed at a ball that there was scarcely a woman in Paris who would not have been ready to forget her duties to satisfy the desire of any of the Russian sailors.

And all this passed unremarked as something quite in the order of things. There were also cases of unmistakable insanity brought about by the excitement.

Thus one woman, having put on a dress composed of the colors of the Franco-Russian flags, awaited on a bridge the arrival of the Russian sailors, and shouting "Vive la Russie," threw herself into the river, and was drowned.

In general the women on all these occasions played the leading part, and even directed the men. Besides the throwing of flowers and various little ribbons and the presenting of gifts and addresses, the French women in the streets threw themselves into the arms of the Russian sailors and kissed them.

Some women brought their children, for some reason or other, to be kissed, and when the Russian sailors had granted this request, all present were transported with joy and shed tears.

This strange excitement was so contagious that, as one correspondent relates, a Russian sailor who appeared to be in perfect health, after having witnessed these exciting scenes for a fortnight, jumped overboard in the middle of the day, and swam about, crying "Long live France." When pulled out of the water, and questioned as to his conduct, he replied that he had vowed to swim round his ship in honor of France.

Thus the unthwarted excitement grew and grew, like a ball of snow, and finally attained such dimensions that not alone those on the spot, or merely nervously predisposed persons, but strong, healthy men were affected by the general strain and were betrayed into an abnormal condition of mind.

I remember even that whilst reading distractedly a description of these festivities, I was suddenly overcome by strong emotion, and was almost on the verge of tears, having to check with an effort this expression of my feelings.

III

A PROFESSOR of psychiatry, Sikorsky by name, not long ago described in the *Kief University Review* what he calls the psychopathic epidemic of Malevanshchina, which he studied in the district of Vasilkof. The essence of this epidemic, according to Sikorsky, was that the peasants of certain villages, under the influence of their leader, Malevanni, became convinced that the end of the world was at hand; in consequence of which they changed their mode of life, began to dispose of their property, to wear gay clothing, to eat and drink of the best, and ceased to work. The professor considered this condition abnormal. He says:

"Their remarkable good humor often attained to exaltation, a condition of gaiety lacking all external motives. They were sentimentally inclined, polite to excess, talkative, excitable, tears of happiness being readily summoned to their eyes, and disappearing without leaving a trace. They sold the necessities of life in order to buy parasols, silk handkerchiefs, and similar articles, which, however, they only wore as ornaments. They ate a great quantity of sweets. Their condition of mind was always joyous, they led a perfectly idle life, visiting one another and

walking about together. . . . When chided for the insanity
of their conduct and their idleness, they replied invariably
with the same phrase: 'If it pleases me, I will work; if it
does not, why compel myself to?' "

The learned professor regards the condition of these
people as a well-defined psychopathic epidemic, and in
advising the government to adopt measures to prevent
its extension, concludes, "Malevanshchina is the cry of
a sick population, a prayer for deliverance from drunkenness, and for improved educational and sanitary conditions."

But if malevanshchina is the cry of a sick population
for deliverance from inebriety and from pernicious social
conditions, what a terrible clamor of a sick people, and
what a petition for a rescue from the effects of wine and
of a false social existence, is this new disease which
appeared in Paris with such fearful suddenness, infect-
ing the greater part of the urban population of France,
and almost the entire governmental, privileged, and civilized classes of Russia?

But if we admit that danger exists in the psychical
conditions of malevanshchina, and that the government
did well in following the professor's advice, by confin-
ing some of the leaders of the malevanshchina in asylums
and monasteries, and by banishing others into distant
places; how much more dangerous must we consider this
new epidemic which has appeared in Toulon and Paris,
and spread thence throughout Russia and France, and
how much more needful is it that society—if the government refuse to interfere—should take decisive measures
to prevent the epidemic from spreading?

The analogy between the two diseases is complete.
The same remarkable good humor, passing into a vague

and joyous ecstasy, the same sentimental, exaggerated politeness, loquacity, emotional weeping, without reason for its commencement or cessation, the same festal mood, the same promenading and paying calls, the same wearing of gorgeous clothes and fancy for choice food, the same misty and senseless speeches, the same indolence, the same singing and music, the same direction on the part of the women, the same clownish state of *attitudes passionnées*, which Sikorsky observed, and which corresponds, as I understand it, with the various unnatural physical attitudes adopted by people during triumphal receptions, acclamations, and after-dinner speeches.

The resemblance is absolute. The difference, an enormous one for the society in which these things take place, is merely that in one case it is the madness of a few scores of poor peaceful country people who, living on their own small earnings, cannot do any violence to their neighbors, and infect others only by personal and vocal communication of their condition; whereas in the other case it is the madness of millions of people who possess immense sums of money and means of violence—rifles, cannon, fortresses, ironclads, melinite, dynamite—and having, moreover, at their disposal the most effective means for communicating their insanity: the post, telegraph, telephone, the entire press, and every class of magazine, which print the infection with the utmost haste, and distribute it throughout the world.

Another difference is that the former not only remain sober, but abstain from all intoxicating drinks, while the latter are in a constant state of semi-drunkenness which they do their best to foster.

Hence for the society in which such epidemics take place, the difference between that at Kief, when, according to Sikorsky, no violence nor manslaughter was recorded, and that of Paris, where in one procession more than twenty women were crushed to death, is equivalent to that between the falling of a small piece of smoldering coal from the fireplace upon the floor, and a fire which has already obtained possession of the floors and walls of the house.

At its worst the result of the epidemic at Kief will be that the peasants of a millionth part of Russia may spend the earnings of their own labor, and be unable to meet the government taxes; but the consequences of the Paris-Toulon epidemic, which has affected people who have great power, immense sums of money, weapons of violence, and means for the propagation of their insanity, may and must be terrible.

IV

ONE MAY listen with compassion to the mouthings of a feeble, old, and unarmed idiot in his cap and nightshirt, not contradicting and even humorously acquiescing with him; but when a crowd of able-bodied madmen escape from confinement, armed to the teeth with knives, swords, and revolvers, wild with excitement, waving their murderous weapons, one not only ceases to acquiesce, but one is unable to feel secure for an instant.

It is the same with the condition of excitement which has been evoked by the French festivities and which is now carrying French and Russian society away. Those who have succumbed to this psychopathic epidemic are the masters of the most terrible weapons of slaughter and destruction.

It is true that it was constantly proclaimed in all the speeches, in all the toasts pronounced at these festivities, and in all the articles upon them, that the object of what was taking place was the establishment of peace. Even the partisans of war, the Russian correspondent previously cited amongst them, speak not of any hatred toward the conquerors of the lost provinces, but of a love which somehow hates.

However, we are well aware of the cunning of those that suffer from mental diseases, and this constant iteration of a desire for peace, and silence as to the sentiments in every man's mind, is precisely a threat of the worst significance.

In his reply at the dinner at the Elysée the Russian ambassador said:—

"Before proposing a toast to which every one will respond from the depths of his soul, not only those within these walls, but also, and with the same enthusiasm, all those whose hearts are at the present moment beating in unison with ours, far away or around us in great and beautiful France, as in Russia, permit me to offer an expression of the deepest gratitude for the welcome, addressed by you to the admiral whom the Tsar deputed to return the Kronstadt visit. In the high position which you occupy, your words express the full meaning of the glorious and peaceful festivities which are now being celebrated with such remarkable unanimity, loyalty, and sincerity."

The same entirely baseless reference to peace may be found in the speech of the French president.

"The links of love which unite Russia and France," he said, "were strengthened two years ago by the touching manifestations of which our fleet was the object at Kronstadt, and are becoming every day more binding; and the *honest* interchange of our friendly sentiments must inspire all those who have at heart the welfare of peace, security, and confidence," etc.

In both speeches the benefits of peace, and of peaceful festivities, are alluded to quite unexpectedly and without any occasion.

The same thing is observable in the interchange of telegrams between the Russian emperor and the president of the Republic.

The emperor telegraphs:—

"At the moment when the Russian fleet is leaving France it is my ardent wish to express to you how touched and gratified I am by the chivalrous and splendid reception which my sailors have everywhere experienced on French soil. The expressions of warm sympathy which have been manifested once again with so much eloquence will add a fresh bond to those which unite the two countries, and will, I trust, contribute to strengthen the general *peace* which is the object of our most constant efforts and desires."

The French president replies:—

"The telegram, for which I thank your majesty, reached me when on the point of leaving Toulon to return to Paris.

"The magnificent fleet on which I had the great satisfaction of saluting the Russian pennant in French waters, the cordial and spontaneous reception which your brave sailors have everywhere received in France, prove gloriously once again the sincere sympathies which unite our two countries. They show at the same time a deep faith in the beneficent influence which may weld together two great nations devoted to the cause of *peace*."

Again, in both telegrams, without the slightest occasion,

are allusions to peace which have nothing at all to do with the reception of the sailors.

There is no single speech or article in which it is not said that the purpose of all these orgies is the peace of Europe. At a dinner given by the representatives of the Russian press, all speak of peace. M. Zola, who, a short time previously, had written that war was inevitable, and even serviceable; M. de Vogüé, who more than once has stated the same in print—say, neither of them, a word as to war, but speak only of peace. The sessions of parliament open with speeches upon the past festivities; the speakers mention that such festivities are an assurance of peace to Europe.

It is as if a man should come into a peaceful company, and commence energetically to assure every one present that he has not the least intention of knocking out any one's teeth, blackening their eyes, or breaking their arms, but has only the most peaceful ideas for passing the evening.

"But no one doubts it," one is inclined to say, "and if you really have such evil intentions, at least do not presume to mention them."

In many of the articles describing the festivities a naïve satisfaction is clearly expressed that no one during them alluded to what it was determined, by silent consent, to hide from everybody, and that only one incautious fellow, who was immediately removed by the police, voiced what all had in their minds by shouting, "A bas l'Allemagne!"—Down with Germany!

In the same way children are often so delighted at being able to conceal an escapade that their very high spirits betray them.

Why, indeed, be so glad that no one said anything about war, if the subject were not uppermost in our minds?

V

No ONE is thinking of war; only milliards are being spent upon preparations for it, and millions of men are under arms in France and Russia.

"But all this is done to insure peace. *Si vis pacem para bellum. L'empire c'est la paix. La République c'est la paix.*"

But if such be the case, why are the military advantages of a Franco-Russian alliance in the event of a war with Germany not only explained in every paper and magazine published for a so-called educated people, but also in the *Village Messenger*, a paper published for the people by the Russian government? Why is it inculcated to this unfortunate people, cheated by its own government, that "to be in friendly relations with France is profitable to Russia, because if, unexpectedly, the before-mentioned states (Germany, Austria, and Italy) made up their minds to declare war with Russia, then though with God's help she might be able to withstand them by herself, and defeat even so considerable an alliance, the feat would not be an easy one, and great sacrifices and losses would be entailed by success." (*Siel'sky Viestnik*, 1893, No. 43.)

And why in all French schools is history taught from the primer of M. Lavisse (twenty-first edition, 1889,) in which the following is inserted:—

"Since the insurrection of the Commune was put down

France has had no further troubles. The day following the war she again resumed work. She paid Germany without difficulty the enormous war indemnity of five milliards.

"But France lost her military renown during the war of 1870. She lost part of her territory. More than fifteen thousand inhabitants of our departments of the Upper Rhine, Lower Rhine, and the Moselle who were good Frenchmen have been compelled to become Germans. But they are not resigned to their fate. They detest Germany; they continue to hope that they may once more be Frenchmen.

"But Germany appreciates its victory, and it is a great country, all the inhabitants of which sincerely love their fatherland, and whose soldiers are brave and well disciplined. In order to recover from Germany what she took from us we must be good citizens and soldiers. It is to make you good soldiers that your teachers instruct you in the history of France.

"The history of France proves that in our country the sons have always avenged the disasters of their fathers.

"Frenchmen in the time of Charles VII, avenged the defeat of their fathers at Crécy, at Poitiers, at Agincourt.

"It is for you, boys being educated in our schools, to avenge the defeat of your fathers at Sedan and at Metz.

"It is your duty—the great duty of your life. You must ever bear that in mind."

At the foot of the page is a series of questions upon the preceding paragraphs. The questions are the following:—

"What has France lost by losing part of her territory?"

"How many Frenchmen have become Germans by the loss of this territory?"

"Do these Frenchmen love Germany?"

"What must we do to recover some day what Germany has taken from us?"

In addition to these there are certain "Reflections on Book VII.," where it is said that "the children of France must not forget her defeat of 1870"; that they must bear on their hearts "the burden of this remembrance," but that "this memory must not discourage them, on the contrary, it must excite their courage."

So that if, in official speeches, peace is mentioned with such emphasis, behind the scenes the lawfulness, profit, and necessity of war is incessantly urged upon the people, the rising generation, and in general upon all Frenchmen and Russians.

"We do not think of war, we are only working for peace."

One feels inclined to inquire, *"Qui diable trompe-t-on ici?"* if the question were worth asking, and it were not too evident who are the unhappy deluded ones.

The deluded ones are always the same eternally deluded, foolish working-folk, those who, with horny hands, make all these ships, forts, arsenals, barracks, cannon, steamers, harbors, piers, palaces, halls, and places with triumphal arches, and who print all these books and papers, and who procure and transport all these pheasants and ortolans and oysters and wines which are to be eaten and drunk by those who are brought up, educated, and maintained by the working-class, and who, in turn, deceive and prepare for it the worst disasters.

Always the same good-natured, foolish working-folk, who, yawning, showing their white, healthy teeth, childishly and naïvely pleased at the sight of admirals and presidents in full dress, of flags waving above their heads, and fireworks, and triumphal music; for whom, before they can look round, there will be no more admirals, or presidents, or flags, or music; but only a damp and empty field of battle, cold, hunger, and pain; before them a murderous enemy; behind, relentless officers preventing their escape; blood, wounds, putrefying bodies, and senseless, unnecessary death.

While, on the other hand, those who have been made much of at Paris and Toulon will be seated, after a good dinner, with glasses of choice wine beside them and cigars between their teeth, in a warm cloth tent, marking upon a map with pins such and such places upon which a certain amount of "food for cannon" is to be expended —"food" composed of those same foolish people—in order finally to capture this fortified place or the other, and to obtain a certain little ribbon or grade.

VI

"But nothing of the kind exists; we have no bellicose intentions," it is replied. "All that has happened is the expression of mutual sympathy between two nations. What can be amiss in the triumphal and honorable reception of the representatives of a friendly nation by the representatives of another nation? What can be wrong in this, even if we admit that the alliance is significant of a protection from a dangerous neighbor who threatens Europe with war?"

It is wrong, because it is false—a most evident and insolent falsehood, inexcusable, iniquitous.

It is false, this suddenly begotten love of Russians for French and French for Russians. And it is false, this insinuation of our dislike to the Germans, and our distrust of them. And more false still is it that the aim of all these indecent and insane orgies is supposed to be the preservation of the peace of Europe.

We are all aware that we neither felt before, nor have felt since, any special love for the French, or any animosity toward the Germans.

We are told that Germany has projects against Russia, that the Triple Alliance threatens to destroy our peace and that of Europe, and that our alliance with France will secure an equal balance of power and be a guarantee of peace. But the assertion is so manifestly stupid that I am ashamed to refute it seriously. For this to be so —that is, for the alliance to guarantee peace—it would be necessary to make the Powers mathematically equal. If the preponderance were on the side of the Franco-Russian alliance, the danger would be the same, or even greater, because if Wilhelm, who is at the head of the Triple Alliance, is a menace to peace, France, who cannot be reconciled to the loss of her provinces, would be a still greater menace. The Triple Alliance was called an alliance of peace, whereas for us it proved an alliance of war. Just so now the Franco-Russian alliance can only be viewed truly as an alliance for war.

Moreover, if peace depend upon an even balance of power, how are those units to be defined between which the balance is to be established?

England asserts that the Franco-Russian alliance is a menace to her security, which necessitates a new alliance on her part. And into precisely how many units is Europe to be divided that this even balance may be attained?

Indeed, if there be such a necessity for equilibrium, then in every society of men a man stronger than his fellows is already dangerous, and the rest must join defensive alliances in order to resist him.

It is asked, "What is wrong in France and Russia expressing their mutual sympathies for the preservation of peace?" The expression is wrong because it is false, and a falsehood once pronounced never ends harmlessly.

The devil was a murderer and the father of lies. Falsehood always leads to murder; and most of all in such a case as this.

Just what is now taking place occurred before our last Turkish war, when a sudden love on our part was supposed to have been awakened toward certain Slavonic brethren none had heard of for centuries; though French, Germans, and English always have been, and are, incomparably nearer and dearer to us than a few Bulgarians, Servians, or Montenegrins. And on that occasion just the same enthusiasm, receptions, and solemnities were to be observed, blown into existence by men like Aksakof and Katkof, who are already mentioned in Paris as model patriots. Then, as now, the suddenly begotten love of Russ for Slav was only a thing of words.

Then in Moscow as now in Paris, when the affair began, people ate, drank, talked nonsense to one another, were much affected by their noble feelings, spoke of union and of peace, passing over in silence the main business—the project against Turkey.

The press goaded on the excitement, and by degrees the government took a hand in the game. Servia revolted. Diplomatic notes began to circulate and semiofficial articles to appear. The press lied, invented, and fumed more and more, and in the end Alexander II., who really did not desire war, was obliged to consent to it; and what we know took place, the loss of hundreds of thousands of innocent men, and the brutalizing and befooling of millions.

What took place at Paris and Toulon, and has since been fomented by the press, is evidently leading to a like or a worse calamity.

At first, in the same manner, to the strains of the "Marseillaise" and "God save the Tsar," certain generals and ministers drink to France and Russia in honor of various regiments and fleets; the press publishes its falsehoods; idle crowds of wealthy people, not knowing how to apply their strength and time, chatter patriotic speeches, stirring up animosity against Germany; and in the end, however peaceful Alexander III may be, circumstances will so combine that he will be unable to avoid war, which will be demanded by all who surround him, by the press, and, as always seems in such cases, by the entire public opinion of the nation. And before we can look round, the usual ominous absurd proclamation will appear in the papers:—

"We, by God's grace, the autocratic great Emperor of all Russia, King of Poland, Grand Duke of Finland, etc., etc., proclaim to all our true subjects, that, for the welfare of these our beloved subjects, bequeathed by God into our care, we have found it our duty before God to send them to slaughter. God be with us."

The bells will peal, long-haired men will dress in golden sacks and pray for successful slaughter. And the old story will begin again, the awful customary acts.

The editors of the daily press, happy in the receipt of an increased income, will begin virulently to stir men up to hatred and manslaughter in the name of patriotism. Manufacturers, merchants, contractors for military stores will hurry joyously about their business, in the hope of double receipts.

All sorts of government functionaries will buzz about, foreseeing a possibility of purloining something more than usual. The military authorities will hurry hither and thither, drawing double pay and rations, and with the expectation of receiving for the slaughter of other men various silly little ornaments which they so highly prize, as ribbons, crosses, orders, and stars. Idle ladies and gentlemen will make a great fuss, entering their names in advance for the Red Cross Society, and ready to bind up the wounds of those whom their husbands and brothers will mutilate, and they will imagine that in so doing they are performing a most Christian work.

And, smothering despair within their souls by songs, licentiousness, and wine, men will trail along, torn from peaceful labor, from their wives, mothers, and children, —hundreds of thousands of simple-minded, good-natured men with murderous weapons in their hands—anywhere they may be driven.

They will march, freeze, hunger, suffer sickness, and die from it, or finally come to some place where they will be slain by thousands, or kill thousands themselves with no reason—men whom they have never seen before, and who neither have done nor could do them any mischief.

And when the number of sick, wounded, and killed becomes so great that there are not hands enough left to pick them up, and when the air is so infected with the putrefying scent of the "food for cannon" that even the authorities find it disagreeable, a truce will be made, the wounded will be picked up anyhow, the sick will be brought in and huddled together in heaps, the killed will be covered with earth and lime, and once more all the crowd of deluded men will be led on and on till those who have devised the project weary of it, or till those who thought to find it profitable receive their spoil.

And so once more men will be made savage, fierce, and brutal, and love will wane in the world, and the Christianizing of mankind, which has already begun, will lapse for scores and hundreds of years. And so once more the men who reaped profit from it all will assert with assurance that since there has been a war there must needs have been one, and that other wars must follow, and they will again prepare future generations for a continuance of slaughter, depraving them from their childhood.

VII

HENCE, when such patriotic demonstrations as the Toulon festivities take place—though they only constrain from a distance the wills of men, and bind them to those accustomed villainies which are always the outcome of patriotism—every one who realizes the true import of these festivities cannot but protest against what is tacitly included in them. And, therefore, when those gentlemen, the journalists, assert that every Russian sympathizes with what took place at Kronstadt, Toulon, and Paris, and that this alliance for life and death is sealed by the desire of the entire nation; and when the Russian Minister of Education assures the French minister that all his brigade of children, clerks, and scientists share his feelings; or when the commander of a Russian squadron assures the French that all Russia will be grateful to them for their reception; and when protopresbyters answer for their flock, and assert that the prayers of Frenchmen for the welfare of the imperial house are joyously echoed in the hearts of the Russian *Tsar-loving* nation; and when the Russian ambassador in Paris, as the representative of the Russian people, states, after a dish of *ortolans à la soubise*, or *lagopèdes glacés*, with a glass of Grand Moët champagne in his hand, that all Russian hearts, beating in unison with his heart, are filled with sudden and exclusive love for *la belle France*—then we, men not yet idiots, regard it as a sacred duty, not only for ourselves, but for tens of millions of Russians, to protest most energetically against such a statement, and to affirm that our hearts do not beat in unison with those of these gentlemen—the journalists, ministers of education, commanders of squadrons, protopresbyters, and ambassadors; but on the contrary, are filled with indignation and disgust at the pernicious falsehood and wrong which, consciously or unconsciously, they are spreading by their words and deeds. Let them drink as much Moët as they please; let them write articles and make speeches from themselves and for themselves; but we who regard ourselves as Christians, cannot admit that what all these gentlemen write and say is binding upon us.

This we cannot admit because we know what lies hidden beneath at these tipsy ecstasies, speeches, and embracings, which resemble, not a confirmation of peace as we are assured, but rather those orgies and revelings to which criminals are addicted when planning their joint crimes.

VIII

ABOUT four years ago the first swallow of this Toulon spring, a well-known French agitator for a war with Germany, came to Russia to prepare the way for the

Franco-Russian alliance, and paid a visit to us in the country. He came to us when we were all engaged cutting the hay crop, and when we had come in to lunch and made our guest's acquaintance, he began at once to tell us how he had fought, been taken prisoner, made his escape, and finally pledged himself as a patriot—a fact of which he was evidently proud—never to cease agitating for a war with Germany until the boundaries and glory of France had been reëstablished.

All our guest's arguments as to the necessity of an alliance of France with Russia in order to reconstruct the former boundary, power, and glory of his country, and to assure our security against the evil intentions of Germany, had no success in our circle.

To his arguments that France could never settle down until she had recaptured her lost provinces, we replied that neither could Russia be at rest till she had been avenged for Jena, and that if the *revanche* of France should happen to be successful, Germany in her turn would desire revenge, and so on without end.

To his arguments that it was the duty of France to recover the sons that had been snatched from her, we replied that the condition of the majority of the working population of Alsace-Lorraine under the rule of Germany had probably suffered no change for the worse since the days when it was ruled by France, and the fact that some of the Alsatians preferred to be registered as Frenchmen and not as Germans, and that he, our guest, wished to reëstablish the fame of the French arms, was no reason to renew the awful calamities which a war would cause, or even to sacrifice a single human life.

To his arguments that it was very well for us to talk like that, who had never endured what France had, and

that we would speak very differently if the Baltic provinces, or Poland, were to be taken from us, we replied
that, even from the imperial standpoint, the loss of the
Baltic provinces or Poland could in no wise be considered
as a calamity, but rather as an advantage, as it would
decrease the necessity of armed forces and State expenses;
and that from the Christian point of view one can never
admit the justice of war, as war demands murder; while
Christianity not only prohibits all killing, but demands
of us the betterment of all men, regarding all men as
brothers, without distinction of nationalities.

A Christian nation, we said, which engages in war,
ought, in order to be logical, not only to take down the
cross from its church steeples, turn the churches to some
other use, give the clergy other duties, having first prohibited the preaching of the Gospel, but also ought to
abandon all the requirements of morality which flow
from the Christian law.

"*C'est à prendre ou à laisser,*" we said. Until Christianity be abolished it is only possible to attract mankind
toward war by cunning and fraud, as now practised. We
who see this fraud and cunning cannot give way to it.

Since, during this conversation, there was no music
or champagne, or anything to confuse our senses, our
guest merely shrugged his shoulders, and, with the amia-
bility of a Frenchman, said he was very grateful for the
cordial welcome he had experienced in our house, but
was sorry that his views were not as well received.

IX

AFTER this conversation we went out into the hay-field, where our guest, hoping to find the peasants more in sympathy with his ideas, asked me to translate to an old, sickly muzhik, Prokophy by name—who, though suffering from severe hernia, was still working energetically, mowing with us—his plan for putting pressure on Germany from both sides, the Russian and the French.

The Frenchman explained this to him graphically, by pressing with his white fingers on either side of the mower's coarse shirt, which was damp with perspiration.

I well remember Prokophy's good-humored smile of astonishment when I explained the meaning of the Frenchman's words and action. He evidently took the proposal to squeeze the Germans as a joke, not conceiving that a full-grown and educated man would quietly and soberly speak of war as being desirable.

"Well, but, if we squeeze him from both sides," he answered, smiling, giving one pleasantry for another, as he supposed, "he will be fixed too fast to move. We shall have to let him out somewhere."

I translated this answer to my guest.

"Tell him we love the Russians," he said.

These words astonished Prokophy even more than the proposal to squeeze the Germans, and awoke in him a certain feeling of suspicion.

"Whence does he come?" he inquired.

I replied that he was a wealthy Frenchman.

"And what business has brought him here?" he asked.

When I replied that the Frenchman had come in the hope of persuading the Russians to enter into an alliance with the French in the event of a war with Germany, Porkophy was clearly entirely displeased, and, turning to the women who were sitting close by on a cock of hay, called out to them, in an angry voice, which unwittingly displayed the feelings which had been aroused in him, to go and stack the rest of the hay.

"Well, you crows," he cried, "you are all asleep! Go and stack! A nice time for squeezing the Germans! Look there, the hay has not been turned yet, and it looks as if we might have to begin on the corn on Wednesday." And then, as if afraid of having offended our visitor, he added, smiling good-naturedly and showing his worn teeth, "Better come and work with us, and bring the Germans too. And when we have finished we will have some feasting, and make the Germans join us. They are men like ourselves."

And so saying Prokophy took his sinewy hand from the fork of the rake on which he had been leaning, lifted it on to his shoulder, and went to join the women.

"Oh, le brave homme!" exclaimed the polite Frenchman, laughing. And thus was concluded for the time his diplomatic mission to the Russian people.

The different aspects of these two men—one shining with freshness and high spirits, dressed in a coat of the latest cut, displaying with his white hands, which had never known labor, how the Germans should be squeezed; the other coarse, with haydust in his hair, shrunken with hard work, sunburnt, always weary, and, notwithstanding his severe complaint, always at work: Prokophy, with his fingers swollen with toil, in his large home-made trousers, worn-out shoes, and a great heap of hay upon his shoulders, moving slowly along with that careful economy of stride common to all workingmen—the different aspects of these two men made much clear to me at the time, which has come back to me vividly since the Toulon-Paris festivities.

One of them represented the class fed and maintained by the people's labor, who in return use up that people as "food for cannon"; while the other was that very "food for cannon" which feeds and maintains those who afterwards so dispose of it.

X

"But France has lost two provinces—children torn from a beloved mother. And Russia cannot permit Germany to make laws for her and rob her of her historical mission in the East, nor risk the chance of losing, like France, her Baltic provinces, Poland, or the Caucasus.

"And Germany cannot hear of the loss of those advantages which she has won at such a sacrifice. And England will yield to none her naval supremacy."

After such word it is generally supposed that a Frenchman, Russian, German, or Englishman should be ready to sacrifice anything, to regain his lost provinces, establish his influence in the East, secure national unity, or keep his control of the seas.

It is assumed that patriotism is, to start with, a sentiment natural to all men, and that, secondly, it is so highly moral a sentiment that it should be induced in all who have it not.

But neither one nor the other is true. I have lived half-a-century amid the Russian people, and in the great mass of laborers, during that period, I have never once seen or heard any manifestation or expression of this sentiment of patriotism, unless one should count those patriotic phrases which are learned by heart in the army, and repeated from books by the more superficial and degraded of the populace. I have never heard from the people any expression of patriotism, but, on the contrary, I have often listened to expressions of indifference, and even contempt, for any kind of patriotism, by the most venerable and serious of working-folk. I have observed the same thing amongst the laboring classes of other nations, and have received confirmation from educated Frenchmen, Germans, and Englishmen, from observation of their respective working-classes.

The working-classes are too much occupied support-ing the lives of themselves and of their families, a duty which engrosses all their attention, to be able to take an interest in those political questions which are the chief motives of patriotism.

Questions as to the influence of Russia in the East, the unity of Germany, the recovery by France of her lost provinces, or the concession of such a part of one state to another state, do not interest the working-man, not only because, for the most part, he is unacquainted with the circumstances which evoke such questions, but also because the interests of his life are altogether inde-pendent of the state and of politics. For a laboring man is altogether indifferent where such-and-such a frontier may be established, to whom Constantinople may belong, whether Saxony or Brunswick shall or shall not be a member of the German Federation, whether Australia or Montebello shall belong to England, or even to what gov-ernment they may have to pay taxes, or into what army send their sons.

But it is always a matter of importance to them to know what taxes they will have to pay, how long to serve in the army, how much to pay for their land, and how much to receive for their labor—all questions entirely independent of State and political interest. This is the reason why, notwithstanding the energetic means employed by governments to inculcate patriotism, which is not natural to the people, and to destroy socialism, the latter continues to penetrate further into the laboring masses; whereas patriotism, though so assiduously inculcated, not only makes no headway, but disappears constantly more and more, and is now solely a possession of the upper classes, to whom it is profitable. And if, as sometimes happens, that patriotism takes hold of the masses as lately in Paris, it is only when the masses have been subjected to some special hypnotic influence by the government and ruling class, and such patriotism lasts only as long as the influence is continued.

Thus, for instance, in Russia, where patriotism, in the form of love for and devotion to the faith, Tsar, and country, is instilled into the people, with extraordinary energy by every means in the hands of the government, —the Church, schools, literature, and every sort of pompous ceremony—the Russian working-man, the hundred millions of the working people, in spite of their undeserved reputation for devotion to faith, Tsar, and country, are a people singularly unduped by patriotism and such devotion.

They are not, for the most part, even acquainted with the orthodox official faith to which they are supposed to be so attached, and whenever they do make acquaintance with it they leave it and become rationalists—that is, they adopt a creed which cannot be attacked and need not be defended; and notwithstanding the constant, energetic insistence of devotion to the Tsar, they regard in

general all authority founded on violence either with
condemnation or with total indifference; their country,
if by that word anything is meant outside their village and
district, they either do not realize at all, or, if they do,
would make no distinctions between it and other countries. So that where formerly Russians would emigrate
into Austria or Turkey, they now go with equal indifference in Russia or outside of Russia, in Turkey, or China.

XI

AN OLD friend of mine, who passed the winters alone
in the country while his wife, whom he visited from
time to time, lived in Paris, often conversed during the
long autumn evening with his steward, an illiterate but
shrewd and venerable peasant, who used to come to him
in the evening to receive his orders; and my friend once
mentioned amongst other things the advantages of the
French system of government compared with our own.
The occasion was a short time previous to the last Polish
insurrection and the intervention of the French government in our affairs. At that time the patriotic Russian press
was burning with indignation at this interference, and
so excited the ruling classes that our political relations
became very strained, and there were rumors of an
approaching war with France.

My friend, having read the papers, explained to this
peasant the misunderstanding between France and
Russia; and coming under the influence of the journal,
and being an old military man, said that were war to
be declared he would reënter the army and fight with
France. At that time a *revanche* against the French

for Sevastopol was considered a necessity by patriotic Russians.

"Why should we fight with them?" asked the peasant.

"Why, how can we permit France to dictate to us?"

"Well, you said yourself that they were better governed than we, replied the peasant quite seriously; "let them arrange things as well in Russia."

And my friend told me that he was so taken aback by this argument that he did not know what to reply, and burst into laughter, as one who has just awakened from a delusive dream.

The same argument, may be heard from every Russian workman if he has not come under the hypnotic influence of the government. People speak of the Russian's love for his faith, Tsar, and country; and yet a single community of peasants could not be found in Russia which would hesitate one moment had they to choose of two places for emigration—one in Russia, under the "Father-Tsar" (as he is termed only in books), and the holy orthodox faith of his idolized country, but with less or worse land; and the other without the "White-father-Tsar," and without the orthodox faith, somewhere outside Russia, in Prussia, China, Turkey, Austria, only with more and better land—the choice would be in favor of the latter, as we have often had opportunity to observe.

The question as to who shall govern him (and he knows that under any government he will be equally robbed) is for the Russian peasant of infinitely less significance than the question (setting aside even the matter of water), Is the clay soft and will cabbage thrive in it?

But it might be supposed that this indifference on the part of Russians arises from the fact that any government under which they might live would be an improvement on their own, because in Europe there is none worse. But that is not so; for as far as I can judge, one may witness the same indifference among English, Dutch, and German peasants emigrating to America, and among the various nationalities which have emigrated to Russia.

Passing from the control of one European government to another—from Turkish to Austrian, or from French to German—alters so slightly the position of the genuine working-classes, that in no case would the change excite any discontent, if only it be not effected artificially by the government and the ruling classes.

XII

USUALLY, FOR a proof of the existence of patriotism one is referred to the display of patriotic sentiment by the people on certain solemn occasions, as in Russia, at the coronation of the Tsar, or his reception after the railway accident on October 29; in France, on the proclamation of war with Prussia; in Germany at the rejoicings after the war; or during the Franco-Russian festivities.

But one ought to take into consideration the way these manifestations are arranged. In Russia, for example, during every progress of the sovereign, delegates are commanded to appear from every peasant community, and materials requisitioned for the reception and welcome of the Tsar.

The enthusiasm of the crowd is for the most part artificially prepared by those who require it, and the degree of enthusiasm exhibited by the crowd is only a clue to the refinements in the art of those who organize such exhibitions. The art has been practised ·for long, hence the specialists in it have acquired great adroitness in its preparation.

When Alexander II was still heir apparent, and commanded, as is usual, the Preobrazhensky Regiment, he once paid an after-dinner visit to the regiment, which was in camp at the time.

As soon as his calash came in sight, the soldiers, who were only in their shirts at the time, ran out to welcome their "august commander," as the phrase is, with such enthusiasm, that they all followed the carriage, and many, while running, made the sign of the cross, gazing upon the prince. All who witnessed this reception were deeply moved by this simple attachment of the Russian soldier to the Tsar and his son, and by the genuinely religious, and evidently spontaneous, enthusiasm expressed in their faces, movements, and especially by the signing of the cross.

And yet all this had been artificially prepared in the following manner:—

After a review on the previous day the prince told the commander of the brigade that he would revisit the regiment on the following day.

"When are we to expect your imperial highness?"

"Probably in the evening, only, pray, do not expect me: and let there be no preparation."

As soon as the prince was gone, the commander of the brigade called all the captains of companies together, and gave orders that on the following day all the men should have clean shirts, and the moment the prince's carriage should come in sight (special signalmen were to be sent out to give warning of it) every one should run to meet it, and with shouts of "Hurrah!" run after it, and, moreover, that every tenth man in each company should cross himself whilst running. The color-sergeants drew up the companies, and told off every tenth man to cross himself. "One, two, three, . . . eight, nine, ten. Sidorenko, you are to cross yourself. One, two, three, . . . Ivanof, to cross yourself."

Thus, what was ordered was accomplished, and an impression of spontaneous enthusiasm was produced upon the prince and upon all who saw it, even upon the soldiers and officers, and even upon the commander of the brigade himself.

The same thing is done, though less peremptorily, wherever patriotic manifestations take place. Thus the Franco-Russian festivities, which strike us as the spontaneous outcome of the nation's feelings, did not happen of their own accord, but were very cleverly prepared and arranged for by the foresight of the French government.

As soon as the advent of the Russian fleet was settled, "at once," I again quote from that official organ, the *Village Messenger*, "not only in large towns upon the somewhat lengthy route from Toulon to Paris, but in many places far removed from it, the organization of festivities was commenced by special committees.

"Contributions were everywhere received to defray the expenses of the welcome. Many towns sent deputations to our ambassador in Paris, praying that our sailors should be permitted to visit them even for a day or an hour.

"The municipalities of all those towns which our sailors were directed to visit voted vast sums of money—more than a hundred thousands rubles—to promote various festivities and merrymakings, and expressed their readiness to devote even a larger sum to the purpose, if necessary, to make the welcome as magnificent as possible.

"In Paris itself, in addition to the sum voted by the

town municipality, a large amount was collected in voluntary contributions by a private committee for the series of entertainments, and the French government decreed over a hundred thousand rubles for the reception of the Russian visitors by the ministers and other authorities. In many places which our sailors were unable to visit it was decided to keep October 13 as a festal day in honor of Russia. A number of towns and departments decided to send to Toulon and Paris special deputies to welcome the Russian visitors, to give them presents in memory of France, or to send them addresses and telegrams of welcome.

"It was decided everywhere to regard October 13 as a national feast-day, and to give a day's holiday to all the school children, and in Paris two days.

"Soldiers undergoing certain sentences were pardoned, in order that they might remember with thankfulness the joyous October 13 in the annals of France.

"To enable the public who wished to visit Toulon to participate in the reception of the Russian squadron, the railways reduced their fares to one-half, and arranged for special trains."

And thus when, by a series of measures undertaken everywhere and at the same time—always thanks to the power in its hands at the command of the government— a certain portion of people, chiefly the froth, the town crowds, is brought into an unnaturally excited state, it is said: Look at this spontaneous action of the will of the whole nation!

Such manifestations as those of Toulon and Paris, as those which take place in Germany at the receptions of the emperor or of Bismarck, or at the manœuvers in Lothringen, as those which are always repeated in Russia at all pompously arranged receptions, only prove that the means of exciting a nation artificially which are at present in the hands of the governments and ruling classes, can always evoke any patriotic manifestation they choose, and afterward label it as the outcome of the patriotic sentiments of the people.

Nothing, on the contrary, proves so clearly the absence of patriotism in the people, as these same excessive measures now used for its artificial excitement and the small results attained with so much effort.

If patriotic sentiments are so natural to a people, why then is it not allowed to express itself of its own accord, instead of being stirred up by every ordinary and extraordinary means?

If only the attempt were made for a time in Russia to abolish at the coronation of the Tsar the taking of the oath of allegiance by the people, the solemn repetition of the prayers for the Tsar during every church service; to forgo the festivals of his birth and saints' days, with illuminations, the pealing of bells, and compulsory idleness, to cease the public exhibition of his portrait and in prayer-books, calendars, and books of study to print no more the family names of himself and of his family, and of even the pronouns alluding to them, in large letters; to cease to honor him by special books and papers published for that purpose; to put an end to imprisonment for the least word of disrespect concerning him—let us see these things altered for a time, and then we could know how far it is inherent in the people, in the genuine working-class. Prokophy and Ivan the village elder, as they are always assured, and as every foreigner is assured, idolize the Tsar, who one way or another betrays them into the hands of landowners and of the rich in general.

So it is in Russia. But if only in like manner the ruling classes in Germany, France, Italy, England, and America were to do what they so persistently accomplish in the inculcation of patriotism, attachment, and obedience to the existing government, we should be able to see how far this supposed patriotism is natural to the nations of our time.

From infancy, by every possible means—class-books, church-services, sermons, speeches, books, papers, songs, poetry, monuments—the people is stupefied in one direction; and then either by force or by bribe, several thousands of the people are assembled, and when these, joined by the idlers always present at every sight, to the sound of cannon and music, and inflamed by the glitter and brilliance about them, will commence to shout out what others are shouting in front of them, we are told that this is the expression of the sentiment of the entire nation.

But, in the first place, these thousands, or even tens of thousands, who shout something or other on these occasions, are only a mere ten-thousandth part of the whole nation; and, in the second, of these ten thousand men who shout and wave their hats, the greater part, if not collected by the authorities, as in Russia, is artificially attracted by some kind of bait; and in the third place, of all these thousands there are scarcely a hundred who know the real meaning of what is taking place, and the majority would shout and wave their hats in just the same way for an exactly opposite intention; and in the fourth place, the police is present with power to quiet and silence at once any who might attempt to shout in a fashion not desired or demanded by government, as was energetically done during the Franco-Russian festivities.

In France, war with Russia was welcomed with just the same zest in the reign of Napoleon I, then the war against Alexander I, then that of the allied forces under Napoleon III; the Bourbons have been welcomed in the same fashion as the House of Orléans, the Republic, Napoleon III, and Boulanger. And in Russia the same welcome has been accorded to Peter, Catherine, Paul, Alexander, Constantine, Nicolas, the Duke of Lichtenberg, the "brotherly Slavonians," the King of Prussia, the French sailors, and any others the authorities desired to welcome. And just the same thing has taken place in England, America, Germany, and Italy.

What is called patriotism in our time is, on the one hand, only a certain disposition of mind, constantly produced and sustained in the minds of the people in a direction desired by the existing government, by schools, religion, and a subsidized press; and on the other hand it is a temporary excitement of the lowest stratum, morally and intellectually, of the people, produced by special means by the ruling classes, and finally acclaimed as the permanent expression of the people's will.

The patriotism of states oppressed by a foreign power presents no exception. It is equally unnatural to the working masses, and artificially induced by the higher classes.

XIII

"BUT IF the common people have no sentiment of patriotism, it is because they have not yet developed this elevated feeling natural to every educated man. If they do not possess this nobility of sentiment, it must be cultivated in them. And this the government does."

So say, generally, the ruling classes, with such assurance that patriotism is a noble feeling, that the simple populace, who are ignorant of it, think themselves, in consequence, at fault, and try to persuade themselves that they really possess it, or at least pretend to have it.

But what is this elevated sentiment which, according to the opinion of the ruling classes, must be educated in the people?

The sentiment, in its simplest definition, is merely the preference for one's own country or nation above the country or nation of any one else; a sentiment perfectly expressed in the German patriotic song, "Deutschland, Deutschland über Alles," in which one need only substitute for the first two words, "Russland," "Frankreich," "Italien," or the name of any other country, to obtain a formula of the elevated sentiment of patriotism for that country.

It is quite possible that governments regard this sentiment as both useful and desirable, and of service to the unity of the State; but one must see that this sentiment is by no means elevated, but, on the contrary, very stupid and immoral. Stupid, because if every country were to consider itself superior to others, it is evident that all but one would be in error; and immoral because it leads all who possess it to aim at benefiting their own country or nation at the expense of every other—an inclination exactly at variance with the fundamental moral law, which all admit, "Do not unto others as you would not wish them to do unto you."

Patriotism may have been a virtue in the ancient world when it compelled men to serve the highest idea of those days—the fatherland. But how can patriotism be a virtue in these days when it requires of men an ideal exactly opposite to that of our religion and morality—an admission, not of the equality and fraternity of all men, but of the dominance of one country or nation over all others? But not only is this sentiment no virtue in our times, but it is indubitably a vice; for this sentiment of patriotism cannot now exist, because there is neither material nor moral foundation for its conception.

Patriotism might have had some meaning in the ancient world, when every nation was more or less uniform in composition, professing one national faith, and subject to the unrestrained authority of its great and adored sovereign, representing, as it were, an island, in an ocean of barbarians who sought to overflow it.

It is conceivable that in such circumstances patriotism —the desire of protection from barbarian assault, ready not only to destroy the social order, but threatening it with plunder, slaughter, captivity, slavery, and the violation of its women—was a natural feeling; and it is conceivable that men, in order to defend themselves and their fellow-countrymen, might prefer their own nation to any other, and cherish a feeling of hatred toward the surrounding barbarians, and destroy them for self-protection.

But what significance can this feeling have in these Christian days?

On what grounds and for what reason can a man of our time follow this example—a Russian, for instance, kill Frenchmen; or a Frenchman, Germans—when he is well aware, however uneducated he may be, that the men of the country or nation against whom his patriotic animosity is excited are no barbarians, but men, Christians like himself, often of the same faith as himself, and, like him, desirous of peace and the peaceful interchange of labor; and besides, bound to him, for the most part, either by the interest of a common effort, or by mercantile or spiritual endeavors, or even by both? So that very often people of one country are nearer and more needful to their neighbors than are these latter to one another, as in the case of laborers in the service of foreign employers of labor, of commercial houses, scientists, and the followers of art.

Moreover, the very conditions of life are now so changed, that what we call fatherland, what we are asked to distinguish from everything else, has ceased to be clearly defined, as it was with the ancients, when men of the same country were of one nationality, one state, and one religion.

The patriotism of an Egyptian, a Jew, a Greek is comprehensible, for in defending his country he defended his religion, his nationality, his fatherland, and his state.

But in what terms can one express to-day the patriotism of an Irishman in the United States, who by his religion belongs to Rome, by his nationality to Ireland, by his citizenship to the United States? In the same position is a Bohemian in Austria, a Pole in Russia, Prussia, or Austria; a Hindu in England; a Tartar or Armenian in Russia or Turkey. Not to mention the people of these particular conquered nations, the people of the most homogeneous countries, Russia, France, Prussia, can no longer possess the sentiment of patriotism which was natural to the ancients, because very often the chief interest of their lives—of the family, for instance, where a man is married to a woman of another nationality; commercial, where his capital is invested abroad; spiritual, scientific, or artistic—are no longer contained within the limits of his country, but outside it, in the very state, perhaps, against which his patriotic animosity is being excited.

But patriotism is chiefly impossible to-day because, however much we may have endeavored during eighteen hundred years to conceal the meaning of Christianity, it has nevertheless leaked into our lives, and controls them to such an extent that the dullest and most unrefined of men must see today the complete incompatibility of patriotism with the moral law by which we live.

XIV

PATRIOTISM WAS a necessity in the formation and consolidation of powerful states composed of different nationalities and acting in mutual defense against barbarians. But as soon as Christian enlightenment transformed these states from within, giving to all an equal standing, patriotism became not only needless, but the sole impediment to a union between nations for which, by reason of their Christian consciousness, they were prepared.

Patriotism today is the cruel tradition of an outlived period, which exists not merely by its inertia, but because the governments and ruling classes, aware that not their power only, but their very existence, depends upon it, persistently excite and maintain it among the people, both by cunning and violence.

Patriotism today is like a scaffolding which was needful once to raise the walls of the building, but which, though it presents the only obstacle to the house being inhabited, is none the less retained, because its existence is of profit to certain persons.

For a long while there has not been and cannot be any reason for dissension between Christian nations. It is even impossible to imagine, how and for what, Russian and German workmen, peacefully and conjointly working on the frontiers or in the capitals, should quarrel. And much less easily can one imagine animosity between some Kazan peasant who supplies Germans with wheat, and a German who supplies him with scythes and machines.

It is the same between French, German, and Italian workmen. And it would be even ridiculous to speak of the possibility of a quarrel between men of science, art, and letters of different nationalities, who have the same objects of common interest independent of nationalities or of governments.

But the various governments cannot leave the nations in peace, because the chief. if not the sole, justification for the existence of governments is the pacification of nations, and the settlement of their hostile relationships. Hence governments evoke such hostile relationships under the aspect of patriotism, in order to exhibit their powers of pacification. Somewhat like a gipsy who, having put some pepper under a horse's tail, and beaten it in its stall, brings it out, and hanging on to the reins, pretends that he can hardly control the excited animal.

We are told that governments are very careful to maintain peace between nations. But how do they maintain it? People live on the Rhine in peaceful communication with one another. Suddenly, owing to certain quarrels and intrigues between kings and emperors, a war commences; and we learn that the French government has considered it necessary to regard this peaceful people as Frenchmen. Centuries pass, the population has become accustomed to their position, when animosity again begins amongst the governments of the great nations, and a war is started upon the most empty pretext, because the German government considers it necessary to regard this population as Germans: and between all Frenchmen and Germans is kindled a mutual feeling of ill-will.

Or else Germans and Russians live in friendly fashion on their frontiers, pacifically exchanging the results of their labor; when all of a sudden those same institutions, which only exist to maintain the peace of nations, begin to quarrel, are guilty of one stupidity after another, and finally are unable to invent anything better than a most childish method of self-punishment in order to have their own way, and do a bad turn to their opponent— which in this case is especially easy, as those who arrange a war of tariffs are not the sufferers from it; it is others who suffer—and so arrange such a war of tariffs as took place not long ago between Russia and Germany. And so between Russians and Germans a feeling of animosity is fostered, which is still more inflamed by the Franco-Russian festivities, and may lead at one moment or another to a bloody war.

I have mentioned these last two examples of the influence of a government over the people used to excite their animosity against another people, because they have occurred in our times: but in all history there is no war which was not hatched by the governments, the governments alone, independent of the interests of the people, to whom war is always pernicious even when successful.

The government assures the people that they are in danger from the invasion of another nation, or from foes in their midst, and that the only way to escape this danger is by the slavish obedience of the people to their government. This fact is seen most prominently during revolutions and dictatorships, but it exists always and everywhere that the power of the government exists. Every government explains its existence, and justifies its deeds of violence, by the argument that if it did not exist the condition of things would be very much worse. After assuring the people of its danger the government subordinates it to control, and when in this condition compels it to attack some other nation. And thus the assurance of the government is corroborated in the eyes of the people, as to the danger of attack from other nations.

"Divide et impera."

Patriotism in its simplest, clearest, and most indubitable signification is nothing else but a means of obtaining for the rulers their ambitions and covetous desires, and for the ruled the abdication of human dignity, reason, and conscience, and a slavish enthralment to those in power. And as such it is recommended wherever it is preached.

Patriotism is slavery.

Those who preach peace by arbitration argue thus: Two animals cannot divide their prey otherwise than by fighting; as also is the case with children, savages, and savage nations. But reasonable people settle their differences by argument, persuasion, and by referring the decision of the question to other impartial and reasonable persons. So the nations should act today. This argument seems quite correct. The nations of our time have reached the period of reasonableness, have no animosity toward one another, and might decide their differences in a peaceful fashion. But this argument applies only so far as it has reference to the people, and only to the people who are not under the control of a government.

But the people that subordinate themselves to a government cannot be reasonable, because the subordination is in itself a sign of a want of reason.

How can we speak of the reasonableness of men who promise in advance to accomplish everything, including murder, that the government—that is, certain men who have attained a certain position—may command? Men who can accept such obligations, and resignedly subordinate themselves to anything that may be prescribed by persons unknown to them in Petersburg, Vienna, Berlin, Paris, cannot be considered reasonable; and the government, that is, those who are in possession of such power, can still less be considered reasonable, and cannot but misuse it, and become dazed by such insane and dreadful power.

This is why peace between nations cannot be attained by reasonable means, by conversations, by arbitration, as long as the subordination of the people to the government continues, a condition always unreasonable and always pernicious.

But the subordination of people to governments will exist as long as patriotism exists, because all governmental authority is founded upon patriotism, that is, upon the readiness of people to subordinate themselves to authority in order to defend their nation, country, or state from dangers which are supposed to threaten.

The power of the French kings over their people before the Revolution was founded on patriotism; upon it too was based the power of the Committee of Public Welfare after the Revolution; upon it was erected the power of Napoleon, both as consul and as emperor; upon it, after the downfall of Napoleon, was based the power of the Bourbons, then that of the Republic, Louis Philippe, and again of the Republic; then of Napoleon III, and again of the Republic, and upon it finally rested the power of M. Boulanger.

It is dreadful to say so, but there is not, nor has there· been, any conjoint violence of one people against another which was not accomplished in the name of patriotism. In its name the Russians fought the French, and the French the·Russians; in its name Russians and French are preparing to fight the Germans, and the Germans to wage war on two frontiers. And such is the case not only with wars. In the name of patriotism the Russians stifle the Poles, the Germans persecute the Slavonians, the men of the Commune killed those of Versailles, and those of Versailles the men of the Commune.

XV

IT WOULD seem that, owing to the spread of education, of speedier locomotion, of greater intercourse between different nations, to the widening of literature, and chiefly to the decrease of danger from other nations, the fraud of patriotism ought daily to become more difficult and at length impossible to practise.

But the truth·is that these very means of general external education, facilitated locomotion and intercourse, and especially the spread of literature, being captured and constantly more and more controlled by government, confer on the latter such possibilities of exciting a feeling of mutual animosity between nations, that in degree as the uselessness and harmfulness of patriotism have become manifest, so also has increased the power of the government and ruling class to excite patriotism among the people.

The difference between that which was and that which
is consists solely in the fact that now a much larger number of men participate in the advantages which patriotism
confers on the upper classes, hence a much larger number
of men are employed in spreading and sustaining this
astounding superstition.

The more difficult the government finds it to retain its
power, the more numerous are the men who share it.

In former times a small band of rulers held the reins
of power, emperors, kings, dukes, their soldiers and
assistants; whereas now the power and its profits are
shared not only by government officials and by the clergy,
but by capitalists—great and small, landowners, bankers,
members of Parliament, professors, village officials, men
of science, and even artists, but particularly by authors
and journalists.

And all these people, consciously or unconsciously,
spread the deceit of patriotism, which is indispensable
to them if the profits of their position are to be preserved.

And the fraud, thanks to the means for its propagation,
and to the participation in it of a much larger number of
people, having become more powerful, is continued so
successfully, that, notwithstanding the increased difficulty
of deceiving, the extent to which the people are deceived
is the same as ever.

A hundred years ago the uneducated classes, who had
no idea of what composed their government, or by what
nations they were surrounded, blindly obeyed the local
government officials and nobles by whom they were enslaved, and it was sufficient for the government, by bribes
and rewards, to remain on good terms with these nobles
and officials, in order to squeeze from the people all that
was required.

Whereas now, when the people can, for the most part, read, know more or less of what their government consists, and what nations surround them; when working-men constantly and easily move from place to place, bringing back information of what is happening in the world—the simple demand that the orders of the government must be accomplished is not sufficient; it is needful as well to cloud those true ideas about life which the people have, and to inculcate unnatural ideas as to the condition of their existence, and the relationship to it of other nations.

And so, thanks to the development of literature, reading, and the facilities of travel, governments which have their agents everywhere, by means of statutes, sermons, schools, and the press, inculcate everywhere upon the people the most barbarous and erroneous ideas as to their advantages, the relationship of nations, their qualities and intentions; and the people, so crushed by labor that they have neither the time nor the power to understand the significance or test the truth of the ideas which are forced upon them or of the demands made upon them in the name of their welfare, put themselves unmurmuringly under the yoke.

Whereas working-men who have freed themselves from unremitting labor and become educated, and who have, therefore, it might be supposed, the power of seeing through the fraud which is practised upon them, are subjected to such a coercion of threats, bribes, and all the hypnotic influence of governments, that, almost without exception, they desert to the side of the government, and by entering some well-paid and profitable employment, as priest, schoolmaster, officer, or functionary, become participators in spreading the deceit which is destroying their comrades.

It is as if nets were laid at the entrances to education, in which those who by some means or other escape from the masses bowed down by labor, are inevitably caught.

At first, when one understands the cruelty of all this deceit, one feels indignant in spite of oneself against those who from personal ambition or greedy advantage propagate this cruel fraud which destroys the souls as well as the bodies of men, and one feels inclined to accuse them of a sly craftiness; but the fact is that they are deceitful with no wish to deceive, but because they cannot be otherwise. And they deceive, not like Machiavellians, but with no consciousness of their deceit, and usually with the naïve assurance that they are doing something excellent and elevated, a view in which they are persistently encouraged by the sympathy and approval of all who surround them.

It is true that, being dimly aware that on this fraud is founded their power and advantageous position, they are unconsciously drawn toward it; but their action is not based on any desire to delude the people, but because they believe it to be of service to the people.

Thus emperors, kings, and their ministers, with all their coronations, manœuvers, reviews, visiting one another, dressing up in various uniforms, going from place to place, and deliberating with serious faces as to how they may keep peace between nations supposed to be inimical to each other—nations who would never dream of quarreling—feel quite sure that what they are doing is very reasonable and useful.

In the same way the various ministers, diplomatists, and functionaries—dressed up in uniforms, with all sorts of ribbons and crosses, writing and docketing with great care, upon the best paper, their hazy, involved, altogether needless communications, advices, projects—are quite assured that, without their activity, the entire existence of nations would halt or become deranged.

In the same manner military men, got up in ridiculous costumes, arguing seriously with what rifle or cannon men can be most expeditiously destroyed, are quite certain that their field-days and reviews are most important and essential to the people.

So likewise the priests, journalists, writers of patriotic songs and class-books, who preach patriotism and receive liberal remuneration, are equally satisfied.

And no doubt the organizers of festivities—like the Franco-Russian fêtes—are sincerely affected while pronouncing their patriotic speeches and toasts.

All these people do what they are doing unconsciously, because they must, all their life being founded upon deceit, and because they know not how to do anything else; and coincidently these same acts call forth the sympathy and approbation of all the people amongst whom they are done. Moreover, being all linked together, they approve and justify one another's acts—emperors and kings those of the soldiers, functionaries, and clergymen; and soldiers, functionaries, and clergymen the acts of emperors and kings, while the populace, and especially the town populace, seeing nothing comprehensible in what is done by all these men, unwittingly ascribe to them a special, almost a supernatural, significance.

The people see, for instance, that a triumphal arch is erected; that men bedeck themselves with crowns, uniforms, robes; that fireworks are let off, cannons fired, bells rung, regiments paraded with their bands; that papers and telegrams and messengers fly from place to place, and that strangely arrayed men are busily engaged in hurrying from place to place and much is said and written; and the throng being unable to believe that all this is done (as is indeed the case) without the slightest necessity, attribute to it all a special mysterious significance, and gaze with shouts and hilarity or with silent awe. And on the other hand, this hilarity or silent awe confirms the assurance of those people who are responsible for all these foolish deeds.

Thus, for instance, not long ago, Wilhelm II ordered a new throne for himself, with some special kind of ornamentation, and having dressed up in a white uniform, with a cuirass, tight breeches, and a helmet with a bird on the top, and enveloped himself in a red mantle, came out to his subjects, and sat down on this new throne, perfectly assured that his act was most necessary and important; and his subjects not only saw nothing ridiculous in it, but thought the sight most imposing.

XVI

FOR SOME time the power of the government over the people has not been maintained by force, as was the case when one nation conquered another and ruled it by force of arms, or when the rulers of an unarmed people had separate legions of janizaries or guards.

The power of the government has for some time been maintained by what is termed public opinion.

A public opinion exists that patriotism is a fine moral sentiment, and that it is right and our duty to regard one's own nation, one's own state, as the best in the world; and flowing naturally from this public opinion is another, namely, that it is right and our duty to acquiesce in the

control of a government over ourselves, to subordinate
ourselves to it, to serve in the army and submit ourselves
to discipline, to give our earnings to the government in
the form of taxes, to submit to the decisions of the law-
courts, and to consider the edicts of the government as
divinely right. And when such public opinion exists, a
strong governmental power is formed possessing milliards
of money, an organized mechanism of administration, the
postal service, telegraphs, telephones, disciplined armies,
law-courts, police, submissive clergy, schools, even the
press; and this power maintains in the people the public
opinion which it finds necessary.

The power of the government is maintained by public
opinion, and with this power the government, by means
of its organs—its officials, law-courts, schools, churches,
even the press—can always maintain the public opinion
which they need. Public opinion produces the power, and
the power produces public opinion. And there appears
to be no escape from this position.

Nor indeed would there be, if public opinion were
something fixed, unchangeable, and governments were
able to manufacture the public opinion they needed.

But, fortunately, such is not the case; and public
opinion is not, to begin with, permanent, unchangeable,
stationary; but, on the contrary, is constantly changing,
moving with the advance of humanity; and public opinion
not only cannot be produced at will by a government,
but is that which produces governments and gives them
power, or deprives them of it.

It may seem that public opinion is at present stationary,
and the same today as it was ten years ago; that in
relation to certain questions it merely fluctuates, but
returns again—as when it replaces a monarchy with a

republic, and then the republic with a monarchy; but it has only that appearance when we examine merely the external manifestation or public opinion which is produced artificially by the government.

But we need only take public opinion in its relation to the life of mankind to see that, as with the day or the year, it is never stagnant, but always proceeds along the way by which all humanity advances, as, notwithstanding delays and hesitations, the day or the spring advances by the same path as the sun.

So that, although, judging from external appearances, the position of European nations today is almost as it was fifty years ago, the relationship of the nations to these appearances is quite different from what it was then.

Though now, the same as then, exist rulers, troops, taxes, luxury and poverty, Catholicism, orthodoxy, Lutheranism, in former times these existed because public opinion demanded them, whereas now they exist only because the governments artificially maintain what was once a vital public opinion.

If we as seldom remark this movement of public opinion as we notice the movement of water in a river when we ourselves are descending with the current, this is because the imperceptible changes in public opinion influence ourselves as well.

The nature of public opinion is a constant and irresistible movement. If it appears to us to be stationary it is because there are always some who have utilized a certain phase of public opinion for their own profit, and who, in consequence, use every effort to give it an appearance of permanence, and to conceal the manifestations of real opinion, which is already alive, though not yet perfectly expressed, in the consciousness of men. And such people, who adhere to the outworn opinion and conceal the new one, are at the present time those who compose governments and ruling classes, and who preach patriotism as an indispensable condition of human life.

The means which these people can control are immense; but as public opinion is constantly pouring in upon them their efforts must in the end be in vain: the old falls into decrepitude, the new grows.

The longer the manifestation of nascent public opinion is restrained, the more it accumulates, the more energetically will it burst forth.

Governments and ruling classes try with all their strength to conserve that old public opinion of patriotism upon which their power rest, and to smother the expression of the new, which would destroy it.

But to preserve the old and to check the new is possible only up to a certain point; just as, only to a certain extent, is it possible to check running water with a dam.

However much governments may try to arouse in the people a public opinion, of the past, unnatural to them, as to the merit and virtue of patriotism, those of our day believe in patriotism no longer, but espouse more and more the solidarity and brotherhood of nations.

Patriotism promises men nothing but a terrible future, but the brotherhood of nations represents an ideal which is becoming ever more intelligible and more desirable to humanity. Hence the progress of mankind from the old outworn opinion to the new must inevitably take place. This progression is as inevitable as the falling in the spring of the last dry leaves and the appearance of the new from swollen buds.

And the longer this transition is delayed, the more inevitable it becomes, and the more evident its necessity.

And indeed, one has only to remember what we profess, both as Christians and merely as men of our day, those fundamental moralities by which we are directed in our social, family, and personal existence, and the position in which we place ourselves in the name of patriotism, in order to see what a degree of contradiction we have placed between our conscience and what, thanks to an energetic government influence in this direction, we regard as our public opinion.

One has only thoughtfully to examine the most ordinary demands of patriotism, which are expected of us as the most simple and natural affair, in order to understand to what extent these requirements are at variance with that real public opinion which we already share. We all regard ourselves as free, educated, humane men, or even as Christians, and yet we are all in such a position that were Wilhelm tomorrow to take offense against Alexander, or Mr. N. to write a lively article on the Eastern Question, or Prince So-and-so to plunder some Bulgarians or Servians, or some queen or empress to be put out by something or other, all we educated humane Christians must go and kill people of whom we have no knowledge, and toward whom we are as amicably disposed as to the rest of the world.

And if such an event has not come to pass, it is owing, we are assured, to the love of peace which controls Alexander, or because Nikolaï Alexandrovitch has married the granddaughter of Victoria.

But if another happened to be in the place of Alexander, or if the disposition of Alexander himself were to alter, or if Nicholas the son of Alexander had married Amalia instead of Alice, we should rush at each other like wild beasts, and rip up each other's bellies.

Such is the supposed public opinion of our time, and such arguments are coolly repeated in every liberal and advanced organ of the press.

If we, Christians of a thousands years' standing, have not already cut one another's throats, it is merely because Alexander III does not permit us to do so.

But this is awful!

XVII

No FEATS OF heroism are needed to achieve the greatest and most important changes in the existence of humanity; neither the armament of millions of soldiers, nor the construction of new roads and machines, nor the arrangement of exhibitions, nor the organization of workmen's unions, nor revolutions, nor barricades, nor explosions, nor the perfection of aërial navigation; but a change in public opinion.

And to accomplish this change no exertions of the mind are needed, nor the refutation of anything in existence, nor the invention of any extraordinary novelty; it is only needful that we should not succumb to the erroneous, already defunct, public opinion of the past, which governments have induced artificially; it is only needful that each individual should say what he really feels or thinks, or at least that he should not say what he does not think.

And if only a small body of the people were to do so at once, of their own accord, outworn public opinion would fall off us of itself, and a new, living, real opinion would assert itself. And when public opinion should thus have changed without the slightest effort, the internal condition of men's lives which so torments them would change likewise of its own accord.

One is ashamed to say how little is needed for all men to be delivered from those calamities which now oppress them; it is only needful not to lie.

Let people only be superior to the falsehood which is instilled into them, let them decline to say what they neither feel nor think, and at once such a revolution of all the organization of our life will take place as could not be attained by all the efforts of revolutionists during centuries, even were complete power within their hands.

If people would only believe that strength is not in force but in truth, would only not shrink from it either in world or deed, not say what they do not think, not do what they regard as foolish and as wrong!

"But what is there so gravely serious in shouting Vive la France! or, Hurrah for some emperor, king, or conqueror; in putting on a uniform and a court decoration and going and waiting in the anteroom and bowing low and calling men by strange titles and then giving the young and uncultured to understand that all this sort of thing is very praiseworthy?" Or, "Why is the writing of an article in defence of the Franco-Russian alliance, or of the war of tariffs, or in condemnation of Germans, Russians, or Englishmen, of such moment?" Or, "What harm is there in attendance at some patriotic festivity, or in drinking the health and making a speech in favor of people whom one does not love, and with whom one has no business?" Or, "What is of such importance in admitting the use and excellence of treaties and alliances, or in keeping silence when one's own nation is lauded in one's hearing, and other nations are abused and maligned;

or when Catholicism, Orthodoxy, and Lutheranism are lauded; or some hero of war, as Napoleon, Peter, Boulanger, or Skobelef, is admired?"

All these things seem so unimportant. Yet in these ways which seem unimportant to us, in our refraining from them, in our proving, as far as we can, the unreasonableness that is apparent to us, in this is our chief, our irresistible might, of which that unconquerable force is composed which constitutes real genuine public opinion, that opinion which, while itself advancing, moves all humanity.

The governments know this, and tremble before this force, and strive in every way they can to counteract or become possessed of it.

They know that strength is not in force, but in thought and in clear expression of it, and, therefore, they are more afraid of the expression of independent thought than of armies; hence they institute censorships, bribe the press, and monopolize the control of religion and of the schools. But the spiritual force which moves the world eludes them; it is neither in books nor in papers; it cannot be trapped, and is always free; it is in the depths of consciousness of mankind. The most powerful and untrammeled force of freedom is that which asserts itself in the soul of man when he is alone, and in the sole presence of himself reflects on the facts of the universe, and then naturally communicates his thoughts to wife, brother, friend, with all those with whom he comes in contact, and from whom he would regard it as sinful to conceal the truth.

No milliards of rubles, no millions of troops, no organization, no wars or revolutions will produce what the

simple expression of a free man may, on what he regards
as just, independently of what exists or was instilled
into him.

One free man will say with truth what he thinks and
feels amongst thousands of men who by their acts and
words attest exactly the opposite. It would seem that he
who sincerely expressed his thought must remain alone,
whereas it generally happens that every one else, or
the majority at least, have been thinking and feeling the
same things but without expressing them.

And that which yesterday was the novel opinion of one
man, today becomes the general opinion of the majority.

And as soon as this opinion is established, immediately
by imperceptible degrees, but beyond power of frustra-
tion, the conduct of mankind begins to alter.

Whereas at present, every man, even, if free, asks himself, "What can I do alone against all this ocean of evil
and deceit which overwhelms us? Why should I express
my opinion? Why indeed possess one? It is better not to
reflect on these misty and involved questions. Perhaps
these contradictions are an inevitable condition of our
existence. And why should I struggle alone with all the
evil in the world? Is it not better to go with the stream
which carries me along? If anything can be done, it must
be done not alone but in company with others."

And leaving the most powerful of weapons—thought
and its expression—which move the world, each man
employs the weapon of social activity, not noticing that
every social activity is based on the very foundations
against which he is bound to fight, and that upon entering the social activity which exists in our world every
man is obliged, if only in part, to deviate from the truth
and to make concessions which destroy the force of the

powerful weapon which should assist him in the struggle. It is as if a man, who was given a blade so marvelously keen that it would sever anything, should use its edge for driving in nails.

We all complain of the senseless order of life, which is at variance with our being, and yet we refuse to use the unique and powerful weapon within our hands—the consciousness of truth and its expression; but on the contrary, under the pretext of struggling with evil, we destroy the weapon, and sacrifice it to the exigencies of an imaginary conflict.

One man does not assert the truth which he knows, because he feels himself bound to the people with whom he is engaged; another, because the truth might deprive him of the profitable position by which he maintains his family; a third, because he desires to attain reputation and authority, and then use them in the service of mankind; a fourth, because he does not wish to destroy old sacred traditions; a fifth, because he has no desire to offend people; a sixth, because the expression of the truth would arouse persecution, and disturb the excellent social activity to which he has devoted himself.

One serves as emperor, king, minister, government functionary, or soldier, and assures himself and others that the deviation from truth indispensable to his condition is redeemed by the good he does. Another, who fulfils the duties of a spiritual pastor, does not in the depths of his soul believe all he teaches, but permits the deviation from truth in view of the good he does. A third instructs men by means of literature, and notwithstanding the silence he must observe with regard to the whole truth, in order not to stir up the government and society against himself, has no doubt as to the good he does. A

fourth struggles resolutely with the existing order as revolutionist or anarchist, and is quite assured that the aims
he pursues are so beneficial that the neglect of the truth,
or even of the falsehood, by silence, indispensable to the
success of his activity, does not destroy the utility of his
work.

In order that the conditions of a life contrary to the
consciousness of humanity should change and be replaced
by one which is in accord with it, the outworn public
opinion must be superseded by a new and living one.

And in order that the old outworn opinion should yield
its place to the new living one all who are conscious of
the new requirements of existence should openly express
them. And yet all those who are conscious of these new
requirements, one in the name of one thing, and one in
the name of another, not only pass them over in silence,
but both by word and deed attest their exact opposites.

Only the truth and its expression can establish that new
public opinion which will reform the ancient obsolete
and pernicious order of life; and yet we not only do not
express the truth we know, but often even distinctly give
expression to what we ourselves regard as false.

If only free men would not rely on that which has no
power, and is always fettered—upon external aids; but
would trust in that which is always powerful and free—
the truth and its expression!

If only men were boldly and clearly to express the truth
already manifest to them of the brotherhood of all nations,
and the crime of exclusive devotion to one's own people,
that defunct, false public opinion would slough off of
itself like a dried skin—and upon it depends the power
of governments, and all the evil produced by them; and

the new public opinion would stand forth, which is even now but awaiting that dropping off of the old to put forth manifestly and powerfully its demand, and establish new forms of existence in conformity with the consciousness of mankind.

XVIII

It is sufficient that people should understand that what is enunciated to them as public opinion, and maintained by such complex, energetic, and artificial means, is not public opinion, but only the lifeless outcome of what was once public opinion; and, what is more important, it is sufficient that they should have faith in themselves, that they should believe that what they are conscious of in the depths of their souls, what in every one is pressing for expression, and is only not expressed because it contradicts the public opinion supposed to exist, is the power which transforms the world, and to express which is the mission of mankind: it is sufficient to believe that truth is not what men talk of, but what is told by his own conscience, that is, by God,—and at once the whole artificially maintained public opinion will disappear, and a new and true one be established in its place.

If people would only speak what they think, and not what they do not think, all the superstitions emanating from patriotism would at once drop away with the cruel feelings and violence founded upon it. The hatred and animosity between nations and peoples, fanned by their governments, would cease; the extolling of military heroism, that is of murder, would be at an end; and, what is of most importance, respect for authorities, abandonment to them of the fruits of one's labor, and subordination to them, would cease, since there is no other reason for them but patriotism.

And if merely this were to take place, that vast mass of feeble people who are controlled by externals would sway at once to the side of the new public opinion, which should reign henceforth in place of the old.

Let the government keep the schools, Church, press, its milliards of money and millions of armed men transformed into machines: all this apparently terrible organization of brute force is as nothing compared to the consciousness of truth, which surges in the soul of one man who knows the power of truth, which is communicated from him to a second and a third, as one candle lights an innumerable quantity of others.

The light needs only to be kindled, and, like wax in the face of fire, this organization, which seems so powerful, will melt, and be consumed.

Only let men understand the vast power which is given them in the word which expresses truth; only let them refuse to sell their birthright for a mess of pottage; only let people use their power—and their rulers will not dare, as now, to threaten men with universal slaughter, to which, at their discretion, they may or may not subject them, nor dare before the eyes of a peaceful populace to hold reviews and manœuvers of disciplined murderers; nor would the governments dare for their own profit and the advantage of their assistance to arrange and derange custom-house agreements, nor to collect from the people those millions of rubles which they distribute among their assistants, and by the help of which their murders are planned.

And such a transformation is not only possible, but it

is as impossible that it should not be accomplished as that a lifeless, decaying tree should not fall, and a younger take its place.

"Peace I leave with you; my peace I give unto you: not as the world giveth, give I unto you. Let not your heart be troubled, neither let it be afraid," said Christ. And this peace is indeed among us, and depends on us for its attainment.

If only the hearts of individuals would not be troubled by the seductions with which they are hourly seduced, nor afraid of those imaginary terrors by which they are intimidated; if people only knew wherein their chiefest, all-conquering power consists—a peace which men have always desired, not the peace attainable by diplomatic negotiations, imperial or kingly progresses, dinners, speeches, fortresses, cannon, dynamite, and melinite, by the exhaustion of the people under taxes, and the abduction from labor of the flower of the population, but the peace attainable by a voluntary profession of the truth by every man, would long ago have been established in our midst.

CARTHAGO DELENDA EST

A *Vita internationale* and *L'Humanité nouvelle* have sent me the following letter:—

"Sɪʀ—With the object of furthering the development of humanitarian ideas and civilization, *La Vita internationale* (of Milan), with the support of *L'Humanité nouvelle* (of Paris and Brussels), has deemed it necessary to concern itself with the difficult problem which has of late arisen in all its gravity and importance, owing to the delicate question about which France and the whole world has become so ardently impassioned—we mean the problem of war and militarism. With this aim in view, we beg all those in Europe that take part in politics, science, art, and the labor movement, and even those that occupy the foremost positions in the army, to contribute to this most civilizing task by replying to the following questions:—

"1. Is war among civilized nations still required by history, law, and progress?

"2. What are the intellectual, moral, physical, economical, and political effects of militarism?

"3. What, in the interests of the world's future civilization, are the solutions which should be given to the grave problems of war and militarism?

"4. What means would most rapidly lead to these solutions?"

I cannot conceal the feelings of disgust, indignation, and even despair which were aroused in me by this letter. Enlightened, sensible, good Christian people, who inculcate the principle of love and brotherhood, who regard murder as an awful crime, who, with very few exceptions, are unable to kill an animal—all these people suddenly, provided that these crimes are called war, not only acknowledge the destruction, plunder, and killing of people to be right and legal, but themselves contribute toward these robberies and murders, prepare themselves for them, take part in them, are proud of them.

Moreover, always and everywhere one and the same phenomenon repeats itself, viz., that the great majority of people—all working-people—those same people who carry out the robberies and murders, and on whom the burden falls—neither devise, nor prepare, nor desire these things, but take part in them against their will, merely because they are placed in such a position and are so instigated that it appears to them, to each individual, that they would suffer more were they to refuse. Whereas those who devise and prepare for these plunders and murders, and who compel the working-people to carry them out, are but an insignificant minority, who live in luxury and idleness, upon the labor of the workers.

This deceit has already been going on for a long time, but lately the insolence of the impostors has reached its extremest development, and a great share of what labor produces is being taken away from the workers, and used for making preparations for plundering and killing. In all the constitutional countries of Europe the workers themselves—all, without exception—are called upon to take part in these robberies and murders; international relations are purposely always more and more complicated, and this leads on to war; peaceful countries are being plundered without the least cause; every year, in some place or other, people murder and rob; and all live in constant dread of general mutual robbery and murder.

It seems evident that, if these things are done, it can only be because the great mass of people are deceived by the minority to whom this deceit is advantageous, and therefore that the first task of those who are anxious to free people from the evils caused by this mutual murdering and plundering should be to expose the deception under which the masses are laboring; to point out to them how the deceit is perpetrated, by what means it is being upheld, and how to get rid of it.

The enlightened people of Europe, however, do nothing of the kind, but, under the pretext of furthering the establishment of peace, they assemble now in one, now in another city of Europe, and, seated at tables, with most serious faces, they discuss the question how best to persuade those brigands who live by their plunder to give up robbing, and become peaceful citizens; and then they put the profound questions: first, whether war is still desirable from the standpoint of history, law, and progress (as if such fictions, invented by us, could demand from us deviation from the fundamental moral law of our life); secondly, as to what are the consequences of war (as if there could be any doubt that the consequences of war are always general distress and corruption); and finally, as to how to solve the problem of war (as if it were a difficult problem how to free deluded people from a delusion which we clearly see.)

This is terrible! We see, for instance, how healthy, calm, and frequently happy people year after year arrive at some gambling-den like Monte Carlo, and, benefiting no one but the keepers of those dens, leave there their health, peace, honor, and often their lives. We pity these people; we see clearly that the deceit to which they are subjected consists in those temptations whereby gamblers are allured, in the inequality of the chances, and in the infatuation of gamblers who, though fully aware that in general they are sure to be losers, nevertheless hope for once at least to be more fortunate than the rest. All this is perfectly clear.

And then, in order to free people from these miseries, we—instead of pointing out to them the temptations to which they are subjected, the fact that they are sure to lose, and the immorality of gambling, which is based on the expectation of other people's misfortunes—assemble with grave faces at meetings, and discuss how to arrange that the keepers of gambling-houses should of their own accord shut up their establishments; we write books about it, and we put questions to ourselves as to whether history, law, and progress require the existence of gambling-houses, and as to what are the economical, intellectual, moral, and other consequences of roulette.

If a man is given to drink, and I tell him that he himself can leave off drinking and that he must do so, there is a hope that he will listen to me; but if I tell him that his drunkenness is a complicated and difficult problem which we learned men are trying to solve at our meetings, then in all probability he will, while awaiting the solution of this problem, continue to drink.

Thus also with these false and refined external, scientific means of abolishing war, such as international tribunals, arbitration, and similar absurdities with which we occupy ourselves, while all the time carefully omitting to mention the most simple, essential, and self-evident method of causing war to cease—a method plain for all to see.

In order that people who do not want war should not fight, it is not necessary to have either international law, arbitration, international tribunals, or solutions of problems; but it is merely necessary that those who are subjected to the deceit should awake and free themselves from the spell or enchantment under which they find themselves. The way to do away with war is for those who do not want war, who regard participation in it as a sin, to refrain from fighting. This method has been preached from the earliest times by Christian writers such as Tertullian and Origen, as well as by the Paulicians, and by their successors, the Mennonites, Quakers, and Herrnhuters. The sin, harmfulness, and senselessness of military service have been written about and exposed in every way by Dymond, Garrison, and, twenty years ago, by Ballou, as well as by myself. The method I have mentioned has been adopted in the past, and of late has been frequently resorted to by isolated individuals in Austria, Prussia, Holland, Switzerland, and Russia, as well as by whole societies like the Quakers, Mennonites, and Nazarenes, and recently by the Dukhobors, of whom a whole population of fifteen thousand are now for the third year resisting the powerful Russian government, and, notwith-

standing all the sufferings to which they have been subjected, do not submit to its demands that they should take
part in the crimes of military service.

But the enlightened friends of peace not only refrain
from recommending this method, but cannot bear the
mention of it; when it is brought before them they pretend not to have noticed it, or, if they cannot help noticing
it, they gravely shrug their shoulders and express their
pity for those uneducated and unreasonable men who
adopt such an ineffectual, silly method, when such a good
one exists—namely, to sprinkle salt on the bird one wishes
to catch, *i.e.* to persuade the governments, who only exist
by violence and deceit, to forsake both the one and
the other.

They tell us that the misunderstandings which arise
between governments will be settled by tribunals or arbitration. But the governments do not at all desire the
settlement of misunderstandings. On the contrary, if there
be none they invent some, it being only by such misunderstanding with the governments that they are afforded a
pretext for keeping up the army upon which their power
is based. Thus the enlightened friends of peace strive to
divert the attention of the working, suffering masses from
the only method that can deliver them from the slavery
in which they are held (from their youth upward), first
by patriotism, next by oaths administered by the mer-
cenary priests of a perverted Christianity, and lastly, by
the fear of punishment.

In our days of close and peaceful relations between
peoples of different nationalities and countries, the deceit
called patriotism (which always claims the preeminence
of one state or nationality over the rest, and which is
therefore always involving people in useless and perni-

cious wars) is too evident for reasonable people of our age not to free themselves from it; and the religious deceit of the obligation of the oath (which is distinctly forbidden by that very gospel which the governments profess) is, thank God, ever less and less believed in. So that what really prevents the great majority from refusing to take part in military service is merely fear of the punishments which are inflicted by the governments for such refusals. This fear, however, is only a result of the government deceit, and has no other basis than hypnotism.

The governments may and should fear those who refuse to serve, and, indeed, they are afraid of them because every refusal undermines the prestige of the deceit by which the governments have the people in their power. But those who refuse have no ground whatever to fear a government that demands crimes from them. In refusing military service every man risks much less than he would were he to enter it.

The refusal of military service and the punishment —imprisonment, exile—is only an advantageous insurance of oneself against the dangers of the military service. In entering the service every man risks having to take part in war (for which he is being prepared), and during war he may be like a man sentenced to death, placed in a position in which under the most difficult and painful circumstances he will almost certainly be killed or crippled, as I have seen in Sevastopol, where a regiment marched to a fort where two regiments had already been destroyed, and stood there until it too was entirely exterminated. Another, more profitable, chance is that the man who enters the army will not be killed, but will only fall ill and die in the unhealthy conditions of military service. A third chance is that, having been insulted by his superior, he will be unable to contain himself, will answer sharply, will break the discipline, and will be subjected to punishment much worse than that to which he would have been liable had he refused military service.

The best chance, however, is that instead of the imprisonment or exile to which a person refusing military service is liable, he will pass three or five years of his life amid vicious surroundings, practising the art of killing, being all the while in the same captivity as in prison, and in humiliating submission to depraved people. This in the first place.

Secondly, in refusing military service, every man, however strange it may seem, can yet always hope to escape punishment—upon his refusal being that last exposure of the governments' deceit which will render any further punishment for such a deed, the punishment of one who refuses to participate in their oppression, impossible. So that submission to the demands of military service is evidently only submission to the hypnotization of the masses—the utterly futile rush of Panurge's sheep into the water, to their evident destruction.

Moreover, besides the consideration of advantage, there is yet another reason which should impel every man to refuse military service who is not hypnotized and is conscious of the importance of his actions. No one can help desiring that his life should not be an aimless and useless existence, but that it should be of service to God and man; yet frequently a man spends his life without finding an opportunity for such service. The summons to accept the military service presents precisely such an opportunity to every man of our time.

Every man, in refusing to take part in military service

or to pay taxes to a government which uses them for military purposes, is, by this refusal, rendering a great service to God and man, for he is thereby making use of the most efficacious means of furthering the progressive movement of mankind toward that better social order which it is striving after and must eventually attain. But not only is it advantageous to refuse the participation in the military service, and not only should the majority of the men of our time so refuse; it is, moreover, *impossible* not to refuse, if only they are not hypnotized. To every man there are some actions which are morally impossible —as impossible as are certain physical actions. And the promise of slavish obedience to strangers, and to immoral people who have the murder of men as their acknowledged object, is, to the majority of men, if only they be free from hypnotism, just such a morally impossible action. And therefore it is not only advantageous to and obligatory on every man to refuse to participate in the military service, but it is also impossible for him not to do so if only he be free from the stupefaction of hypnotism.

"But what will happen when all people refuse military service, and there is no check nor hold over the wicked, and the wicked triumph, and there is no protection against savage people—against the yellow race—who will come and conquer us?"

I will say nothing about the fact that, as it is, the wicked have long been triumphing, that they are still triumphing, and that while fighting one another they have long dominated the Christians, so that there is no need to fear what has already been accomplished; nor will I say anything with regard to the dread of the savage yellow race, whom we persistently provoke and instruct in war—that being a mere excuse, and one-hundredth part of the army now kept up in Europe being sufficient for the imaginary protection against them—I will say nothing about all this, because the consideration of the general result to the world of such or such actions cannot serve as a guide for our conduct and activity.

To man is given another guide, and that an unfailing one—the guide of his conscience, following which he indubitably knows that he is doing what he should do. Therefore, all considerations of the danger that threatens every individual who refuses military service, as well as what menaces the world in consequence of such refusals —all these are but a particle of that enormous and monstrous deceit in which Christian mankind is enmeshed, and which is being carefully maintained by the governments who exist by the power of this deceit.

If man act in accordance with what is dictated to him by his reason, his conscience, and his God, only the very best can result for himself as well as for the world.

People complain of the evil conditions of life in our Christian world. But is it possible for it to be otherwise, when all of us acknowledge not only that fundamental divine law proclaimed some thousands of years ago, "Thou shalt not kill," but also the law of love and brotherhood of all men, and yet, notwithstanding this, every man in the European world practically disavows this fundamental divine law acknowledged by him, and at the command of president, emperor, or minister, of Nicholas or William, arrays himself in a ridiculous costume, takes an instrument of murder and says, "Here I am, ready to injure, ruin, or kill any one I am ordered to"?

What must a society be like which is composed of such men? Such a society must be dreadful, and indeed it is so!

Awake, brethren! Listen neither to those villains who, from your childhood, infect you with the diabolic spirit of patriotism, opposed to righteousness and truth, and only necessary in order to deprive you of your property, your freedom, and your human dignity; nor to those ancient impostors who preach war in the name of a cruel and vindictive God invented by them, and in the name of a perverted and false Christianity; nor, even less, to those modern Sadducees who, in the name of science and civilization, aiming only at the continuation of the present state of things, assemble at meetings, write books, and make speeches, promising to organize a good and peaceful life for people without their making any effort! Do not believe them. Believe only the consciousness which tells you that you are neither beasts nor slaves, but free men, responsible for your actions, and therefore unable to be murderers either of your own accord or at the will of those who live by these murders.

And it is only necessary for you to awake in order to realize all the horror and insanity of that which you have been and are doing, and, having realized this, to cease that evil which you yourselves abhor, and which is ruining you. If only you were to refrain from the evil which you yourselves detest, those ruling impostors, who first corrupt and then oppress you, would disappear like owls before the daylight, and then those new, human, brotherly conditions of life would be established for which Christendom—weary of suffering, exhausted by deceit, and lost in insolvable contradictions—is longing. Only let every man without any intricate or sophisticated arguments accomplish that which today his conscience unfailingly bids him do, and he will recognize the truth of the Gospel words:—

"If any man will do his will, he shall know of the teaching, whether it be of God, or whether I speak of myself." (John vii. 17.)

PATRIOTISM, OR PEACE?

OU write asking me to state my opinion on the case between the United States and England, "in the cause of Christian consistency and true peace," and you express the hope "that the nations may soon be awakened to the only means of insuring international peace."

I entertain the same hope; and for this reason. The complication which, in our time, involves the nations: exalting patriotism as they do, educating the young generation in that superstition, and at the same time shirking that inevitable consequence of patriotism, war—has, it seems to me, reached that last degree at which the very simplest consideration, such as suggests itself to every unbiased person, may suffice to show to men the extreme contradiction in which they are placed.

Often, when one asks children which they choose of two incompatible but eagerly desired things, they will answer, "Both." "Which do you wish—to go for a drive, or to play at home?" "To go for a drive and to play at home."

Exactly so with the Christian nations, when life itself

puts the question to them, "Which do you choose—patriotism or peace?" They answer, "Patriotism and peace." And yet to combine patriotism and peace is just as impossible as to go for a drive and to stay at home at one and the same time.

The other day a conflict arose between the United States and England over the frontier of Venezuela. Salisbury did not agree to something; Cleveland wrote a message to the Senate; patriotic, warlike cries were raised on both sides; a panic occurred on the Stock market; people lost millions of pounds and dollars; Edison said he was devising machines to kill more men in an hour than were killed by Attila in all his wars; and both nations began to make energetic preparations for war.

But, together with these preparations for war, alike in England and America, various writers, princes, and statesmen began to counsel the governments of both nations to keep from war, insisting that the matter in dispute was not sufficiently serious for war, especially as between two Anglo-Saxon nations, peoples of one language, who ought not to go to war with each other, but ought rather in amity together to domineer over others. Whether because of this, or because all kinds of bishops, clergymen, and ministers prayed and preached over the matter in their churches, or because both sides considered they were not yet ready; for one cause or another, it has turned out there is to be no war this time. And people have calmed down.

But one would have too little penetration not to see that the causes which have thus led to dispute between England and the States still remain the same; that if the present difficulty is settled without war, yet, inevitably, tomorrow or next day, disputes must arise between England and the States, between England and Germany,

England and Russia, England and Turkey, disputes in all possible combinations. Such arise daily; and one or other of them will surely bring war.

For, if there live side by side two armed men, who have from childhood been taught that power, riches, and glory are the highest goods, and that to obtain these by arms, to the loss of one's neighbors, is a most praise-worthy thing; and if, further, there is for these men no moral, religious, or political bond—then is it not clear that they will always seek war, that their normal relations will be warlike, and that having once caught each other by the throat, they separate again only, as the French proverb has it, *pour mieux sauter*—they draw back to take a better spring, to rush upon each other with more ferocity?

The egoism of the individual is terrible. But the egoists of private life are not armed; they do not count it good to prepare, or to use, arms against their competitors; their egoism is controlled by the powers of the state and of public opinion. A private person who should, arm in hand, deprive his neighbor of a cow or an acre of field would be at once seized by the police and imprisoned. Moreover, he would be condemned by public opinion, called a thief and a robber. Quite otherwise with states. All are armed. Influence over them there is none; more than those absurd attempts to catch a bird by sprinkling salt on its tail, such as are the efforts to establish international congresses, which armed states (armed, forsooth, that they may be above taking advice) will clearly never accept. And above all, the public opinion which punishes every violent act of the private individual, praises, exalts as the virtue of patriotism, every appropriation of other people's property made with a view of increasing the power of one's own country.

Open the newspapers on any day you like, and you will always see, every moment, some black spot, a possible cause for war. Now it is Korea; again the Pamirs, Africa, Abyssinia, Armenia, Turkey, Venezuela, or the Transvaal. The work of robbery ceases not for an instant; now here, now there, some small war is going on incessantly, like the exchange of shots in the first line; and a great real war may, must, begin at some moment.

If the American desires the greatness and prosperity of the States before all nations, and the Englishman desires the same for his nation, and the Russian, Turk, Dutchman, Abyssinian, Venezuelan, Boer, Armenian, Pole, Czech, each have a similar desire; if all are convinced that these desires ought not to be concealed and suppressed, but, on the contrary, are something to be proud of, and to be encouraged in oneself and in others; and if one's country's greatness and prosperity can be obtained only at the expense of another, or at times of many other countries and nations—then how can war not be?

Obviously, to avoid war, it is necessary, not to preach sermons and pray God for peace, not to adjure the English-speaking nations to live in peace together in order to domineer over other nations, not to make double and triple counter-alliances, not to intermarry princes and princesses, but to destroy the root of war. And that is, the exclusive desire for the well-being of one's own people; it is patriotism. Therefore, to destroy war, destroy patriotism. But to destroy patriotism, it is first necessary to produce conviction that it is an evil; and that is difficult to do. Tell people that war is an evil, and they will laugh; for who does not know it? Tell them that patriotism is an evil, and most of them will agree, but with a reservation.

"Yes," they will say, "wrong patriotism is an evil; but there is another kind, the kind we hold." But just what this good patriotism is, no one explains. If good patriotism consists in inaggressiveness, as many say, still all patriotism, even if not aggressive, is necessarily retentive; that is, people wish to keep what they have previously conquered. The nation does not exist which was founded without conquest; and conquest can only be retained by the means which achieved it—namely, violence, murder. But if patriotism be not even retentive, it is then the restoring patriotism of conquered and oppressed nations, of Armenians, Poles, Czechs, Irish, and so on. And this patriotism is about the very worst; for it is the most embittered and the most provocative of violence.

Patriotism cannot be good. Why do not people say that egoism may be good? For this might more easily be maintained as to egoism, which is a natural and inborn feeling, than as to patriotism, which is an unnatural feeling, artificially grafted on man.

It will be said, "Patriotism has welded mankind into states, and maintains the unity of states." But men are now united in states; that work is done; why now maintain exclusive devotion to one's own state, when this produces terrible evils for all states and nations? For this same patriotism which welded mankind into states is now destroying those same states. If there·were but one patriotism—say of the English only— then it were possible to regard that as conciliatory, or beneficent. But when, as now, there is American patriotism, English, German, French, Russian, all opposed to one another, in this event, patriotism no longer, unites but disunites. To say that patriotism was beneficent, unifying the states, when it flourished in Greece and Rome, and that it is also similarly and equally beneficent now, after eighteen centuries of life under Christianity, is as much as to say that, because plowing was useful and good for the field before the sowing, it is equally so now, when the crop has come up.

It might, indeed, be well to let patriotism survive, in memory of the benefits it once brought, in the way we have preserved ancient monuments, like temples, tombs, and so on. But temples and tombs endure without causing any harm; while patriotism ceases not to inflict incalculable woes.

Why are Armenians and Turks now agitated, being massacred, becoming like wild beasts? Why are England and Russia, each anxious for its own share of the inheritance from Turkey, waiting upon, and not ending, these butcheries of Armenians? Why are Abyssinians and Italians being massacred? Why was a terrible war within an ace of outbreak over Venezuela; and since, another over the Transvaal? And the Chino-Japanese war, the Russo-Turkish, the Franco-German? And the bitterness of conquered nations: Armenians, Poles, Irish? And the preparations for a war of all nations? All this is the fruit of patriotism. Seas of blood have been shed over this passion; and will yet be shed for it, unless people free themselves of this obsolete relic of antiquity.

Several times now I have had occasion to write about patriotism; about its entire incompatibility, not only with the truly understood teaching of Christ, but with the very lowest demands of morality in a Christian society. Each time my arguments have been met either with silence, or with a lofty suggestion that my ideas, as expressed, are Utopian utterances of mysticism, anarchism, and cosmopolitanism. Often my ideas are summed up, and then, instead of counter-arguments, the remark only is added, that "this is nothing less than cosmopolitanism!" As if this word, cosmopolitanism, had indisputably refuted all my arguments.

Men who are serious, mature, clever, kind, and who—this is the most important matter—stand like a city on a mountain top; men who by their example involuntarily lead the masses; such men assume that the legitimacy and beneficence of patriotism are so far evident and certain, that it is not worth while answering the frivolous and foolish attacks on the sacred feeling. And the majority of people, misled from childhood, and infected with patriotism, accept this lofty silence as the most convincing argument; and they continue to walk in the darkness of ignorance.

Those who, from their position, can help to free the masses from their sufferings, and do not do so, commit a vast sin.

The most fearful evil in the world is hypocrisy. Not in vain did Christ, once only, show anger; and that against the hypocrisy of the Pharisees.

But what was the Pharisaic hypocrisy compared with the hypocrisy of our own time? In comparison with our hypocrites, those among the Pharisees were the justest of men; and their art of hypocrisy was child's play, beside ours. It cannot be otherwise. All our lives, with their profession of Christianity, of the doctrine of humility and love, lived in an armed robber camp, cannot be other than one unbroken, frightful hypocrisy. It is very convenient to profess a doctrine which has, at one end, Christian holiness and consequent infallibility, and at the other end, the heathen sword and gallows; so that, when it is possible to deceive and impose by holiness, holiness is brought in play, while, when the deceit fails, the sword and gallows are set to work. Such a doctrine is very convenient. But a time comes when the cobweb of lies gives way, and it is no longer possible to keep up both ends; one or the other has to go. This is about to happen with the doctrine of patriotism.

Whether people wish it or do not wish it, the question stands clear to mankind, *How can this patriotism, whence come human sufferings incalculable, sufferings both physical and moral, be necessary, and be a virtue?* This question, of compulsion, must be answered.

It is needful, either to show that patriotism is so beneficent that it redeems all those terrible sufferings which it causes to mankind; or else, to acknowledge that patriotism is an evil, which, instead of being grafted upon and suggested to people, should be struggled against with all one's might, to escape from it.

C'est à prendre ou à laisser, as the French say. If patriotism be good, then Christianity, as giving peace, is an idle dream, and the sooner we root it out, the better. But if Christianity really gives peace, and if we really want peace, then patriotism is a survival of barbarism, and it is not only wrong to excite and develop it, as we do now, but it ought to be rooted out by every means, by preaching, persuasion, contempt, ridicule. If Christianity be truth, and we wish to live in peace, then must we more than cease to take pleasure in the power of our country; we must rejoice in the weakening of that power, and help thereto.

A Russian should rejoice if Poland, the Baltic Provinces, Finland, Armenia, should be separated, freed from Russia; so with an Englishman in regard to Ireland, India, and other possessions; and each should help to this, because, the greater the state, the more wrong and cruel is its patriotism, and the greater is the sum of suffering upon which its power is founded. Therefore, if we really wish to be what we profess to be, we must not only cease our present desire for the growth of our state, but we must desire its decrease, its weakening, and help this forward with all our might. And in this way we must train the rising generation; we must educate them so that, just as now a young man is ashamed to show his rude egoism by eating everything and leaving nothing for others, by pushing the weak out of the way that he may pass himself, by forcibly taking that which another needs: so he may then be equally ashamed of desiring increased power for his own country; and so that, just as it is now considered stupid, foolish, to praise oneself, it shall then be seen to be equally foolish to praise one's own nation, as it is now done in divers of the best national histories, pictures, monuments, text-books, articles, verses, sermons, and silly national hymns. It must be understood that, as long as we praise patriotism, and cultivate it in the young, so long will there be armaments to destroy the physical and spiritual life of nations; and wars, vast, awful wars, such as we are preparing for, and into the circle of which we are drawing, debauching them in our patriotism, the new and to be dreaded combatants of the far East.

The Emperor Wilhelm, one of the most absurd personages of our time—orator, poet, musician, dramatist, and painter, chief of all, patriot—lately had made a sketch representing all the nations of Europe, standing, with drawn swords, on the sea-shore; there, under direction of the Archangel Michael, gazing at figures of Buddha and Confucius, seated in the distance. In Wilhelm's intention, this denotes that the nations of Europe must unite, to oppose the danger moving upon them from the quarter shown. And he is perfectly right; that is, from his pagan, gross, patriotic point of view, obsolete these eighteen hundred years.

The European nations, forgetful of Christ for the sake of patriotism, have ever more and more excited and incited these peaceful peoples to patriotism; and now have roused them to such a degree that really, if only Japan and China as completely forget the teaching of Buddha and Confucius as we have forgotten the teaching of Christ, they would soon master the art of killing (soon learned, as Japan has shown); and being brave, skilful, strong, and numerous, they would inevitably do with Europe what the European countries are doing with Africa; unless Europe can oppose to them something stronger than armaments and Edisonian devices. "The discipline is not above his master: but every one that is perfect shall be as his master."

To the question of a petty king, as to how many men, and in what way, he should add to his troops, in order to conquer a southern tribe which refused submission to him, Confucius replied, "Disband all your army, use what you now spend on troops for the education of your people, and for the improvement of agriculture; and the southern tribe will expel its king, and, without war, submit to thy authority."

Thus taught Confucius, whom we are counseled to fear.

And we, having forgotten the teaching of Christ, having renounced him, wish to subdue nations by violence; thereby only to prepare for ourselves new enemies, still more powerful than our present neighbors.

A friend of mine, having seen Wilhelm's picture, said: "The picture is excellent, only it does not at all signify what is written below. It really shows the Archangel Michael

pointing out to all the governments of Europe, represented as brigands hung round with arms, that which is
to destroy, annihilate them; namely, the meekness of
Buddha and the reasonableness of Confucius." He might
have added, "and the humility of Lao-Tse." And indeed
we, in our hypocrisy, have so far forgotten Christ, and
corroded out of our lives all that is Christian, that the
teachings of Buddha and Confucius rise incomparably
higher than that bestial patriotism which guides our
pseudo-Christian nations.

The salvation of Europe, of the whole Christian world,
comes not by being girt with swords, like brigands, as in
Wilhelm's picture; not by rushing across seas to kill our
brethren: but, oppositely, by casting off that survival of
barbarism, patriotism; and having renounced it, by dis-
arming; showing the Oriental nations an example, not of
savage patriotism and ferocity, but that one of brotherly
life which has been taught to us by Christ.

LETTER ON THE PEACE CONFERENCE

HE opinion expressed in your estimable letter, that the easiest and surest way to universal disarmament is by individuals refusing to take part in military service, is most just. I am even of opinion that this is the only way to escape from the terrible and ever increasing miseries of wardom (militarism). But your opinion that at the Conference which is about to assemble at the Tsar's invitation, the question should be debated whether men who refuse military service may not be employed on public works instead, appears to me quite mistaken—in the first place, because the Conference itself can be nothing but one of those hypocritical arrangements which aim not at peace, but, on the contrary, at hiding from men the one means of obtaining universal peace, which the most advanced men begin to discern.

The Conference, it is said, will aim, if not at disarmament, then at checking the increase of armaments. It is supposed that at this Conference the representatives of governments will agree to cease increasing their forces. If so, the question involuntarily presents itself: How will the governments of those countries act which at the time of this meeting happen to be weaker than their neighbors? Such governments will hardly agree to remain in that condition—weaker than their neighbors. Or, if they have such firm belief in the validity of the stipulations made by the Conference as to agree to remain weaker, why should they not be weaker still? Why spend money on an army at all?

If, again, the business of the Conference will be to equalize the fighting forces of the various states, and to keep them stationary, then, even could such an impossible balance be arrived at, the question involuntarily arises: Why need the governments stop at such armaments as now exist? Why not decrease them? Why need Germany, France, and Russia have, say, for instance, 1,000,000 men each, and not 500,000, or why not 10,000 each, or why not 1000 each? If diminution is possible, why not reduce to a minimum? And, finally, why not, instead of armies, have champions—David and Goliath—and settle international questions according to the results of their combats?

It is said that the conflicts between governments are to be decided by arbitration. But, apart from the fact that the disputes will be settled, not by representatives of the people, but by representatives of the governments, and that there is no guarantee that the decisions will be just ones, who is to carry out the decisions of the court? The army? Whose army? That of all the Powers? But the strength of those armies is unequal. Who, for instance, on the Continent is to carry out a decision which is disadvantageous, say, for Germany, Russia, and France allied together? Or who, at sea, will carry out a decision contrary to the interests of England, America, and France?

The arbitrator's sentence against the military violence of states will be carried out by military violence—that is to say, the thing that has to be checked is to be the instrument by which it is to be checked. To catch a bird, put salt on its tail.

I recollect, during the siege of Sevastopol, sitting one day with the Adjutant of Von Saken, commander of the garrison, when Prince S. S. Urusof, a very brave officer, a very eccentric man, and one of the best chess-players of that day in Europe, entered the room. He said he wished to see the general. One of the adjutants took him to the general's cabinet. Ten minutes later Urusof passed out again, looking discontented. The adjutant who had accompanied him returned to us and recounted, laughing, on what business Urusof had come to Von Saken. He had proposed to challenge the English to play a game of chess for the possession of the advanced trench of the fifth bastion, which had been lost and regained several times, and had already cost some hundreds of lives.

Undoubtedly it would have been far better to play chess for the trench than to kill people. But Von Saken did not agree to Urusof's proposal, for he knew well that it would be useless to play at chess for the trench unless both sides trusted each other implicitly, and knew that what was agreed upon would be carried out. But the presence of the soldiers before the trench, and the cannon pointed at it, were signs that no such mutual confidence existed. While there were armies on both sides it was clear that the matter would be decided, not by chess, but by charges. And the same consideration applies to international questions. For them to be decided by courts of arbitration there must be, among the Powers, full mutual confidence that the decisions of the court will be re-

spected. If there is such confidence, no armies are necessary. But if armies exist, it is obvious that this confidence
is lacking, and that international questions can be decided
only by the strength of the armies. As long as armies exist
they are necessary, not only for acquiring fresh territories,
as all the states are now doing, in Asia, in Africa, or in
Europe, but also in order to maintain by force what has
been obtained by force.

Obtaining or retaining by force can be done only by
conquering. And it is always *les gros bataillons* which
conquer. And, therefore, if a government has an army, it
should have as large a one as possible. That is its business.
If a government does not do that, it is unnecessary. A
government may undertake many things in internal
affairs; it may emancipate, civilize, enrich a people, build
roads and canals, colonize waste lands, or organize public
works, but there is one thing it cannot do—viz., the very
thing which this Conference is summoned to do, *i.e.*
reduce its fighting force.

But if, as appeared from the explanations that followed
the manifesto, it will be an aim of the Conference to prohibit implements of destruction which seem particularly
cruel (and why, while they are about it, not try to prohibit the seizure of letters, the falsification of telegrams,
the spy system, and all the terrible meannesses which
form an integral part of military defense?), such prohibition to use in strife all the means that exist is just as
impracticable as it is to forbid people fighting for their
lives to strike the most sensitive parts of the body. And
why is a wound, or death, from an explosive bullet worse
than a wound from the most ordinary bullet or splinter,
inflicted on a very tender part? The suffering in that

case also reaches the utmost limit, and is followed by just the same death as results from any other weapon.

It is amazing that sane adults can seriously express such queer ideas. No doubt diplomatists, who devote their lives to lying, are so accustomed to that vice, and live and act in so dense an atmosphere of lies, that they themselves do not see all the absurdity and mendacity of their proposals. But how can honest private people (not such as curry favor with the Tsar, by extolling his ridiculous proposals)—how is it that they do not see that the result of this Conference can be nothing but the strengthening of the deception in which governments keep their subjects, as was the case with Alexander the First's "Holy Alliance"?

The aim of the Conference will be, not to establish peace, but to hide from men the sole means of escape from the miseries of war, which lies in the refusal by private individuals of all participation in the murders of war. And, therefore, the Conference can on no account accept for discussion the question suggested.

With those who refuse military service on conscientious grounds, governments will always behave as the Russian government behaved with the Dukhobors. At the very time when it was professing to the whole world its peaceful intentions, it was (with every effort to keep the matter secret) torturing and ruining and banishing the most peaceable people in Russia, merely because they were peaceable, not in words only, but in deeds, and therefore refused to be soldiers. All the European governments have met, and still meet, refusals of military service in the same way, though less brutally. That is how the governments of Austria, Germany, France, Sweden

Switzerland, and Holland have acted, and are still acting, and they cannot act otherwise.

They cannot act otherwise because they govern their own subjects by force—*i.e.* by means of a disciplined army—and can, therefore, on no account leave the reduction of that force (and consequently of their own power) to the casual inclination of private people, especially because nobody likes to kill or to be killed; and should they tolerate such refusals, the great majority of people probably would prefer to do other work instead of being soldiers. So that, as soon as people were permitted to refuse army service, and do work instead, there would soon be so many laborers that there would not be soldiers enough to make the workers work.

Liberals entangled in their much talking, socialists, and other so-called advanced people may think that their speeches in Parliament and at meetings, their unions, strikes, and pamphlets, are of great importance; while the refusals of military service by private individuals are unimportant occurrences not worthy of attention. The governments, however, know very well what is important to them and what is not. And the governments readily allow all sorts of liberal and radical speeches in Reichstags, as well as workmen's associations and socialist demonstrations, and they even pretend themselves to sympathize with these things, knowing that they are of great use to them in diverting people's attention from the great and only means of emancipation. But governments never openly tolerate refusals of military service, or refusals of war taxes, which are the same thing, because they know that such refusals expose the fraud of governments and strike at the root of their power.

As long as governments continue to rule their people

by force, and continue to desire, as now, to obtain new possessions (Philippines, Port Arthur, etc.), and to retain what they already posses (Poland, Alsace, India, Algeria, etc.), so long will they not voluntarily decrease their armies, but will, on the contrary, continue to increase them.

It was recently reported that an American regiment refused to go to Iloilo. This news was given as something astonishing. But the really astonishing thing is that such things do not occur continually. How could all those Russians, Germans, Frenchmen, Italians, and Americans who have fought in recent times, set off to kill men of another country at the whim of strangers, whom in most cases they did not respect, and submit themselves to suffering and death?

It seems plain and natural that all these men should recollect themselves, if not when they are enlisted as soldiers, then at the last moment when they are being led against the enemy, and should stop, fling away their weapons, and call to their opponents to do the same.

It seems so plain and natural that every one should do this, and if they do not do so it is only because they believe in the governments that assure them that all the burdens people bear for war are laid upon them for their own good. With amazing effrontery, all governments have always declared, and still go on declaring, that all the preparations for war, and even the very wars themselves, that they undertake, are necessary to preserve peace. In this sphere of hypocrisy and deception a fresh step is being made now, consisting in this: That the very governments for whose support the armies and the wars are essential pretend that they are concerned to discover means to diminish the armies and to abolish war. The governments wish to persuade the peoples that there is no need for private individuals to trouble about freeing themselves from wars; the governments themselves, at their conferences, will arrange first to reduce and presently quite to abolish armies. But this is—untrue.

Armies can be reduced and abolished only in opposition to the will, but never by the will, of governments.

Armies will only be diminished and abolished when people cease to trust governments, and themselves seek salvation from the miseries that oppress them, and seek that safety, not by the complicated and delicate combinations of diplomatists, but in the simple fulfilment of that law, binding upon every man, inscribed in all religious teachings, and present in every heart, not to do to others what you wish them not to do to you—above all, not to slay your neighbors.

Armies will first diminish, and then disappear, only when public opinion brands with contempt those who, whether from fear, or for advantage, sell their liberty and enter the ranks of those murderers, called soldiers; and when the men now ignored and even blamed—who, in despite of all the persecution and suffering they have borne—have refused to yield the control of their actions into the hands of others, and become the tools of murder—are recognized by public opinion, to be the foremost champions and benefactors of mankind. Only then will armies first diminish and then quite disappear, and a new era in the life of mankind will commence. And that time is near.

And that is why I think that your opinion that the refusals to serve in the army are facts of immense importance, and that they will emancipate mankind from the miseries or war, is perfectly just. But your opinion that the Conference may conduce toward this is quite an error. The Conference can only divert people's eyes from the sole path leading to safety and liberty.*

* A number of Swedish gentlemen addressed a letter to Tolstoï concerning the Tsar's Peace Conference, in reply to which he wrote them a letter.

Tolstoï is always most careful in the arrangement of the thoughts he puts before the world. His works are written over and over again before they are published. On this occasion, after he had despatched the letter, he felt that the manner in which he had expressed his opinion was not satisfactory. Eventually he rewrote the article, in such a way that the whole letter was recast in a fresh form, and hardly a paragraph of the original remained unaltered.—TR.

LETTER TO A
NON-COMMISSIONED OFFICER

OU are surprised that soldiers are taught that it is right to kill people in certain cases and in war, while in the books admitted to be holy by those who so teach, there is nothing like such a permission, but, on the contrary, not only is all murder forbidden, but all insulting of others is forbidden also, and we are told not to do to others what we do not wish done to us. And you ask, is not this a fraud? And if it is a fraud, then for whose sake is it done?

Yes, it is a fraud, committed for the sake of those accustomed to live on the sweat and blood of other men, and who have therefore perverted, and still pervert, Christ's teaching, which was given to man for his good, but which has now, in its perverted form, become the chief source of human misery.

The thing has come about in this way:—

The government, and all those people of the upper classes that are near the government, and that live by the work of others, need some means of dominating the workers, and this means they find in their control of the army. Defence against foreign enemies is only an excuse. The German government frightens its subjects about the Russians and the French, the French government frightens its people about the Germans, the Russian government frightens its people about the French and the Germans, and that is the way with all governments. But neither the Germans, nor the Russians, nor the French, desire to fight their neighbors and other people; but, living in peace, they dread war more than anything else in the world. The government and the upper governing classes, to excuse their domination of the laborers, behave like a gipsy who whips his horse before he turns a corner and then pretends he cannot hold it in. They provoke their own people and some foreign government, and then pretend that for the well-being or for the defense of their people they must declare war, which again brings profit only to generals, officers, functionaries, merchants, and, in general, to the rich. In reality war is an inevitable result of the existence of armies; and armies are only needed by governments in order to dominate their own working-classes.

The thing is a crime, but the worst of it is that the government, in order to have a plausible basis for its domination of the people, has to pretend that it holds the highest religious teaching known to man (*i.e.* the Christian), and that it brings up its subjects in this teaching. That teaching, however, is in its nature opposed not only to murder, but to all violence, and, therefore, the governments, in order to dominate the people and to be considered Christian, had to pervert Christianity and to hide its true meaning from the people, and thus deprive men of the well-being Christ brought them.

This perversion was accomplished long ago, in the time

of that scoundrel the Emperor Constantine, who for doing it was enrolled among the saints.* All subsequent governments, especially our Russian government, do their utmost to preserve this perverted understanding, and not to allow the people to see the real meaning of Christianity; because, having seen the real meaning of Christianity, the people would perceive that the governments, with their taxes, soldiers, prisons, gallows, and false priests, are not only not the pillars of Christianity they profess to be, but are its greatest enemies.

In consequence of this perversion those frauds which have surprised you are possible, and all those terrible misfortunes occur from which people suffer.

The people are oppressed, robbed, poor, ignorant, dying of hunger. Why? Because the land is in the hands of the rich; the people are enslaved in mills and in factories, obliged to earn money because taxes are demanded from them, and the price of their labor is diminished while the price of things they need is increased.

How are they to escape? By taking the land from the rich? But if this is done, soldiers will come and will kill the rebels or put them in prison. Take the mills and factories? The same will happen. Organize and support a strike? But it is sure to fail. The rich will hold out longer than the workers, and the armies are always on the side of the capitalists. The people will never extricate themselves from the want in which they are kept, as long as the army is in the hands of the governing classes.

But who compose these armies that keep the people in

---

* Constantine the Great was decreed to be a god by the Roman Senate, and was made a Christian saint by the Eastern Church.—Tr.

this state of slavery? Who are these soldiers that will fire at the peasants who take the land, or at the strikers who will not disperse, and at the smugglers who bring in goods without paying taxes, that put in prison and there guard those who refuse to pay taxes? The soldiers are these same peasants who are deprived of land, these same strikers who want better wages, these same taxpayers who want to be rid of these taxes.

And why do these people shoot at their brothers? Because it has been instilled into them that the oath they were obliged to take on entering the service is binding, and that, though it is generally wrong to murder people, it is right to do so at the command of their superiors. That is to say that that fraud is played off upon them which has occurred to you. But here we meet the question: How is it that sensible people—often people who can read, and even educated people—believe in such an evident lie? However little education a man may have, he cannot but know that Christ did not sanction murder, but taught kindness, meekness, forgiveness of injuries, love of one's enemies—and therefore he cannot help seeing that on the basis of Christian teaching he cannot pledge himself in advance to kill all whom he may be ordered to kill.

The question is: How can sensible people believe, as all now serving in the army have believed and still believe, such an evident fraud? The answer is that it is not this one fraud by itself that takes people in, but they have from childhood been deprived of the proper use of their reason by a whole series of frauds, a whole system of frauds, called the Orthodox Faith, which is nothing but the grossest idolatry. In this faith people are taught that God is triple, that besides this triple God

there is a Queen of Heaven,* and besides this queen
there are various saints whose corpses have not de-
cayed,** and besides these saints there are ikons*** of
the Gods and of the Queen of Heaven, to which one
should offer candles and pray with one's hands; and that
the most important and holy thing on earth is the
pap,**** which the parson makes of wine and white
bread on Sundays behind a railing; and that after the
parson has whispered over it, the wine is no longer wine,
and the white bread is not bread, but they are the blood
and flesh of one of the triple Gods, etc.

All this is so stupid and senseless that it is quite impossible to understand what it all means. And the very
people who teach this faith do not tell you to understand

---

* The Holy Virgin, the "Mother of God," and "Queen of
Heaven," plays a prominent part in the Orthodox Eastern Church,
i.e. the Russo-Greek Church.—TR.

** One proof of holiness adduced as justifying admission to the
rank of sainthood is the non-decomposition of the holy person's
corpse. These miraculously preserved bodies are enshrined in
chapels, monasteries, and cathedrals, and are there visited by
pilgrims who offer up prayers at the shrine, place candles before
it, and usually leave some contribution for the benefit of the
establishment. The inspection allowed is not very close, and there
are stories of people being employed to stuff the saints with straw.
These tales are, however, considered irreligious.—TR.

*** The *ikons* of the Eastern Church are not "graven images,"
but are pictures painted in a conventional cadaverous manner on
wood; these are often covered with an embossed metal cover allowing only the hands and face to be seen, and making the ikon as
much like an image as a picture.—TR.

**** "The pap" is the author's irreverent way of referring to
the mixture of bread and wine administered by the priests of
the Orthodox Eastern Church at the celebration of the Holy
Eucharist.—TR.

it, but only tell you to believe it; and people trained to it
from childhood can believe any kind of nonsense that is
told them. And when men have been so befooled that
they believe that God hangs in the corner,* or sits in a
morsel of pap which the parson gives out in a spoon; that
to kiss a board or some relics, and to put candles in
front of them, is useful for life here and hereafter—they
are called on to enter the military service, where they are
humbugged to any extent, being made to swear on the
Gospels (in which swearing is prohibited) that they will
do just what is forbidden in those Gospels, and then
taught that to kill people at the word of those in command is not a sin, but that to refuse to submit to those in
command is a sin. So that the fraud played off on soldiers,
when it is instilled into them that they may without sin
kill people at the wish of those in command, is not an
isolated fraud, but is bound up with a whole system of
fraud, without which this one fraud would not deceive
them.

Only a man·who is quite befooled by the false faith
called Orthodoxy, palmed off upon him for the true Christian faith, can believe that there is no sin in a Christian
entering the army, promising blindly to obey any man
who ranks above him in the service, and, at the will of
others, learning to kill, and committing that most terrible
crime, forbidden by all laws.

A man free from the pseudo-Christian faith called
Orthodox will not believe that.

---

* This refers to the common practice of hanging an ikon in the
corner of each dwelling-room. These ikons are called "Gods," and
are prayed to in a way that among common and devout people
often amounts to idolatry.—TR.

And that is why the so-called Sectarians—*i.e.* Christians who have repudiated the Orthodox teaching and acknowledge Christ's teaching as explained in the Gospels, and especially in the Sermon on the Mount—are not tricked by this deception, but have frequently refused, and still do refuse, to be soldiers, considering such occupation incompatible with Christianity and preferring to bear all kinds of persecution, as hundreds and thousands of people are doing; in Russia among the Dukhobors and Molokans, in Austria the Nazarenes, and in Sweden, Switzerland, and Germany among members of the Evangelical sects. The government knows this, and is therefore exceedingly anxious that the general Church fraud, without which its power could not be maintained, should be commenced with every child from early infancy, and should be continually maintained in such a way that none may avoid it. The government tolerates anything else, drunkenness and vice (and not only tolerates, but even organizes drunkenness and vice—they help to stupefy people), but by all the means in its power it hinders those who have escaped from its trap from assisting others to escape.

The Russian government perpetrates this fraud with special craft and cruelty. It orders all its subjects to baptize their children during infancy into the false faith called Orthodoxy, and it threatens to punish them if they disobey. And when the children are baptized, *i.e.* are reckoned as Orthodox, then under threats of criminal penalties they are forbidden to discuss the faith into which, without their wish, they were baptized; and for such discussion of that faith, as well as for renouncing it and passing to another, they are actually punished. So that about all Russians it cannot be said that they believe the Orthodox faith—they do not know whether they believe it or not, but were converted to it during infancy and kept in it by violence, *i.e.* by the fear of punishment. All Russians were entrapped into Orthodoxy by a cunning fraud, and are kept in it by cruel force. Using the power it wields, the government perpetrates and maintains this fraud, and the fraud upholds its power.

And, therefore, the only means to free people from their many miseries lies in freeing them from the false faith instilled in them by government, and in their imbibing the true Christian teaching which is hidden by this false teaching. The true Christian teaching is very simple, clear, and obvious to all, as Christ said. But it is simple and accessible only when man is freed from that falsehood in which we were all educated. and which is passed off upon us as God's truth.

Nothing needful can be poured into a vessel full of what is useless. We must first empty out what it useless. So it is with the acquirement of true Christian teaching. We have first to understand that all the stories telling how God six thousand years ago made the world; how Adam sinned and the human race fell; and how the Son of God, a God born of a virgin, came on earth and redeemed man; and all the fables in the Old Testament and in the Gospels, and all the lives of the saints with their stories of miracles and relics—are nothing but a gross hash of Jewish superstitions and priestly frauds. Only to a man quite free from this deception can the clear and simple teaching of Christ, which needs no explanation, be accessible and comprehensible. That teaching tells us nothing of the beginning, or of the end, of the world, or about God and His purpose, or in general about things which we cannot, and need not, know; but it speaks only of what man must do to save himself, *i.e.* how best to live the life he has come into, in this world, from birth to death. For this purpose it is only necessary to act to others as we wish them to act to us. In that is all the law and the prophets, as Christ said. And to act in that way we need neither ikons, nor relics, nor church services, nor priests, nor catechisms, nor governments, but on the contrary, we need perfect freedom from all that; for to do to others as we wish them to do to us is only possible when a man is free from the fables which the priests give out as the only truth, and is not bound by promises to act as other people may order. Only such a man will be capable of fulfilling—not his own will nor that of other men—but the will of God.

And the will of God is not that we should fight and oppress the weak, but that we should acknowledge all men to be our brothers and should serve one another.

These are the thoughts your letter has aroused in me. I shall be very glad if they help to clear up the questions you are thinking about.

LETTER TO
DR. EUGEN HEINRICH SCHMITT

OU write to me that people seem quite unable to understand that to serve the government is incompatible with Christianity.

In just the same way people were long unable to see that indulgences, inquisitions, slavery, and tortures were incompatible with Christianity. But a time came when it was comprehensible; and a time will come when men will understand the incompatibility with Christianity, first of war service (that already is beginning to be felt), and then of service to government in general.

It is now fifty years since a not widely known, but very remarkable, American writer—Thoreau—not only clearly expressed that incompatibility in his admirable essay on "Civil Disobedience." but gave a practical example of such disobedience. Not wishing to be an accomplice or supporter of a government which legalized slavery, he declined to pay a tax demanded of him, and went to prison for it.

Thoreau refused to pay taxes to government, and evidently the same motives as actuated him would prevent men from serving a government. As, in your letter to the minister, you have admirably expressed it: you do not consider it compatible with your moral dignity to work for an institution which represents legalized murder and robbery.

Thoreau was, I think, the first to express this view. People paid scant attention to either his refusal or his article fifty years ago—the thing seemed so strange. It was put down to his eccentricity. Today your refusal attracts some attention, and, as is always the case when new truth is clearly expressed, it evokes a double surprise—first, surprise that a man should say such queer things, and then, surprise that I had not myself discovered what this man is saying; it is so certain and so obvious.

Such a truth as that a Christian must not be a soldier —*i.e.* a murderer—and must not be the servant of an institution maintained by violence and murder, is so certain, so clear and irrefutable, that to enable people to grasp it, discussion, proof, or eloquence are not necessary. For the majority of men to hear and understand this truth, it is only needful that it should be constantly repeated.

The truth that a Christian should not take part in murdering, or serve the chiefs of the murderers for a salary collected from the poor by force, is so plain and indisputable that those who hear it cannot but agree with it. And if a man continues to act contrary to these truths after hearing them, it is only because he is accustomed to act contrary to them, and it is difficult to break the habit. Moreover, as long as most people act as he does, he will not, by acting contrary to the truth, lose the regard of the majority of those who are most respected.

The case is the same as it is with the question of vegetarianism. "A man can live and be healthy without killing animals for food; therefore, if he eats meat, he participates in taking animal life merely for the sake of his appetite. And to act so is immoral." It is so simple and indubitable that it is impossible not to agree with it. But because most people do eat meat, people, on hearing the case stated, admit its justice, and then, laughing, say; "But a good beefsteak is a good thing all the same; and I shall eat one at dinner today with pleasure."

Just in the same way officers in the army, and officials employed in the civil service, treat statements of the incompatibility of Christianity and humanitarianism with military and civil service. "Yes, of course, it's true," says such a man, "but, all the same, it is nice to wear a uniform and epaulets, which serve as an introduction anywhere, and which people respect; and it is still better to know that, whatever happens, your salary will be paid punctually and accurately on the first of each month. So that though your statement of the case is correct, I am nevertheless bent on getting a rise of salary and securing a pension."

The position is admitted to be indubitable; but, in the first place, one need not oneself kill an ox to get beefsteaks. It has already been killed. And one need not oneself collect taxes or murder. The taxes are already collected, and the army already exists. And, secondly, most people have not yet heard this view of things, and do not know that it is wrong to do these things. So that, for the present, one need not refuse a well-cooked beefsteak, or a uniform, and all its advantages, or medals and orders; or, above all, a secure monthly salary; "and as for the future, we shall see when the time comes."

At the root of the matter lies the fact that people have not yet heard the injustice and wickedness of such a way of life stated. And, therefore, it is necessary continually to repeat "Carthago delenda est," and Carthage will certainly fall.

I do not say that government and its power will be destroyed. It will not fall to pieces quickly; there are still too many gross elements among the people to support it. But the Christian support of government will be destroyed—*i.e.* those who do violence will cease to find support for their authority in the sanctity of Christianity. Those who employ violence will be simply violators, and nothing else. And when that is so—when they can no longer cloak themselves with pseudo-Christianity—then the end of all violence will be near.

Let us seek to hasten that end. "Carthago delenda est." Government is violence, Christianity is meekness, non-resistance, love. And, therefore, government cannot be Christian, and a man who wishes to be a Christian must not serve government. Government cannot be Christian. A Christian cannot serve government. Government cannot . . . and so on.

A REPLY TO CRITICISMS

RECEIVED your letter, and hastened to read your article in *The Northern Messenger*. I am much obliged to you for drawing my attention to this. The article is excellent, and I have learned from it much that was new and joyful to me. I knew about Micskiewicz and Tovianski. But I ascribed their religious direction to the exceptional dispositions of these two individuals. From your article I learn that they are only the forerunners of a Christian movement, deeply touching in its nobility and sincerity, which has been called forth by patriotism, and which still endures.

My article, "Christianity and Patriotism," evoked very many objections. I received them from philosophers and journalists, Russian, French, German, and Austrian; and now from you. All the objections, yours among them, amount to this: That my condemnation of patriotism is justly applied to bad patriotism, but has no foundation as regards good and useful patriotism. But, as to what constitutes this latter, and how it is distinguishable from bad patriotism, no one has yet troubled to explain.

You say in your letter, that "as well as the militant,

inhumane patriotism of strong nations, there is also the opposite patriotism of enslaved nations, who seek only to defend their native faith and language against the enemy." You thus identify good patriotism as the patriotism of the oppressed. But the oppression or the dominance of nations makes no essential difference in what is called patriotism. Fire is always the same burning and dangerous fire, whether it blaze up in a bonfire or flicker in a match.

By "patriotism" is really meant a love for one's own nation above other nations; just as by "egoism" is meant a love for oneself more than for others. It is hard to imagine how such preference for one nation above others can be deemed a good, and therefore a desirable, disposition. If you say that patriotism is more pardonable in the oppressed than in the oppressor, just as a manifestation of egoism is more pardonable in a man who is being strangled than in one who is left in peace, then it is impossible to disagree with you; nevertheless, patriotism cannot change its nature, whether it is displayed in oppressor or oppressed. This disposition of preference for one nation over all others, like egoism, can in nowise be good.

But not only is patriotism a bad disposition, it is unreasonable in principle.

By patriotism is meant, not only spontaneous, instinctive love for one's own nation, and preference for it above all other nations, but also the belief that such love and preference are good and useful. This belief is especially unreasonable in Christian nations.

It is unreasonable, not only because it runs counter to the first principles of Christ's teachings, but also because Christianity gains, by its own method, everything for

which patriotism seeks; thus making patriotism superfluous, unnecessary, and a hindrance, like a lamp by daylight.

A man who, like Krasinski, believes that "the Church
of God is not in this or that place, this or that rite, but
in the whole planet, and in all the relations which can
exist between individuals and nations"—such a man can
no longer be a patriot; but he will, in the name of Christianity, do all that patriotism can demand of him. For
example, patriotism demands of its votary the devotion of
his life for the sake of his fellow-countrymen. But Christianity, demanding the same devotion for the good of all
men, demands it all the more forcibly and naturally for
those of one's own nation.

You write of the terrible acts of violence perpetrated
by the savage, stupid, and cruel Russian authorities,
directed against the belief and language of the Poles;
and you exhibit these as providing a motive for patriotic
action. But I do not see this. To feel indignation at these
deeds, and to oppose them with all one's might, it is not
necessary to be either a Pole or a patriot; to be a Christian
is enough.

Upon this point I, for instance, who am not a Pole,
will yet vie with any Pole in the degree of my abhorrence
of, my indignation at, those savage and stupid measures
which Russian government officials direct against the
Poles. I will go as far also, in my desire to oppose those
measures; and this, not because I care for Catholicism
above other religions, or for the Polish language above
other tongues, but because I strive to be a Christian. In
like manner, for the abolition of such evils, whether in
Poland, or Alsace, or Bohemia, we need the spread, not
of patriotism, but of true Christianity.

Some may say, "We do not wish to accept Christianity, and we are therefore free to exalt patriotism." But when once men have acknowledged Christianity, or at least the perception of human equality and respect for human dignity which flow from Christianity, there is then no longer room for patriotism. What, again, most astonishes me in all this is, that the upholders of the patriotism of the oppressed do not see how harmful patriotism, however perfect and refined they may represent it to be, is to their own particular cause.

Those attacks upon language and religion in Poland, the Baltic provinces, Alsace, Bohemia, upon the Jews in Russia, in every place where such acts ·of violence occur—in what name have they been, and are they, perpetrated? In none other than the name of that patriotism which you defend.

Ask our savage Russifiers of Poland and the Baltic provinces, ask the persecutors of the Jews, why they act thus. They will tell you it is in defence of their native religion and language; they will tell you that if they do not act thus, their religion and language will suffer—the Russians will be Polonized, Teutonized, Judaized.

Were there no doctrine that patriotism is beneficial, men of the end of the nineteenth century would never be found sunken so low as to determine upon the abominations they at present enact.

Now, learned men (our most savage religious persecutor is an ex-professor) find standing-ground upon patriotism. They know history, they know of all the fruitless horrors of persecution for the sake of language and religion; but, thanks to the doctrine of patriotism, they have a justification.

Patriotism gives them a standing-ground, which Christianity takes from under their feet. Therefore it behooves conquered nations, sufferers from oppression, to destroy patriotism, to destroy its doctrinal foundations, to ridicule it, and not to exalt it.

Defending patriotism, people go on to talk of the individuality of nations, of patriotism aiming to save the individuality of a nation; while the individuality of nations is assumed to be a necessary condition of progress.

But, to begin with, who says that such individuality is necessary to progress? This is in no way proved, and we have no right to take such an arbitrary assumption as an axiom. In the next place, even if it be accepted, even then, the way for a nation to assert its individuality is, not to struggle to do so, but, on the contrary, to forget about its individuality, and then to accomplish with all its power that which its people feel themselves most able, and therefore most called upon, to do. Just as an individual will, most assert his individuality, not when he pays heed to it, but when, having forgotten about it, he, to the limit of his strength and capacity, does that to which his nature attracts him. So matters would be arranged among a people who, working for their support as a community, must choose different kinds of work and different places. Only let each one follow his strength and capacity in doing what is most necessary to the community, and do this as well as he can, and all will inevitably work differently, with different tools and in different places.

One of the commonest sophisms used in defending immorality consists in wilfully confusing what is with what should be, and, having begun to speak of one thing, substituting another. This very sophism is employed above all in relation to patriotism. It is a fact, that to every Pole, the Pole is nearest and dearest; to the German, the German; to the Jew; the Jew; to the Russian, the Russian. It is even true that, through historical causes and bad education, the people of one nation instinctively feel aversion and ill-will to those of another. All this is so; but to admit it, like admitting the fact that each man loves himself more than he loves others, can in no way prove that it ought so to be. On the contrary, the whole concern of all humanity, and of every individual, lies in suppressing these preferences and aversions, in battling with them, and in deliberately behaving toward other nations and toward individual foreigners, exactly as toward one's own nation and fellow-countrymen.

To care for patriotism as an emotion worthy to be cultivated in every man is wholly superfluous. God, or nature, has already, without our care, so provided for this feeling that every man has it, leaving us no cause to trouble about cultivating it in ourselves and others. We must concern ourselves, not about patriotism, but to bring into life that light which is within us; to change the character of life, and approach it to the ideal which stands before us. That ideal, presented in our time before every man, and illumined with the true light from Christ, has not to do with the resuscitation of Poland, Bohemia, Ireland, Armenia; has not to do with the preservation of the unity and greatness of Russia, England, Germany, Austria; but, on the contrary, is concerned to destroy this unity and greatness of Russia, England, Germany, Austria, by the destruction of those force-maintained anti-Christian combinations called states, which stand in the way of all true progress, and occasion the sufferings of oppressed and conquered nations; occasion all those evils from which contemporary humanity suffers. Such destruc-

tion is only possible through true enlightenment, resulting in the avowal that we, before being Russians, Poles,
Germans, are men, the followers of one teacher, the children of one Father, brothers; and this the best representatives of the Polish nation understand, as you have
so excellently shown in your article. Day by day this is
understood by a greater and greater number of people
throughout the whole world. So that the days of State
violence are already numbered, and the liberation, not
only of conquered nations, but of the crushed working-
people, is by this time near, if only we ourselves will not
delay the time of liberation, by sharing with deed and
word in the violent measures of governments. The
approval of patriotism of any kind as a good quality, and
the incitement of the people to patriotism, are chief
hindrances to the attainment of those ideals which rise
before us.

Once more, I thank you very much for your letter, for
the excellent article, and for the opportunity you have
given me of again reconsidering, verifying, and expressing
my ideas on patriotism.

REPLY TO CRITICS

A LETTER ADDRESSED TO "THE DAILY CHRONICLE"

INCE the appearance of my book, "The Kingdom of God is within Us," and my article on "Patriotism and Christianity," I often hear and read in articles and letters addressed to me, arguments against, I will not say the ideas expressed in those books, but against such misconstructions as are put upon them. This is done sometimes consciously, but very often unwittingly, and is wholly due to a want of understanding of the spirit of the Christian religion.

"It is all very well," they say; "despotism, capital punishments, wars, the arming of all Europe, the precarious state of the working-classes, are indeed great evils, and you are right in condemning all this; but how can we do without government? What will you give instead of it? Being ourselves men, with a limited knowledge and intellect, have we the right, just because it seems best to us, to destroy that order of things which has helped our forefathers to attain the present state of civilization and its advantages? If you destroy the State, you must put something in its place. How can we run the risk of all the calamities which might ensue if government was abolished?"

But the fact is that the Christian doctrine, in its true sense, never proposed to abolish anything, nor to change any human organization. The very thing which distinguishes Christian religion from all other religions and social doctrines is that it gives men the possibilities of a real and good life, not by means of general laws regulating the lives of all men, but by enlightening each individual man with regard to the sense of his own life, by showing him wherein consists the evil and the real good of his life. And the sense of life thus imparted to man by the Christian doctrine is so simple, so convincing, and leaves so little room for doubt, that if once man understands it, and, therefore, conceives wherein is the real good and the real evil of his life, he can never again consciously do what he considers to be the evil of his life, nor abstain from doing what he considers to be the real good of it, as surely as a plant cannot help turning toward light, and water cannot help running downward.

The sense of life, as shown by the Christian religion, consists in living so as to do the will of Him who sent us into life, from whom we are come, and to whom we shall return. The evil of our life consists in acting against this will, and the good in fulfilling it. And the rule given to us for the fulfilment of this will is so very plain and simple that it is impossible not to understand, or to misunderstand it.

If you cannot do unto others what you would that they should do to you, at least do not unto them what you would not that they should do unto you.

If you would not be made to work ten hours at a stretch in factories or in mines, if you would not have your children hungry, cold, and ignorant, if you would not be robbed of the land that feeds you, if you would not be shut up in prisons and sent to the gallows or hanged for committing an unlawful deed through passion or ignorance, if you would not suffer wounds nor be killed in war—do not do this to others. All this is so simple and straightforward, and admits of so little doubt, that it is impossible for the simplest child not to understand, nor for the cleverest man to refute it. It is impossible to refute this law, especially because this law is given to us, not only by all the wisest men of the world, not only by the Man who is considered to be God by the majority of Christians, but because it is written in our minds and hearts.

Let us imagine a servant in his lord's power, appointed by his master to a task he loves and understands. If this man were to be addressed by men whom he knows to be dependent on his master in the same way as he is, to whom similar tasks are set at which they will not work, and who would entreat him for his own good and for the good of other men to do what is directly opposed to his lord's plain commandments, what answer can any reasonable servant give to such entreaties? But this simile is far from fully expressing what a Christian must feel when he is called upon to take an active part in oppressing, robbing people of their land, in executing them, in waging war, and so on, all things which governments call upon us to do; for, however binding the commands of that master may have been to his servant, they can never be compared to that unquestionable knowledge which every man, as long as he is not corrupted by false doctrines, does possess, that he cannot and must not do unto others what he does not wish to be done unto him, and therefore cannot and must not take part in all things opposed to the rule of his Master, which are imposed upon him by governments.

Therefore the question for a Christian does not lie in this: whether or no a man has the right to destroy the existing order of things, and to establish another in its stead, or to decide which kind of government will be the best, as the question is sometimes purposely and very often unintentionally put by the enemies of Christianity (the Christian does not think about the general order of things, but leaves the guidance of them to God, for he firmly believes God has implanted His law in our minds and hearts, that there may be order, not disorder, and that nothing but good can arise from our following the unquestionable law of God, which has been so plainly manifested to us); but the question, the decision of which is not optional, but unavoidable, and which daily presents itself for a Christian to decide, is: How am I to act in the dilemma which is constantly before me? Shall I form part of a government which recognizes the right to own landed property by men who never work on it, which levies taxes on the poor in order to give them to the rich, which condemns erring men to gallows and death, which sends out soldiers to commit murder, which depraves whole races of men by means of opium and brandy, etc., or shall I refuse to take a share in a government, the doings of which are contrary to my conscience? But what will come of it, what sort of State will there be, if I act in this way, is a thing I do not know and which I shall not say I do not wish to know, but which I cannot know.

The main strength of Christ's teaching consists especially in this: that He brought the question of conduct from a world of conjecture and eternal doubt, down to a firm and indisputable ground. Some people say, "But we also do not deny the evils of the existing order and the necessity of changing it, but we wish to change it, not suddenly, by means of refusing to take any part in the government, but, on the contrary, by participating in the government, by gaining more and more freedom, political rights, and obtaining the election of the true friends of the people and the enemies of all violence."

This would be very well, if taking part in one's government and trying to improve it, could coincide with the aim of human life. But, unfortunately, it not only does not coincide, but is quite opposed to it.

Supposing human life to be limited to this world, its aim can consist only in man's individual happiness; if, on the other hand, life does not end in this world, its aim can consist only in doing the will of God. In both cases it does not coincide with the progress of governments. If it lies here, in man's personal happiness, and if life ends here, what should I care about the future prosperity of a government which will come about when, in all probability, I shall be there no more? But if my life is immortal, then the prosperity of the English, the Russian, the German, or any other state, which is to come in the twentieth century, is too paltry an aim for me, and can never satisfy the cravings of my immortal soul. A sufficient aim for my life is either my immediate personal good, which does not coincide with the government measures and improvements, or the fulfilment of the will of God, which also not only cannot be conciliated with the requirements of government, but is quite opposed to them. The vital question not only for a Christian, but, I think, for any reasonable being, when he is summoned to take part in governmental acts, lies not in the prosperity of his state or government, but in this question:—

"Wilt thou, a being of reason and goodness, who comes today and may vanish tomorrow, wilt thou, if thou believest in the existence of God, act against His law and His will, knowing that any moment thou canst return to Him; or, if thou dost not believe in Him, wilt thou, knowing that if thou errest thou shalt never be able to redeem thy error, wilt thou, nevertheless, act in opposition to the principles of reason and love, by which alone thou canst be guided in life? Wilt thou, at the request of thy government, take oaths, defend, by compulsion, the owner of land or capital, wilt thou pay taxes for keeping policemen, soldiers, warships, wilt thou take part in parliaments, law courts, condemnations, and wars?"

And to all this—I will not say for a Christian, but for a reasonable being—there can be but one answer: "No, I cannot, and will not." But they say, "This will destroy the State and the existing order." If the fulfilment of the will of God is destroying the existing order, is it not a proof that this existing order is contrary to the will of God, and ought to be destroyed?

LETTER TO THE LIBERALS*

 SHOULD be very glad to join you and your associates—whose work I know and appreciate—in standing up for the rights of the "Literature Committee," and in opposing the enemies of popular education. But in the sphere in which you are working, I see no way to resist them.

My only consolation is that I, too, am constantly engaged in struggling against the same enemies of enlightenment, though in another manner.

Concerning the special question with which you are preoccupied, I think that, in place of the "Literature

* This letter was addressed to a Russian lady who wrote to Tolstoï asking his advice or assistance when the "Literature Committee," *Komitet Gramotnosti*, in which she was actively engaged, was closed. The circumstances were as follows: A "Voluntary Economic Society" (founded in the reign of Catherine the Great) existed, and was allowed to debate economic problems within certain limits. Its existence was sanctioned by, and it was under the control of, the Ministry of the Interior. A branch of this society was formed called the "Literature Committee." This branch aimed at spreading good and wholesome literature among the people

Committee" which has been prohibited, a number of other "Literature Associations," to pursue the same objects, should be formed without consulting the government, and without asking permission from any censor. Let government, if it likes, prosecute these "Literature Associations," punish the members, banish them, etc. If government does that it will merely cause people to attach special importance to good books and to libraries, and it will strengthen the trend toward enlightenment.

It seems to me that it is now specially important to do what is right quietly and persistently, not only without asking permission from government, but consciously avoiding its participation. The strength of the government lies in the people's ignorance, and government knows this, and will, therefore, always oppose true enlightenment. It is time we realized that fact. And it is most undesirable to let government, while it is diffusing darkness, pretend it is busy with the enlightenment of the people. It is doing this now, by means of all sorts of pseudo-educational establishments which it controls: schools, high schools, universities, academies, and all kinds of committees and congresses. But good is good, and enlightenment is enlightenment, only when it is quite good and quite enlightened, and not when it is toned

---

and in the schools, by establishing libraries or in other ways. However, their views as to what books it is good for people to read did not tally with those of the government, and in 1896 it was decreed that the "Voluntary Economic Society" should be transferred from the supervision of the Ministry of the Interior to that of the Ministry of Education. This sounded harmless, but translated into unofficial language it meant that the activity of the Committee was to terminate, and the proceeding of the whole Society was to be reduced to a formality.—TR.

down to meet the requirements of Delyanof's or Dur-
novo's circulars. And I am extremely sorry when I see
valuable, disinterested, and self-sacrificing efforts spent
unprofitably. Sometimes it seems to me quite comical to
see good, wise people spending their strength in a struggle
against government, to be maintained on the basis of
laws which that very government itself makes just what
it likes.

The matter is, it seems to me, this:—

There are people (we ourselves are such) who realize
that our government is very bad, and who struggle against
it. From before the days of Radishchef* and the Decembrists** there have been two ways of carrying on the
struggle; one way is that of Stenka Razin,*** Pugatchef,†
the Decembrists, the Revolutionary party†† of the years

* Radishchef, the author of "A Journey from Petersburg to Moscow," was a Liberal whose efforts toward the abolition of serfdom
displeased the government. He committed suicide in 1802.—Tr.

** The Decembrists were members of the organization which
attempted, by force, to terminate autocratic government in Russia
when Nicholas I. ascended the throne in 1825.—Tr.

*** Stenka Razin was a Cossack who raised a formidable insurrection in the seventeenth century. He was eventually defeated
and captured, and was executed in Moscow in 1671.—Tr.

† Pugatchef headed the most formidable Russian insurrection of
the eighteenth century. He was executed in Moscow in 1775.—Tr.

†† The series of reforms, including the abolition of serfdom,
which followed the Crimean War and the death of Nicholas I,
were, from the first, adopted half-heartedly. Since about the time
of the Polish insurrection (1863) the reactionary party obtained
control of the government and has kept it ever since. The more
vehement members of the Liberal party, losing hope of constitutional reform, organized a Revolutionary party in the sixties, and
later on the Terrorist party was formed, which organized assassi-
nations as a means toward liberty, equality, and fraternity.—Tr.

sixty, the Terrorists° of the thirteenth of March, and others.

The other way is that which is preached and practised by you—the method of the "Gradualists," which consists in carrying on the struggle without violence and within the limits of the law, conquering constitutional rights bit by bit.

Both these methods have been employed unceasingly within my memory for more than half a century, and yet the state of things grows worse and worse. Even such signs of improvement as do show themselves have come, not from either of these kinds of activity, but from causes of which I will speak later on, and in spite of the harm done by these two kinds of activity. Meanwhile, the power against which we struggle grows ever greater, stronger, and more insolent. The last rays of self-government—the *zemstvos* (local government boards), public trial, your Literature Committee, etc.—are all being done away with.

Now that both methods have been ineffectually tried for so long a time, we may, it seems to me, see clearly that neither the one nor the other will do—and why this is so. To me, at least, who have always disliked our government, but have never adopted either of the above methods of resisting it, the defects of both methods are apparent.

The first way is unsatisfactory because (even could an attempt to alter the existing régime by violent means succeed) there would be no guarantee that the new or-

---

° Alexander II was killed by a bomb thrown at him in the streets of Petersburg on the thirteenth of March (N.S.), 1881. This assassination was organized by the Terrorist party.—Tr.

ganization would be durable, and that the enemies of that new order would not, at some convenient opportunity, triumph by using violence such as has been used against them, as has happened over and over again in France and wherever else there have been revolutions. And so the new order of things, established by violence, would have continually to be supported by violence, *i.e.* by wrong-doing. And, consequently, it would inevitably and very quickly be vitiated like the order it replaced. And in case of failure, all the violence of the revolutionists only strengthens the order of things they strive against (as has always been the case, in our Russian experience, from Pugatchef's rebellion to the attempt of the thirteenth of March), for it drives the whole crowd of undecided people, who stand wavering between the two parties, into the camp of the conservative and retrograde party. So I think that, guided by both reason and experience, we may boldly say that this means, besides being immoral, is also irrational and ineffective.

The other method is, in my opinion, even less effective or rational. It is ineffective and irrational because government, having in its hands the whole power (the army, the administration, the Church, the schools, and police), and framing what are called the laws, on the basis of which the Liberals wish to resist it—this government knows very well what is really dangerous to it, and will never let people who submit to it, and act under its guidance, do anything that will undermine its authority. For instance, take the case before us: a government such as ours (or any other), which rests on the ignorance of the people, will never consent to their being really enlightened. It will sanction all kinds of pseudo-educational organizations, controlled by itself: schools, high schools, universities, academies, and all kinds of committees and congresses and publications sanctioned by the censor—as long as those organizations and publications serve its purpose, *i.e.* stupefy people, or, at least, do not hinder the stupefaction of people. But as soon as those organizations, or publications, attempt to cure that on which the power of government rests, *i.e.* the blindness of the people, the government will simply, and without rendering account to any one, or saying why it acts so and not otherwise, pronounce its "veto" and will rearrange, or close, the establishments and organizations and will forbid the publications. And therefore, as both reason and experience clearly show, such an illusory, gradual conquest of rights is a self-deception which suits the government admirably, and which it, therefore, is even ready to encourage.

But not only is this activity irrational and ineffectual, it is also harmful. It is harmful because enlightened, good, and honest people by entering the ranks of the government give it a moral authority which but for them it would not possess. If the government were made up entirely of that coarse element—the violators, self-seekers, and flatterers—who form its core, it could not continue to exist. The fact that honest and enlightened people are found who participate in the affairs of the government gives government whatever it possesses of moral prestige.

That is one evil resulting from the activity of Liberals who participate in the affairs of government, or who come to terms with it. Another evil of such activity is that, in order to secure opportunities to carry on their work, these highly enlightened and honest people have to begin to compromise, and so, little by little, come to consider that, for a good end, one may swerve somewhat from truth in word and deed. For instance, that one may, though not believing in the established Church, go through its ceremonies; may take oaths; and may, when necessary for the success of some affair, present petitions couched in language which is untrue and offensive to man's natural dignity: may enter the army; may take part in a local government which has been stripped of all its powers; may serve as a master or a professor, teaching not what one considers necessary oneself, but what one is told to preach by government; and that one may even become a Zemsky Nachalnik,° submitting to governmental demands and instructions which violate one's conscience; may edit newspapers and periodicals, remaining silent about what ought to be mentioned. and printing what one is ordered to print; and entering into these compromises—the limits of which cannot be foreseen—enlightened and honest people (who alone could form some barrier to the infringements of human liberty by the government, imperceptibly retreating ever farther and farther from the demands of conscience) fall at last into a position of complete dependency on government. They receive rewards and salaries from it, and, continuing to

° During the Reform period, in the reign of Alexander II, many iniquities of the old judicial system were abolished. Among other innovations "Judges of the Peace" were appointed to act as magistrates. They were elected (indirectly); if possessed of a certain property qualification, men of any class were eligible. and the regulations under which they acted were drawn up in a comparatively liberal spirit. Under Alexander III the office of "Judge of the Peace" was abolished, and was replaced by "Zemsky Nachalniks." Only members of the aristocracy were eligible; they were not elected, but appointed by government, and they were armed with authority to have peasants flogged. They were less like magistrates and more like government officials than the "Judges of the Peace" had been.—TR.

imagine they are forwarding liberal ideas, they become
the humble servants and supporters of the very order
against which they set out to fight.

It is true that there are also better, sincere people in
the Liberal camp, whom the government cannot bribe,
and who remain unbought and free from salaries and
position. But even these people have been insnared in
the nets spread by government, beat their wings in their
cages (as you are now doing with your Committee),
unable to advance from the spot they are on. Or else,
becoming enraged, they go over to the revolutionary
camp; or they shoot themselves, or take to drink, or they
abandon the whole struggle in despair, and, oftenest of
all, retire into literary activity, in which, yielding to the
demands of the censor, they say only what they are
allowed to say, and—by that very silence about what is
most important—convey to the public distorted views
which just suit the government. But they continue to
imagine that they are serving society by the writings
which give them the means of subsistence.

Thus, both reflection and experience alike show me
that both the means of combating government, hereto-
fore believed in, are not only ineffectual, but actually
tend to strengthen the power and the irresponsibility of
government.

What is to be done? Evidently not what for seventy
years past has proved fruitless, and has only produced
inverse result. What is to be done? Just what those have
done, thanks to whose activity is due that progress toward
light and good which has been achieved since the world
began, and is still being achieved today. That is what
must be done. And what is it?

Merely the simple, quiet, truthful carrying on of what

you consider good and needful, quite independently of government, and of whether it likes it or not. In other words: standing up for your rights, not as a member of the Literature Committee, not as a deputy, not as a landowner, not as a merchant, not even as a member of Parliament; but standing up for your rights as a rational and free man, and defending them, not as the rights of local boards or committees are defended, with concessions and compromises, but without any concessions and compromises, in the only way in which moral and human dignity can be defended.

Successfully to defend a fortress one has to burn all the houses in the suburbs, and to leave only what is strong and what we intend not to surrender on any account. Only from the basis of this firm stronghold can we conquer all we require. True, the rights of a member of Parliament, or even of a member of a local board, are greater than the rights of a plain man; and it seems as if we could do much by using those rights. But the hitch is that in order to obtain the rights of a member of Parliament, or of a committeeman, one has to abandon part of one's rights as a man. And having abandoned part of one's rights as a man, there is no longer any fixed point of leverage, and one can no longer either conquer or maintain any real right. In order to lift others out of a quagmire one must stand on firm ground oneself, and if, hoping the better to assist others, you go into the quagmire, you will not pull others out, but will yourself sink in.

It may be very desirable and useful to get an eight-hour day legalized by Parliament, or to get a liberal program for school libraries sanctioned by your Committee; but if, as a means to this end, a member of Parliament must publicly lift up his hand and lie, lie when taking an oath, by expressing in words respect for what he does not respect; or (in our own case) if, in order to pass most liberal programs, it is necessary to take part in public worship, to be sworn, to wear a uniform, to write mendacious and flattering petitions, and to make speeches of a similar character, etc.—then by doing these things and forgoing our dignity as men, we lose much more than we gain, and by trying to reach one definite aim (which very often is not reached) we deprive ourselves of the possibility of reaching other aims which are of supreme importance. Only people who have something which they will on no account and under no circumstances yield can resist a government and curb it. To have power to resist you must stand on firm ground.

And the government knows this very well, and is concerned, above all else, to worm out of men that which will not yield, in other words, the dignity of man. When that is wormed out of them, government calmly proceeds to do what it likes, knowing that it will no longer meet any real resistance. A man who consents publicly to swear, pronouncing the degrading and mendacious words of the oath; or submissively to wait several hours, dressed up in a uniform, at a minister's reception; or to inscribe himself as a special constable for the coronation; or to fast and receive communion for respectability's sake; or to ask of the head censor whether he may, or may not, express such and such thoughts, etc.—such a man is no longer feared by government.

Alexander II said he did not fear the Liberals because he knew they could all be bought, if not with money, then with honors.

People who take part in government, or work under its direction, may deceive themselves or their sympathizers by making a show of struggling; but those against whom they struggle—the government—know quite well, by the strength of the resistance experienced, that these people are not really pulling, but are only pretending to. And our government knows this with respect to the Liberals, and constantly tests the quality of the opposition, and finding that genuine resistance is practically non-existent, it continues its course in full assurance that it can do what it likes with such opponents.

The government of Alexander III knew this ver well, and, knowing it, deliberately destroyed all that the Liberals thought they had achieved and were so proud of. It altered and limited trial by jury; it abolished the. "Judges of the Peace"; it canceled the rights of the universities; it perverted the whole system of instruction in the high schools; it reëstablished the cadet corps, and even the state's sale of intoxicants; it established the Zemsky Nachalniks; it legalized flogging; it almost abolished the local government boards (*Zemstvos*); it gave uncontrolled power to the governors of provinces; it encouraged the quartering of troops (*eksekutsia*) on the peasants in punishment; it increased the practice of "administrative"* banishment and imprisonment, and the capital punishment of political offenders; it renewed religious persecutions; it brought to a climax the use of barbarous superstitions; it legalized murder in duels; under the name of a "state of siege"** it established lawlessness with

* Sentenced by *"Administrative Order"* means sentenced by the arbitrary will of government, or the chief of the gendarmes of a province. Administrative sentences are often inflicted without the victim being heard in his own defense, or even knowing what acts (real or supposed) have led to his punishment.—TR.

** The "Statute of Increased Protection," usually translated "state capital punishment, as a normal condition of things—and in all this it met with no protest except from one honorable woman* who boldly told the government the truth as she saw it.

The Liberals whispered among themselves that these things displeased them, but they continued to take part in legal proceedings, and in the local governments, and in the universities, and in government service, and in the press. In the press they hinted at what they were allowed to hint at, and kept silence on matters they had to be silent about, but they printed whatever they were told to print. So that every reader (who was not privy to the whisperings of the editorial rooms), on receiving a Liberal paper or magazine, read the announcement of the most cruel and irrational measure unaccompanied by comment or sign of disapproval, sycophantic and flattering addresses to those guilty of enacting these measures, and frequently even praise of the measures themselves. Thus all the dismal activity of the government of Alexander III—destroying whatever good had begun to take root in the days of Alexander II, and striving to turn Russia back to the barbarity of the commencement of this century—all this dismal activity of gallows, rods, persecutions, and stupefaction of the people has become (even in the lib-

---

of siege," was first applied to Petersburg and Moscow only, but was subsequently extended to Odessa, Kief, Kharkof, and Warsaw. Under this law the power of capital punishment was intrusted to the governor-generals of the provinces in question.—TR.

* Madame Tsebrikof, a well-known writer and literary critic, wrote a polite but honest letter to Alexander III, pointing out what was being done by the government. She was banished to a distant province for a time and was then allowed to reside, not in Petersburg, but in the government of Tver.—TR.

eral papers and magazines) the basis of an insane laudation of Alexander III and of his acclamation as a great
man and a model of human dignity.

This same thing is being continued in the new reign.
The young man who succeeded the late Tsar, having
no understanding of life, was assured, by the men in
power to whom it was profitable to say so, that the best
way to rule a hundred million people is to do as his father
did, *i.e.* not to ask advice from any one but just to do
what comes into one's head, or what the first flatterer
about him advises. And, fancying that unlimited autocracy is a sacred life-principle òf the Russian people, the
young man begins to reign; and, instead of asking the
representatives of the Russian people to help him with
their advice in the task of ruling (about which he, educated in a cavalry regiment, knows nothing, and can know
nothing), he rudely and insolently shouts at those representatives of the Russian people who visit him with congratulations, and he calls the desire, timidly expressed by
some of them,* to be allowed to inform the authorities of
their needs, "nonsensical fancies."

And what followed? Was Russian society shocked? Did
enligtened and honest people—the Liberals—express their
indignation and repulsion? Did they at least refrain from
laudation of this government and from participating in it
and encouraging it? Not at all. From that time a specially
intense competition in adulation commenced, both of the
father and of the son who imitated him. And not a protesting voice was heard, except in one anonymous letter,
cautiously expressing disapproval of the young Tsar's

---

* By the representatives of the Tver Zemstvo and others, at a
reception in the Winter Palace on the accession of Nicholas II.—TR.

conduct. And, from all sides, fulsome and flattering addresses were brought to the Tsar, as well as (for some reason or other) ikons,* which nobody wanted and which served merely as objects of idolatry to benighted people. An insane expenditure of money, the coronation, amazing in its absurdity, was arranged; the arrogance of the rulers and their contempt of the people caused thousands to perish in a fearful calamity, which was regarded as a slight eclipse of the festivities, which should not terminate on that account.** An exhibition was organized, which no one wanted except those who organized it, and which cost millions of rubles. In the Chancery of the Holy Synod, with unparalleled effrontery, a new and supremely stupid means of mystifying people was devised, viz., the enshrinement of the incorruptible body of a saint whom nobody knew anything about. The stringency of the censor was increased. Religious persecution was made more severe. The "state of siege," *i.e.* the legalization of lawlessness, was continued, and the state of things is still becoming worse and worse.

And I think that all this would not have happened if those enlightened, honest people, who are now occupied

* Conventional painting of God, Jesus, Angels, Saints, the Mother of God, etc., usually done on bits of wood, with much gilding. They are hung up in the corners of the rooms as well as in churches, etc., to be prayed to.—TR.

** As part of the coronation festivities a "people's fête" was arranged to take place on the Khodinskoye Field, near Moscow. Owing to the incredible stupidity of the arrangements, some three thousand people were killed when trying to enter the grounds, besides a large number who were injured. This occurred on Saturday, May 18 (O. S.), 1896. That same evening the emperor danced at the grand ball given by the French ambassador in Moscow.—TR.

in Liberal activity on the basis of legality, in local governments, in the committees, in censor-ruled literature, etc.,
had not devoted their energies to the task of circumvent-
ing the government, and, without abandoning the forms
it has itself arranged, of finding ways to make it act so
as to harm and injure itself;* but, abstaining from taking
any part in government or in any business bound up with
government, had merely claimed their rights as men.

"You wish, instead of 'Judges of the Peace,' to institute
Zemsky Nachalniks with birch rods; that is your business,
but we will not go to law before your Zemsky Nachalniks,
and will not ourselves accept appointment to such an
office: you wish to make trial by jury a mere formality;
that is your business, but we will not serve as judges, or
as advocates, or as jurymen: you wish under the name
of a 'state of siege,' to establish despotism; that is your
business, but we will not participate in it, and will plainly
call the 'state of siege' despotism, and capital punishment inflicted without trial, murder: you wish to organize
cadet corps, or classical high schools, in which military
exercises and the Orthodox faith are taught; that is your
affair, but we will not teach in such schools, or send our
children to them, but will educate our children as seems
to us right: you decide to reduce the local government
boards (*zemstvos*) to impotence; we will not take part
in it: you prohibit the publication of literature that
displeases you; you may seize books and punish the

* Sometimes it seems to me simply laughable that people can
occupy themselves with such an evidently hopeless business; it is
like undertaking to cut off an animal's leg without its noticing
it.—Author's Note.

printers, but you cannot prevent our speaking and writing, and we shall continue to do so: you demand an oath of allegiance to the Tsar; we will not accede to what is so stupid, false, and degrading: you order us to serve in the army; we will not do so, because wholesale murder is as opposed to our conscience as individual murder, and above all, because the promise to murder whomsoever a commander may tell us to murder is the meanest act a man can commit: you profess a religion which is a thousand years behind the times, with an 'Iberian Mother of God, ° relics, and coronations; that is your affair, but we do not acknowledge idolatry and superstition to be religion, but call them idolatry and superstition, and we try to free people from them."

And what can government do against such activity? It can banish or imprison a man for preparing a bomb, or even for printing a proclamation to working-men; it can transfer your "Literature Committee" from one ministry to another, or close a Parliament—but what can a government do with a man who is not willing publicly to lie with uplifted hand, or who is not willing to send his children to an establishment which he considers bad, or who is not willing to learn to kill people, or is not willing to take part in idolatry, or is not willing to take part in coronations, deputations, and addresses, or who says and writes what he thinks and feels? By prosecuting such a man, government secures for him general sympathy,

---

° "The Iberian Mother of God" is a wonder-working ikon of the Virgin Mary which draws a large revenue. It is frequently taken to visit the sick, and travels about with six horses; the attendant priest sits in the carriage bareheaded. The smallest fee charged is six shillings for a visit, but more is usually given.—TR.

making him a martyr, and it undermines the foundations on which it is itself built, for in so acting, instead of protecting human rights, it itself infringes them.

And it is only necessary for all those good, enlightened, and honest people, whose strength is now wasted in revolutionary, socialistic, or liberal activity, harmful to themselves and to their cause, to begin to act thus, and a nucleus of honest, enlightened, and moral people would form around them, united in the same thoughts and the same feelings; and to this nucleus the ever wavering crowd of average people would at once gravitate, and public opinion—the only power which subdues governments—would become evident, demanding freedom of speech, freedom of conscience, justice, and humanity. And as soon as public opinion was formulated, not only would it be impossible to close the "Literature Committee," but all those inhuman organizations—the "state of siege," the secret police, the censor, Schlüsselburg,* the Holy Synod, and the rest—against which the revolutionists and the liberals are now struggling would disappear of themselves.

So that two methods of opposing the government have been tried, both unsuccessfully; and it now remains to try a third and a last method, one not yet tried, but one which, I think, cannot but be successful. Briefly, that means this: that all enlightened and honest people should try to be as good as they can, and not even good in all respects, but only in one; namely, in observing one of the most elementary virtues—to be honest, and not to lie, but to act and speak so that your motives should be in-

* The most terrible of the places of imprisonment in Petersburg; the Russian Bastile.—TR.

telligible to an affectionate seven-year-old- boy; to act so that your boy should not say, "But why, papa, did you say so-and-so, and now you do and say something quite different?" This method seems very weak, and yet I am convinced that it is this method, and this method only, that has moved humanity since the race began. Only because there were straight men, truthful and courageous, who made no concessions that infringed their dignity as men, have all those beneficent revolutions been accomplished of which mankind now have the advantage, from the abolition of torture and slavery up to liberty of speech and of conscience. Nor can this be otherwise, for what conscience (the highest forefeeling man possesses of the truth accessible to him) demands, is always, and in all respects, the activity most fruitful and most necessary for humanity at the given time. Only a man who lives according to his conscience can have influence on people, and only activity that accords with one's conscience can be useful.

But I must explain my meaning. To say that the most effectual means of achieving the ends toward which revolutionists and liberals are striving, is by activity in accord with their consciences, does not mean that people can begin to live conscientiously in order to achieve those ends. To begin to live conscientiously on purpose to achieve any external ends is impossible.

To live according to one's conscience is possible only as a result of firm and clear religious convictions; the beneficent result of these in our external life will inevitably follow. Therefore the gist of what I wished to say to you is this: that it is unprofitable for good, sincere people to spend their powers of mind and soul in gaining small practical ends; e.g. in the various struggles of nationalities, or parties, or in Liberal wire-pulling, while they have not reached a clear and firm religious perception, *i.e.* a consciousness of the meaning and purpose of their life. I think that all the powers of soul and of mind of good people, who wish to be of service to men, should be directed to that end. When that is accomplished, all else will be accomplished too.

Forgive me for sending you so long a letter, which perhaps you did not at all need, but I have long wished to express my views on this question. I even began a long article about it, but I shall hardly have time to finish it before death comes, and therefore I wished to get at least part of it said. Forgive me if I am in error about anything.

"THOU SHALT NOT KILL"

ON THE DEATH OF KING HUMBERT

"Thou shalt do no murder."
—Ex. xx. 13.
"The disciple is not above his master: but every one when he is perfected shall be as his master."
Luke vi. 40.
"For all they that take up the sword shall perish with the sword."
Matt. xxvi. 52.
"All things therefore whatsoever ye would that men should do unto you, even so do ye also unto them."
—Matt. vii. 12.

HEN kings are tried and executed like Charles I, Louis XVI, and Maximilian of Mexico; or killed in a palace conspiracy like Peter III, Paul, and all kinds of Sultans, Shahs, and Khans, the event is generally passed over in silence. But when one of them is killed without a trial, and not by a palace conspiracy; like Henry IV, Alexander II, Carnot, the Empress of Austria, the Shah of Persia, and, recently, King Humbert, then such murder causes great surprise

and indignation among Kings and Emperors, and those attached to them, as if they were the great enemies of murder, as if they never profited by murder, never took part in it, and never gave orders to commit it. And yet the kindest of these murdered Kings, such as Alexander II or Humbert, were guilty of the murder of tens of thousands of persons killed on the battle-field, not to mention those executed at home; while hundreds of thousands, and even millions, of people have been killed, hanged, beaten to death, or shot, by the more cruel Kings and Emperors.

Christ's teaching cancels the law "an eye for an eye, a tooth for a tooth"; but those men who have kept to the older law and still keep to it, who act upon it by punishing and carrying on wars, and who not only act on the law "an eye for an eye," but give orders to kill thousands without any provocation, by declaring war—*they* have no right to be indignant when the same law is applied to themselves in so infinitesimal a measure that hardly one King or Emperor gets killed to a hundred thousand, or perhaps to a million ordinary people killed by the order, or with the consent, of Kings and Emperors.

Kings and Emperors should not be indignant when such murders as that of Alexander II or Humbert occur, but should, on the contrary, be surprised that such murders are so rare, considering the continual and universal example of committing murders they themselves set the people.

Kings and Emperors are surprised and horrified when one of themselves is murdered, and yet the whole of their activity consists in managing murder and preparing for murder. The keeping up, the teaching and exercising, of armies with which Kings and Emperors are always so

much occupied, and of which they are the organizers—
what is it but preparation for murder?

The masses are so hypnotized that, though they see
what is continually going on around them, they do not
understand what it means. They see the unceasing care
Kings, Emperors, and Presidents bestow on disciplined
armies, see the parades, reviews, and manœuvers they
hold, and of which they boast to one another, and the
people eagerly crowd to see how their own brothers,
dressed up in bright-colored, glittering clothes, are turned
into machines to the sound of drums and trumpets, and,
obedient to the shouting of one man, all make the same
movements; and they do not understand the meaning
of it all.

Yet the meaning of such drilling is very clear and
simple. It is preparing for murder. It means the stupefying
of men in order to convert them into instruments for
murdering.

And it is just Kings and Emperors and Presidents who
do it, and organize it, and pride themselves on it. And
it is these same people whose special employment is
murder-organizing, who have made murder their profession, who dress in military uniforms, and carry weapons
(swords at their side), who are horror-struck and indignant when one of themselves is killed.

It is not because such murders as the recent murder
of Humbert are exceptionally cruel that they are so
terrible. Things done by the order of Kings and Emperors,
not only in the days of old, such as the massacre of St.
Bartholomew, persecutions for faith, terrible ways of
putting down peasant riots, but also the present executions, the torture of solitary cells and disciplinary battal-

ions, hanging, decapitation, shooting, and slaughter at the wars, are incomparably more cruel than the murders committed by Anarchists.

Nor is it on account of their injustice that these murders are terrible. If Alexander and Humbert did not deserve death, the thousands of Russians who perished at Plevna, and of Italians who perished in Abyssinia, deserved it still less. No, it is not because of their cruelty and injustice these murders are terrible, but because of the want of reason in those who perpetrate them.

If the regicides commit murder under the influence of feelings of indignation evoked by witnessing the sufferings of the enslaved people, for which sufferings they hold Alexander II, Carnot, or Humbert responsible, or because they are influenced by personal desire for revenge—however immoral such conduct may be, still it is comprehensible; but how can an organized body of Anarchists such as those by whom, it is said, Bréssi was sent out, and by whom another Emperor was threatened, how can it, quietly considering means of improving the condition of the people, find nothing better to do than to murder people; the killing of whom is as useful as cutting off one of the Hydra's heads?

Kings and Emperors have long established a system resembling the mechanism of a magazine rifle, *i.e.*, as soon as one bullet flies out another takes its place. *"Le roi est mort—vive le roi!"* Then what is the use of killing them? It is only from a most superficial point of view that the murder of such persons can seem a means of saving the people from oppression and wars, which destroy their lives.

We need only remember that the same kind of oppression and war went on no matter who stood at the head of the Government: Nicholas or Alexander, Louis or Napoleon, Frederic or William, Palmerston or Gladstone, McKinley or any one else, in order to see that it is not some definite person who causes the oppression and the wars from which people suffer.

The misery of the people is not caused by individuals, but by an order of Society by which they are bound together in a way that puts them in the power of a few, or, more often, of one man: a man so depraved by his unnatural position—having the fate and lives of millions of people in his power—that he is always in an unhealthy state and suffering more or less from a mania of self-aggrandizement, which is not noticed in him only because of his exceptional position.

Apart from the fact that such men are surrounded, from the cradle to the grave, by the most insane luxury and its usual accompaniment of flattery and servility, the whole of their education, and all their occupations, are centered on the one object of murder, the study of murder in the past, the best means of murdering in the present, the best ways of preparing for murder in the future. From their earliest years they learn the art of murder in all possible forms, always carry about with them instruments of murder, dress in different uniforms, attend parades, manœuvers, and reviews, visit each other, present orders and the command of regiments to each other. And yet not only does nobody tell them the real name of their actions, not only does nobody tell them that preparing for murder is revolting and criminal, but they hear nothing but praise and words of admiration from all around them for these actions.

The only part of the Press that reaches them, and which seems to them to be the expression of the feelings of the best of the people or their best representatives, exalts all their words and deeds, however silly and wicked they may be, in the most servile manner. All who surround them, men and women, cleric or lay, all these people who do not value human dignity, vie with each other in flattering them in the most refined manner, agree with them in everything, and deceive them continually, making it impossible for them to know life as it is. These men might live to be a hundred and never see a real, free man, and never hear the truth.

We are sometimes appalled by the words and deeds of these men, but if we only consider their state we cannot but see that any man would act in the same way in such a position. A reasonable man can do but one thing in such a position, *i.e.*, leave it. Every one who remains in such a position will act in the same manner.

What, indeed, must be going on in the head of some William of Germany, a man of limited understanding, little education, and with a great deal of ambition, whose ideals are like those of a German "junker," when any silly or horrid thing he may say is always met with an enthusiastic "*Hoch!*" and commented on, as if it were something very important, by the Press of the whole world? He says that the soldier should be prepared to kill their own fathers in obedience to his command. The answer is "Hurrah!" He says the Gospels must be introduced with a fist of iron. "Hurrah!" He says that the Army must not take any prisoners in China, but kill all, and he is not placed in a lunatic asylum, but they cry "Hurrah!" and set sail for China to execute his orders.

Or Nicholas, who, though naturally modest, begins his reign by declaring to venerable old men, in answer to the desire they express of being allowed to discuss their own affairs, that their hope for self-governments it a senseless dream. And the organs of the Press that reach him, and the people whom he meets, praise him for it. He proposes a childish, silly, and untruthful project of universal peace at the same time that he is ordering an increase of the Army, and even then there are no limits to the laudations of his wisdom and his virtue. Without any reason, he senselessly and pitilessly offends the whole of the Finnish nation, and again hears nothing but praise. At last he enters upon the Chinese slaughter, terrible by its injustice, cruelty, and its contrast with his project of peace; and he gets applauded simultaneously from all sides, both for his own conquests and for his adherence to his father's policy of peace. What must indeed be going on in the heads and hearts of such men?

So that it is not Alexanders and Humberts, Williams, Nicholases, and Chamberlains, who are the cause of oppression and war, even though they do organize them, but it is those who have placed them in, and support them in, a position in which they have power over the life and death of men.

Therefore it is not necessary to kill Alexanders and Nicholases, Williams and Humberts, but only to leave off supporting the social condition of which they are the product. It is the selfishness and stupefaction of the people who sell their freedom and their honor for insignificant material advantages, which supports the present state of society.

Those who stand on the lowest rung of the ladder, partly as a consequence of being stupefied by a patriotic and pseudo-religious education, partly for the sake of personal advantages, give up their freedom and their feeling of human dignity to those who stand higher, and who offer them material advantages. In a like position are those standing a little higher. They, too, through being stupefied, and especially for material advantages, give up their freedom and sense of human dignity. The same is true of those standing still higher; and so it continues up to the highest rungs, up to the person or persons who, standing on the very summit of the social cone, have no one to submit to, nor anywhere to rise to, and have no motive for action except ambition and love of power. These are generally so depraved and stupefied by their insane power over life and death, and by the flattery and servility of those around them, which is connected with such power, that while doing evil they feel convinced they are the benefactors of the human race. It is the people themselves who, by sacrificing their human dignity for material profits, produce these men, and are afterwards angry with them for their stupid and cruel acts; murdering such people is like whipping children after spoiling them.

Very little seems needed to stop oppression and useless war, and to prevent any one from being indignant with those who seem to be the cause of such oppression and war.

Only that things should be called by their right names and seen as they are; that it should be understood that an army is an instrument of murder, that the recruiting and drilling of armies which Kings, Emperors, and Presidents carry on with so much self-assurance are preparations for murder.

If only every King, Emperor, and President would understand that his work of organizing armies is not an honorable and important duty, as his flatterers persuade him it is, but a most abominable business, *i.e.*, the preparing for, and the managing of, murder. If only every private individual understood that the payment of taxes which helps to equip soldiers, and above all, military service, are not immaterial but highly immoral actions, by which he not only permits murder, but takes part in it himself—then this power of the Kings and Emperors which arouses indignation, and causes them to be killed, would come to an end of itself.

And so the Alexanders, Carnots, Humberts, and others should not be killed, but it ought to be shown them that they are murderers; and above all, they should not be allowed to kill men; their orders to murder should not be obeyed.

If men do not yet act in this manner, it is only because Governments, to maintain themselves, diligently exercise a hypnotic influence upon the people. Therefore we can help to prevent people killing Kings and each other, not by murder—murders only strengthen this hypnotic state— but by arousing men from the delusion in which they are held.

And it is this that I have tried to do in these remarks.

HELP!

HE facts related in this Appeal,* composed by three of my friends, have been repeatedly verified, revised, and sifted; the Appeal itself has been several times recast and corrected; everything has been rejected from it which, although true, might seem an exaggeration; so that all that is now stated in this Appeal is the real, indubitable truth, as far as the truth is accessible to men guided only by the religious desire, in this revelation of the truth, to serve God and their neighbor, both the oppressors and the oppressed. But, however striking the facts here related, their importance is determined, not by the facts themselves, but by the way in which they will be regarded by those who learn about them. And I fear that the majority of those who read this Appeal will not understand all its importance.

---

*Early in 1897, an Appeal on behalf of the Dukhobors was drawn up by three friends of Count Tolstoï's. The latter added this article to what his friends had written. His three friends were all banished for their offense.

"Why, these fellows are a set of rioters; coarse, illiterate peasants; fanatics who have fallen under evil influence. They are a noxious, anti-governmental sect, which the Government cannot put up with, but evidently must suppress, as it suppresses every movement injurious to the general welfare. If women and children, innocent people, have to suffer thereby, well, what is to be done?"

This is what, with a shrug of the shoulders, people who have not penetrated the importance of this event will say.

On the whole, this phenomenon will, to most people, seem devoid of interest, like every phenomenon whose place is strongly and clearly defined. Smugglers appear —they must be caught; anarchists, terrorists—society must get rid of them; fanatics, self-mutilators—they must be shut up, transported; infringers of public order appear— they must be suppressed. All this seems indisputable, evident, decisive, and therefore uninteresting.

And yet such an attitude toward what is related in this Appeal is a great error.

As in the life of each separate individual (I know this in my own life, and every one will find similar cases in his own), so also in the life of nations and humanity, events occur which constitute turning-points in their whole existence; and these events, like the "still small voice" (not the "great and strong wind") in which Elijah heard God, are always not loud, not striking, hardly remarkable; and in one's personal life one always afterward regrets that at the time one did not guess the importance of what was taking place.

"If I had known it was such an important moment in my life," one afterwards thinks, "I should not have acted in such a way."

It is the same in the life of mankind. A Roman emperor

enters Rome in noisy, pompous triumph—how important this seems; and how insignificant, it then seemed, that a Galilean was preaching a new doctrine, and was executed therefor, just as hundreds of others were executed for apparently similar crimes.

And so now, too, how important in the eyes of refined members of rival parties of the English, French, and Italian parliaments, or of the Austrian and German diets, and in the eyes of all the business men in the city and of the bankers of the whole world, and their press organs, are the questions as to who shall occupy the Bosporus, who shall seize some patch of land in Africa or Asia, who shall triumph in the question of bimetallism, and so on; and how, not only unimportant, but even so insignificant that they are not worth speaking about, seem the stories which tell that, somewhere in the Caucasus, the Russian government has taken measures for crushing certain half-savage fanatics, who deny the obligation to submit to the authorities.

And yet, in reality, how not merely insignificant, but comic, beside the phenomena of such immense importance as are now taking place in the Caucasus, is the strange anxiety of full-grown people, educated, and illuminated by the teaching of Christ (or at least acquainted with this teaching, and capable of being illuminated by it), as to which country shall have this or that patch of land, and what words were uttered by this or that erring, stumbling mortal, who is merely a production of surrounding conditions.

Pilate and Herod, indeed, might not understand the importance of that for which the Galilean, who had disturbed their province, was brought before them for judgment; they did not even think it worth while learning wherein consisted His teaching; even had they known it, they might have been excused for thinking that it would disappear (as Gamaliel said); but we—we cannot but know the teaching itself, as well as the fact that it has not disappeared in the course of eighteen hundred years, and will not disappear until it is realized. And if we know this, then, notwithstanding the insignificance, illiterateness, and obscurity of the Dukhobors, we cannot but see the whole importance of that which is taking place among them. Christ's disciples were just such insignificant, unrefined, unknown people, and other than such the followers of Christ cannot be. Among the Dukhobors, or rather, "Christians of the Universal Brotherhood," as they now call themselves, nothing new is taking place, but merely the germinating of that seed which was sown by Christ eighteen hundred years ago, the resurrection of Christ Himself.

This resurrection must take place, cannot but take place, and it is impossible to shut one's eyes to the fact that it is taking place, merely because it is occurring without the firing of guns, parade of troops, planting of flags, illuminated fountains, music, electric lights, bell-ringing, and the solemn speeches and the cries of people decorated with gold lace and ribbons. Only savages judge of the importance of phenomena by the outward splendor with which they are accompanied.

Whether we wish to see this or not, there has now been manifested in the Caucasus, in the life of the "Universal Brotherhood of Christians," especially since their persecution, a demonstration of that Christian life toward which all that is good and reasonable in the world is striving. For all our State institutions, our parliaments, societies, sciences, arts—all this only exists and operates in order to realize that life which all of us, thinking men, see before us as the highest ideal of perfection. And here we have people who have realized this ideal, probably in part, not wholly, but have realized it in a way we did not dream of doing with our complex State institutions. How, then, can we avoid acknowledging the importance of this phenomenon? For that is being realized toward which we are all striving, toward which all our complex activity is leading us.

It is generally said, that such attempts at the realization of the Christian life have been made more than once already; there have been the Quakers, the Mennonites, and others, all of whom have weakened and degenerated into ordinary people, living the general life under the State. And, therefore, it is said such attempts at the realization of the Christian life are not of importance.

To say so is like saying that the pains of labor which have not yet ended in birth, that the warm rains and the sun-rays which have not as yet brought spring, are of no importance.

What, then, is important for the realization of the Christian life? It is certainly not by diplomatic negotiation about Abyssinia and Constantinople, papal encyclicals, socialistic congresses, and so on, that mankind will approach to that for which the world endures. For, if the kingdom of God, *i.e.* the kingdom on earth of truth and good, is to be realized, it can be realized only by such attempts as were made by the first disciples of Christ, afterwards by the Paulicians, Albigenses, Quakers, Moravian Brethren, Mennonites, all the true Christians of the world, and now by the "Christians of the Universal Brotherhood."

The fact that these pains of labor continue and increase

does not prove that there will be no birth, but, on the contrary, that the birth is near at hand. People say that this will happen, but not in that way—in some other way, by books, newspapers, universities, theaters, speeches, meetings, congresses. But even if it be admitted that all these newspapers and books and meetings and universities help to the realization of the Christian life, yet, after all, the realization must be accomplished by living men, good men, with a Christian spirit, ready for righteous common life. Therefore, the main condition for the realization is the existence and gathering together of such people as shall even now realize that toward which we are all striving. And behold, these people exist!

It may be, although I doubt it, that the movement of the "Christian Universal Brotherhood" will also be stamped out, especially if society itself does not understand all the importance of what is taking place, and does not help them with brotherly aid; but that which this movement represents, that which has been expressed in it, will certainly not die, cannot die, and sooner or later will burst forth to the light, will destroy all that is now crushing it, and will take possession of the world. It is only a question of time.

True, there are people, and, unfortunately, there are many, who hope and say, "But not in our time," and therefore strive to arrest the movement. Yet their efforts are useless, and they do not arrest the movement, but by their efforts only destroy in themselves the life which is given them. For life is life, only when it is the carrying out of God's purpose. But, by opposing Him, people deprive themselves of life, and at the same time, neither for one year, nor for one hour, can they delay the accomplishment of God's purpose.

And it is impossible not to see that, with the outward connection now established among all the inhabitants of the earth, with the awakening of the Christian spirit which is now appearing in all corners of the earth, this accomplishment is near at hand. And that obduracy and blindness of the Russian government, in directing persecution against the "Christians of the Universal Brotherhood," a persecution like those of pagan times, and the wonderful meekness and firmness with which the new Christian martyrs have endured these persecutions—all these facts are undoubted signs of the nearness of this accomplishment.

And therefore, having understood all the importance of the event that is taking place, both for the life of the whole of humanity and for the life of each of us, remembering that the opportunity to act, which is now presented us, will never return, let us do that which the merchant in the Gospel parable did, selling all he possessed that he might obtain the priceless pearl; let us disdain all mean, selfish considerations, and let each of us, in whatever position he be, do all that is in his power, in order—if not directly to help those through whom the work of God is being done, if not to partake in this work— at least not to be the opponents of the work of God which is being accomplished for our good.

THE EMIGRATION OF THE DUKHOBORS

POPULATION of twelve thousand people—"Christians of the Universal Brotherhood," as the Dukhobors, who live in the Caucasus, call themselves—are at the present moment in the most distressing circumstances.

Without entering into argument as to who is right: whether it be the governments who consider that Christianity is compatible with prisons, executions, and above all, with wars and preparations for war; or whether it be the Dukhobors, who acknowledge as binding only the Christian law (which renounces the use of any force whatever, and condemns murder), and who therefore refuse to serve in the army—one cannot fail to see that this controversy is very difficult to settle. No government could allow some people to shun duties which are being fulfilled by all the rest, and to undermine thereby the very basis of the State. The Dukhobors, on the other hand, cannot disregard that very law which they consider as divine, and, consequently, as supremely obligatory.

Governments have hitherto found a way out of this dilemma, either by compelling those who refuse military service on account of their religious convictions) to fulfil other duties, more difficult, but not in conflict with their religious beliefs, as has been done, and is still being done, in Russia with the Mennonites (who are compelled to do the usual term of service at government works); or else the governments do not recognize the legality of a refusal for religious reasons, and punish those that fail to obey a general law of the State, by putting them into prison for the usual term of service, as is done in Austria with the Nazarenes. But the present Russian government has found yet a third way of treating the Dukhobors—a way which one might have expected would be dispensed with in our time. Besides subjecting those that refuse military service to the most painful tortures, it systematically causes suffering to their fathers, mothers, and children, probably with the object of shaking—by the tortures of these innocent families—the resoluteness of the dissentients.

Not to mention the floggings, incarcerations, and every kind of tortures to which the Dukhobors who refused to serve in the army were subjected in the penal battalions, where many died, and their banishment to the worst parts of Siberia; not to mention the two hundred reserves, who, during the course of two years, languished in prison, and are now separated from their families, and exiled, in pairs, to the wildest parts of the Caucasus, where, deprived of every opportunity of earning a living, they are literally dying of starvation—not to mention these punishments of those guilty of having refused to serve in the army, the families of the Dukhobors are being systematically ruined and exterminated.

They are all deprived of the right to leave the place where they live, and are heavily fined and imprisoned for non-compliance with the strangest demands of the authorities; for instance, for calling themselves by a different name from the one they are ordered to adopt, for fetching flour from a neighboring mill, for going from the village to a wood to gather fuel; a mother is even punished for visiting her son. And so the last resources of inhabitants formerly well-to-do are being quickly exhausted. In this way four hundred families have been expelled from their homes and settled in various Tartar and Georgian villages, where they, being obliged to pay for their lodgings and food, and not having any land or other means of subsistence, have found themselves in such difficult circumstances that in the course of the three years since their removal, the fourth part of them, mostly old people and children, have already died from want and disease.

It is difficult to imagine that such a systematic extermination of a whole population of twelve thousand people should enter into the plans of the Russian government. It is probable that the superior authorities are unaware of that which is in reality going on, and even if they suspect it, they would not desire to know the details, feeling that they ought not to allow such a state of things to continue, and yet at the same time recognizing that what is being done is necessary.

At all events, it is certain that the Caucasian administration has been during the last three years regularly torturing, not only those that refuse to serve in the army, but also their families, and that in the same systematic way it is ruining and starving to death all the Dukhobors who were exiled.

All petitions in favor of the Dukhobors, and any assistance rendered them, have hitherto only led to the banishment from Russia of those who have interceded in their behalf, and to the expulsion from the Caucasus of those who have attempted to help these victims. The Caucasian administration has surrounded with a kind of Chinese wall the whole of an unsubmissive population, and this population is gradually dying out; another three or four years and probably not one of the Dukhobors will survive.

This would actually have happened, but for an incident, apparently unforeseen by the Caucasian government—namely, when last year the dowager-empress, having come to the Caucasus on a visit to her son, the Dukhobors succeeded in submitting to her a petition, asking for permission to be settled all together in some remote place, and if this should be impossible, to allow them to emigrate. The empress handed over this petition to the superior authorities, and the latter acknowledged the possibility of allowing the Dukhobors to emigrate.

It seems as if the problem were now solved, and that a way has been found out of a position burdensome for both sides. This, however, is only apparently the case.

The Dukhobors are now in a position which makes it impossible for them to emigrate. At present they have not sufficient means to do so, and being confined within their villages, they are unable to make any preparations. Formerly they were well-to-do, but during the last few years the greater part of their means has been taken away from them by confiscations and fines, or has been spent in maintaining their exiled brethren. As they are not allowed to leave the vicinity of their homes, and as nobody is allowed to see them, there is no possibility whatever for them to confer and decide upon the way of emigrating. The following letter describes, better than anything else could do, the position in which the Dukhobors now find themselves.

This is what a man, highly respected among them, writes to me:—

We inform you that we submitted a petition to her

Imperial Majesty, the Empress Maria Feodorovna, who handed it over to the Senate. The result was the decree expressed in the enclosed official notification.

On February 10, I went to Tiflis, and there met our brother St. John;* but our meeting was of very short duration; they soon arrested both of us. I was put into prison, and he was immediately expelled from Russia.

I intimated to the chief of police that I had come on business to the governor. He said: "We will first imprison you, and afterward we will report you to the governor." On the 12th I was put into prison, and on the 19th I was taken to the governor, escorted by two soldiers. The chief clerk in the governor's office asked me, "Why were you arrested?" I said, "I don't know." "Was it you who were in Signakh lately?" "Yes, I was there." "And what did you come here for?" "I wish to see the governor; last summer we submitted a petition to the Empress Maria Feodorovna during her stay at Abostuman. I received an answer to the petition through the head official of the Signakh district. I asked for a copy, but he refused, saying that he could not give one without the governor's permission—and this is why I have now come here."

He announced me to the governor, the governor called me in, and I explained to him the position of affairs. He said: "Instead of seeing me you made haste to meet the Englishman." I replied: "The Englishman is also our brother."

The governor talked to me kindly, and advised us to emigrate as soon as possible; he added. "You can all go, except those of you who are liable to be summoned at the next call to military service."

---

* This is an ex-captain of the English army who took the Dukhobors some money collected for them in England.

He also gave orders for me to be released from prison, and sent back to Signakh. We are, just now, meeting in council, and, with God's help, we will try to prepare for our emigration to England or America. And in this matter we ask for your brotherly assistance.

As to the position of our brethren, we inform you that Peter Vasilyevitch Verigin° has been ordered to remain for another term of five years. The brethren in the province of Kars are still, as before, being fined at every opportunity; they are still forbidden to leave their places of residence, and for non-compliance with this order they are put into prison for a term of one to two weeks. Diseases continue as before; but there are fewer deaths. Material want is most acutely experienced by the brethren of the Signakh district; those of the other districts, however, are somewhat better off.

And here is the official notification:—

The Fasting-Dukhobors,° ° who were expelled in the year 1895 from the district of Akhalkalak, and transported into other districts of the government of Tiflis, having submitted a petition to her Imperial Majesty the Empress Maria Feodorovna, asking either to be grouped and settled in one place, and to be exempt from the duties of military service, or to be allowed to emigrate, the following instructions have been received:—

1. The request for exemption from military service is refused.

° Verigin is one of their brethren who was at first banished to the government of Archangel, and afterward to Siberia, and who is now for the eleventh year in exile.

° ° The government thus designates those Dukhobors that have not consented to military service, and who also refrain from flesh foods.

2. The Fasting-Dukhobors—with the exception, of course, of those that have reached the age at which they can be summoned to the duties of military service, and of those who have failed to fulfil those duties—may emigrate under these conditions:—(*a*) That they provide themselves with a foreign passport, in accordance with the established order; (*b*) that they leave Russia at their own expense; and (*c*) that before leaving they sign an agreement never to return within the borders of the empire, understanding that in the case of non-compliance with this last point the offender will be condemned to exile to remote places.

As to their request to be settled in one village, it is refused.

This notification is issued by order of the governor of Tiflis to one of the petitioning Fasting-Dukhobors, Vasili Potapof, in answer to his personal application.

TIFLIS, *February 21, 1898.*

People are permitted to emigrate, but they have previously been ruined, so that they have nothing to emigrate with, and the circumstances in which they find themselves are such as to render it absolutely impossible for them to know where to go and how to arrange the migration, and they are even unable to make use of the assistance extended to them from outside, since all those that attempt to help them are immediately expelled, and the Dukhobors themselves are put into prison for each absence from their homes.

Thus, if no assistance can be rendered them from outside, they will in the end be completely ruined, and will all die out, notwithstanding the permission given them to emigrate.

I happen to know the details of the persecutions and sufferings of these people; I am in communication with them, and they ask me to help them. Therefore I consider it my duty to address myself to all good people, whether Russian or not Russian, asking them to help the Dukhobors out of the terrible position in which they now are. I have attempted to address myself, through the medium of a Russian newspaper, to the Russian public, but do not know as yet whether my appeal will be published or not; and I now address myself once more to all sympathizers, asking for their assistance—first, in the form of money, of which much will be needed for the removal to a distant place of ten thousand people; and secondly, of advice and guidance in the difficulties of the coming emigration of people who do not understand any foreign language and have never left Russia before.

I trust that the leading authorities of the Russian government will not prevent such assistance from being rendered, and that they will check the excessive zeal of the Caucasian administration, which is, at the present moment, not admitting any communication whatever with the Dukhobors. . . .*

---

* Count Tolstoï's appeal was heeded. A considerable sum of money was collected; the English and American Quakers with especial alacrity came to the aid of those who were persecuted for practising the Quaker principles of non-resistance; a large tract of land was granted by the Dominion of Canada for their settlement. Ships were chartered to bring the exiles across the ocean, and finally, in the spring of 1899, the Dukhobors were landed on the shores of America and, like the Pilgrim fathers, given freedom to worship God in their own manner and to wrest a living from the abundant though latent resources of the as yet unbroken wilderness.—ED.

NOBEL'S BEQUEST

A LETTER ADDRESSED TO A SWEDISH EDITOR

HERE has lately appeared in the papers information that in connection with Nobel's will the question has been discussed as to who should be chosen to receive the £10,000 bequeathed to the person who has best served the cause of peace. This has called forth certain considerations in me, and you will greatly oblige me by publishing them in your paper.

I think this point in Nobel's will concerning those who have best served the cause of peace is very difficult. Those who do indeed serve this cause do so because they serve God, and are therefore not in need of pecuniary recompense, and will not accept it. But I think the condition expressed in the will would be quite correctly fulfilled if the money were transmitted to the destitute and suffering families of those who have served the cause of peace.

I am alluding to the Caucasian Dukhobors or Spirit-Wrestlers. No one in our time has served, and is continuing to serve, the cause of peace more effectively and powerfully than these people.

Their service of the cause of peace consists in this. A whole population, more than ten thousand persons, having come to the conviction that a Christian cannot be a murderer, decided not to participate in the military service. Thirty-four men who were summoned to enter the service refused to take the oath and serve, for which they have been confined to a penal battalion—one of the most dreadful of punishments. About three hundred men of the reserve returned their certificates * to the authorities, declaring that they could not and would not serve. These three hundred men were incarcerated in the Caucasian prisons, their families being transported from their homes and settled in Tartar and Georgian villages, where they have neither land nor work to live by.

Notwithstanding the admonitions of the authorities, and threats that they and their families will continue to suffer until they consent to fulfil military duties, those who have refused to do so do not change their decision. And their relatives—their fathers, mothers, wives, sisters—not only do not seek to dissuade them from, but encourage them in, this decision. These men say:—

"We are Christians, and therefore cannot consent to be murderers. You may torture and kill us, we cannot hinder that, but we cannot obey you, because we profess that same Christian teaching which you yourself also accept."

These words are very simple, and, so far from being new, it seems strange to repeat them. Nevertheless, these words, spoken in our time and under the conditions in which the Dukhobors find themselves, have a great importance. In our time everybody speaks of peace, and of the means of instituting it. Peace is spoken of by professors, writers, members of Parliament and of peace

---

* Men in the army reserve have certificates showing the position they occupy in the service.—Tr.

societies, and these same professors, writers, members of Parliament and of peace societies, when the occasion offers, express patriotic feelings; and when their time comes they quietly enter the ranks of the army, believing that war will cease, not through their efforts, but through somebody else's, and not in their time, but in some time to come.

Priests and pastors preach about peace in their churches, and zealously pray God for it, but they are careful not to tell their flocks that war is incompatible with Christianity. All the emperors, kings, and presidents, traveling from capital to capital, lose no opportunity to speak of peace. They speak of peace when embracing each other at the railway stations; they speak of peace when receiving deputations and presents; they speak of peace with a glass of wine in their hands, at dinners and suppers; above all they lose no opportunity to speak of peace in front of those same troops which are collected for murder, and of which they boast one before another.

And, therefore, in the midst of this universal falsehood, the conduct of the Dukhobors, who say nothing about peace, but only say that they themselves do not wish to be murderers, has a special significance, because it exhibits to the world that ancient, simple, unerring, and only means of establishing peace long ago revealed to man by Christ, but from which the people of former times were so far off that it seemed impracticable; while in our time it has become so natural that one can only be astonished how it is that all men of the Christian world have not yet adopted it.

This means is simple, because for its application it is not necessary to undertake anything new, but only for each man of our time himself to refrain from doing that which he regards as bad and shameful for himself as well as for others; and not to consent to be the slave of those who prepare men for murder. This means is certain, because, if Christians were only to admit—what they must admit—that a Christian cannot be a murderer, there would then be no soldiers; because all are Christians, and there would be lasting and inviolable peace between them. And this means is the only one, because, as long as Christians will not regard participation in the military service as impossible for themselves, so long will ambitious men involve others in this service, and there will be armies; and if there be armies, there will also be wars.

I know this means has already for long been practised. I know how the ancient Christians who refused the military service were executed by the Romans for doing so (these refusals are described in the lives of the saints). I know how the Paulicians were, every one of them, destroyed for the same conduct. I know how the Bogomili were persecuted, and how the Quakers and Mennonites suffered for this same cause. I know also how, at the present time, in Austria, the Nazarenes are languishing in prisons; and how people have been martyred in Russia.

But the fact that all these martyrdoms have not abolished war in no way proves that they have been useless. To say that this means is not efficacious because it has already been applied for a long time and yet war still exists, is the same as to say that in spring the sun's warmth is not efficacious because the ground has not yet become bare of snow, and flowers have not yet sprung up.

The meaning of these refusals in former times and now is quite different; then they were the first rays of the sun falling on the frozen winter earth, now they are the last touch of warmth necessary to destroy the remains of the seeming winter which has lost its power. And in fact there never was before that which now is; never before was the absurdity so evident that all men, without exception, strong and weak, disposed for war and abhorring it, should be equally obliged to take part in military service; or that the greater part of the national wealth should be spent on continually increasing military preparations; never before was it so clear as in our time that the continual excuse for the gathering and maintenance of armies—the supposed necessity of defense from an imaginary attack of enemies—has no basis in reason, and that all these threats of attack are only the invention of those to whom armies are necessary for their own purpose of maintaining power over the nations.

It has never occurred before, that war threatened man with such dreadful devastations and calamities, and such massacres of whole populations, as it does at the present time. And, lastly, never before have those feelings of unity and good-will among nations owing to which war appears to be something dreadful, immoral, senseless, and fratricidal, been so widely spread. But, above all never, as it is now, was the deceit so evident by which some people compel others to prepare for war, burdensome, unnecessary, and abhorrent to all.

It is said that, to destroy war by this means, too much time would have to elapse; that a long process of the union of all men in the one and the same desire to avoid participation in war would have to be gone through. But love of peace and abhorrence of war, like love of health and abhorrence of disease, have long since been the continual and general desire of all men' not corrupted, intoxicated, and deluded.

So that, if peace has not yet been established, it is not because there does not exist among men the universal desire for it; it is not because there is no love for peace and abhorrence of war; but only because there exists the cunning deceit by which men have been, and are, persuaded that peace is impossible and war indispensable. And therefore, to establish peace amongst men, first of all amongst Christians, and to abolish war, it is not necessary to inculcate in men anything new; it is only necessary to liberate them from the deceit which has been instilled into them, causing them to act contrary to their general desire. This deceit is being more and more revealed by life itself, and in our time it is so far revealed that only a small effort is necessary in order that men should completely free themselves from it. Precisely this effort the Dukhobors are making in our time by their refusal of the military service.

The conduct of the Dukhobors is tearing off the last covering which hides the truth from man. And the Russian government knows this and is endeavoring with all its strength to keep up, if only for a time, that deceit upon which its power is founded; and that government is, for this purpose, using the cruel and secret measures usual, in such cases, to those who know their guilt.

The Dukhobors who have refused the military services are confined to penal battalions and exiled to the worst parts of Siberia and the Caucasus; while their families —old men, children, wives—are driven out of their dwellings and settled in localities where, homeless and without means of earning their food, they are gradually dying out from want and disease. And all this is being done in the greatest secrecy. Those incarcerated in prisons, and those who are being exiled, are kept separate from every one else; the exiled are not allowed to communicate with Russians, they are kept exclusively among non-Russian tribes, true information concerning the Dukhobors is forbidden in the press, letters from them are not forwarded, letters to them do not reach them, special police guard against any communication between the Dukhobors and Russians, forbidding it; and those who have endeavored to help the Dukhobors, and spread information about them among the public, have been banished to distant places or else altogether exiled from Russia. And, as is always the case, these measures only produce the reverse result to that which the government desires.

In our time it is impossible unperceived to sweep off the face of the earth a religious, moral, and industrious population of ten thousands souls. Those same people, soldiers and jailers, who guard the Dukhobors, those tribes amongst whom they are dispersed, also those individuals who, notwithstanding all the efforts of the government, communicate with the Dukhobors—all these discover that for which, and in the name of which, the Dukhobors are suffering; they find out the utterly inexcusable cruelty of the government and its fear of publicity; and men who formerly never doubted the lawfulness of the government and compatibility of Christianity with the military service, not only begin to have doubts, but are becoming completely persuaded of the rightness of the Dukhobors, and of the falsity of the government, and are liberating themselves and others from the deceit which has held them up to this time.

And it is this liberation from deceit and consequent approach toward the effectual establishment of peace on earth which today constitutes the great worth of the Dukhobors.

This is why I believe that no one has served the cause of peace in a greater degree than they have. The dreadful condition in which their families at present find themselves* justifies one in affirming that no one can with greater justice be awarded the money which Nobel bequeathed to those that have best served the cause of peace.

---

* Information concerning them can be found in a book lately published in English, entitled, "Christian Martyrdom in Russia." It is edited by Vladimir Tcherkof, with concluding chapter and letter by Count Tolstoï.—ED.

LETTER TO
ERNEST HOWARD CROSBY

AM very glad to have news of your activity, and to hear that your work begins to attract attention. Fifty years ago Lloyd Garrison's Declaration of Nonresistance only estranged people from him; and Ballou's fifty years' labor in the same direction was constantly met by a conspiracy of silence. I now read with great pleasure, in the *Voice*, admirable thoughts by American writers on this question of nonresistance. I need only demur to the notion expressed by Mr. Bemis. It is an old but unfounded libel upon Christ to suppose that the expulsion of the cattle from the temple indicates that Jesus beat people with a whip, and advised His disciples to behave in a like manner.* The opinions expressed by these writers, especially by Heber Newton and George D. Herron, are quite correct; but unfortunately they do not reply to the problem which Christ put to men, but to another, which has been

* See our Revised Version of John ii. 15, which, as amended in translation, clearly shows that Jesus used the scourge only for "both the sheep and the oxen."—ED.

substituted for it by those chief and most dangerous opponents of Christianity, the so-called "orthodox" ecclesiastical authorities.

Mr. Higginson says: "I do not believe non-resistance admissible as a universal rule." Heber Newton says that people's opinion as to the practical result of the application of Christ's teaching will depend on the extent of people's belief in His authority. Carlos Martyn considers the transition stage in which we live not suited for the application of the doctrine of non-resistance. George D. Herron holds that to obey the law of non-resistance we must learn how to apply it to life. Mrs. Livermore, thinking that the law of non-resistance can be fully obeyed only in the future, says the same. All these views refer to the question, "What would happen if people were all obliged to obey the law of non-resistance?"

But, in the first place, it it impossible to oblige every one to accept the law of non-resistance. Secondly, if it were possible to do so, such compulsion would in itself be a direct negation of the very principle set up. Oblige all men to refrain from violence? Who then should enforce the decision? Thirdly, and this is the chief point, the question, as put by Christ, is not at all, "Can non-resistance become a general law for humanity?" but, "How must each man act to fulfil his allotted task, to save his soul, and to do the will of God, three things which are really one and the same thing?"

Christian teaching does not lay down laws for everybody, and does not say to people, "You all, for fear of punishment, must obey such and such rules, and then you will all be happy"; but it explains to each individual his position in relation to the world, and gives him to see what results, for him individually, inevitably flow from that relation. Christianity says to mankind (and to each man separately), that a man's personal life can have no rational meaning if he counts it as belonging to himself or as having for its aim worldly happiness for himself or for other people. This is so, because the happiness he seeks is unattainable—(1) for the reason that, all beings striving after worldly advantages, the gain of one is the loss of others, and it is most probable that each individual will incur much superfluous suffering in the course of his vain effort to seize unattainable blessings; (2) because, even if a man gains worldly advantages, the more he obtains the less he is satisfied, and the more he hankers after fresh ones; (3) and chiefly because the longer a man lives the more irresistible becomes the approach of old age, sickness, death, destroying all possibility of worldly advantages. So that if man consider his life to be his own, to be spent in seeking worldly happiness for himself as well as for others, then that life can have no rational explanation for him. Life takes a rational meaning only when one understands that, to consider our life our own, or to see its aim in worldly happiness for ourselves or for other people, is a delusion; that a man's life does not belong to him who has received it, but to Him who has given it; and therefore its object should be, not the attainment of worldly happiness, either for one's self or for other individuals, but solely to fulfil the will of Him, the Creator of this life.

This conception alone gives life a rational meaning, and makes life's aim (which is to fulfil the will of God) attainable. And, most important of all, only when enlightened by this conception does man see clearly the right direction for his own activity. Man is then no longer destined to suffer and to despair, as was inevitable under the former conception. "The universe and I in it," says a man of this conception to himself, "exist by the will of God. I cannot know the whole of the universe, for in immensity it transcends my comprehension; nor can I know my own position in it; but I do know with certainty what God, who has sent me into this world, infinite in time and space, and therefore incomprehensible to me, demands from me. This is revealed to me (1) by the collective wisdom of the best men who have gone before me, *i.e.* by tradition; (2) by my own reason; and (3) by my heart, *i.e.* by the highest aspirations of my nature.

Tradition—the collective wisdom of my greatest forerunners—tells me that I should do unto others as I would that they should do unto me. My reason shows me that only by all men acting thus is the highest happiness for all men attainable. Only when I yield myself to that intuition of love which demands obedience to this law is my own heart happy and at rest. And not only can I then know how to act, but I can and do discern that work, to coöperate in which my activity was designed and is required. I cannot fathom God's whole design, for the sake of which the universe exists and lives; but the divine work which is being accomplished in this world, and in which I participate by living, is comprehensible to me.

This work is the annihilation of discord and strife among men, and among all creatures; and the establishment of the highest unity, concord, and love. It is the fulfilment of the promises of the Hebrew prophets, who foretold a time when all men should be taught by truth, when spears should be turned into reaping-hooks, swords be beaten to plowshares, and the lion lie down with the lamb. So that a man of Christian intelligence not only knows what he has to do, but he also understands the work he is doing. He has to act so as to coöperate toward the establishment of the kingdom of God on earth. For this, a man must obey his intuition of God's will, *i.e.* he must act lovingly toward others, as he would that others should act toward him. Thus the intuitive demands of man's soul coincide with the external aim of life which he sees before him.

Man in this world, according to Christian teaching, is God's laborer. A laborer does not know his master's whole design, but he does know the immediate object which he is set to work at. He receives definite instructions what to do, and especially what not to do, lest he hinder the attainment of the very ends toward which his labor must tend. For the rest he has full liberty given him. And therefore, for a man who has grasped the Christian conception of life, the meaning of his life is perfectly plain and reasonable; nor can he have a moment's hesitation as to how he should act, or what he should do to fulfil the object for which he lives.

And yet, in spite of such a twofold indication, clear and indubitable to a man of Christian understanding of what is the real aim and meaning of human life, and of what men should do and should not do, we find people (and people calling themselves Christians) who decide that in such and such circumstances men ought to abandon God's law and reason's guidance, and act in opposition to them; because, according to their conception, the effects of actions performed in submission to God's law may be detrimental or inconvenient.

According to the law, contained alike in tradition, in our reason, and in our hearts, man should always do unto others as he would that they should do unto him; he should always cooperate in the development of love and union among created beings. But on the contrary, in the judgment of these people who look ahead, as long as it is premature, in their opinion, to obey this law, man should do violence, imprison or kill people, and thereby evoke anger and venom instead of loving union in the hearts of men. It is as if a bricklayer, set to do a particular task, and knowing that he was coöperating with others to build a house, after receiving clear and precise instructions from the master himself how to build a certain wall, should receive from some fellow brick-layers (who like himself knew neither the plan of the house nor what would fit in with it) orders to cease build-ing his wall, and instead rather to pull down a wall which other workmen had erected.

Astonishing delusion! A being who breathes one day and vanishes the next receives one definite, indubitable law to guide him through the brief term of his life; but instead of obeying that law he prefers to fancy that he knows what is necessary, advantageous, and well-timed for men, for all the world—this world which continually shifts and evolves; and for the sake of some advantage (which each man pictures after his own fancy) he decides that he and other people should temporarily abandon the indubitable law given to one and to all, and should act, not as they would that others should act toward them, bringing love into the world, but instead do violence, imprison, kill, and bring into the world enmity whenever it seems profitable to do so. And he decides to act thus, though he knows that the most horrible cruelties, martyr-doms, and murders—from the inquisitions, and the mur-ders, and horrors of all the revolutions, down to the violences of contemporary anarchists, and their slaughter by the established authorities—have only occurred because people will imagine that they know what is necessary for mankind and for the world. But are there not always, at any given moment, two opposite parties, each of which declares that it is necessary to use force against the other—the "law and order" party against the "anarchist"; the "anarchist" against the "law and order" men; English against Americans, and Americans against English, and English against Germans; and so forth in all possible combinations and rearrangements?

A man enlightened by Christianity sees that he has no reason to abandon the law of God, given to enable him to walk with sure foot through life, in order to follow the chance, inconstant, and often contradictory demands of men. But besides this, if he has lived a Christian life for some time, and has developed in himself a Christian moral sensibility, he literally cannot act as people demand of him. Not this reason only, but his feeling also, makes it impossible. To many people of our society it would be impossible to torture or kill a baby, even if they were told that by so doing they could save hundreds of people. And in the same way a man, when he has developed a Christian sensibility of heart, finds a whole series of actions are become impossible for him. For instance, a Christian who is obliged to take part in judicial proceedings in which a man may be sentenced to death, or who is obliged to take part in evictions, or in debating a proposal leading to war, or to participate in preparations for war (not to mention war itself), is in a position parallel to that of a kindly man called on to torture or to kill a baby. It is not reason alone that forbids him to do what is demanded of him; he feels instinctively that he cannot do it. For certain actions are morally impossible, just as others are physically impossible. As a man cannot lift a mountain, and as a kindly man cannot kill an infant, so a man living the Christian life cannot take part in deeds of violence. Of what value then to him are arguments about the imaginary advantages of doing what is morally impossible for him to do?

But how is a man to act when he sees clearly an evil in following the law of love and its corollary law of non-resistance? How (to use the stock example) is a man to act when he sees a criminal killing or outraging a child, and he can only save the child by killing the criminal? When such a case is put, it is generally assumed that the only possible reply is that one should kill the assailant to save the child. But this answer is given so quickly and decidedly only because we are all so accustomed to the use of violence, not only to save a child, but even to prevent a neighboring government altering its frontier at the expense of ours, or to prevent some one from smuggling lace across that frontier, or even to defend our garden fruit from a passer-by. It is assumed that to save the child the assailant should be killed.

But it is only necessary to consider the question, "On what grounds ought a man, whether he be or be not a Christian, to act so?" in order to come to the conclusion that such action has no reasonable foundation, and only seems to us necessary because up to two thousand years ago such conduct was considered right, and a habit of acting so had been formed. Why should a non-Christian, not acknowledging God, and not regarding the fulfilment of His will as the aim of life, decide to kill the criminal in order to defend the child? By killing the former he kills for certain; whereas he cannot know positively whether the criminal would have killed the child or not. But letting that pass, who shall say whether the child's life was more

needed, was better, than the other's life? Surely, if the
non-Christian knows not God, and does not see life's
meaning to be in the performance of His will, the only
rule for his actions must be a reckoning, a conception, of
which is more profitable for him and for all men, a continuation of the criminal's life or of the child's. To decide
that, he needs to know what would become of the child
whom he saves, and what, had he not killed him, would
have been the future of the assailant. And as he cannot
know this, the non-Christian has no sufficient rational
ground for killing a robber to save a child.

If a man be a Christian, and consequently acknowledges God, and sees the meaning of life in fulfilling His
will, then, however ferocious the assailant, however innocent and lovely the child, he has even less ground to
abandon the God-given law, and to do to the criminal as
the criminal wishes to do to the child. He may plead with
the assailant, may interpose his own body between the
assailant and the victim; but there is one thing he cannot
do—he cannot deliberately abandon the law he has received from God, the fulfilment of which alone gives
meaning to his life. Very probably bad education, or
his animal nature, may cause a man, Christian or non-
Christian, to kill an assailant, not to save a child, but even
to save himself or to save his purse. But it does not follow
that he is right in acting thus, or that he should accustom
himself or others to think such conduct right. What it
does show is that, notwithstanding a coating of education
and of Christianity, the habits of the stone age are yet
so strong in man that he still commits actions long since
condemned by his reasonable conscience.

I see a criminal killing a child, and I can save the child
by killing the assailant—therefore, in certain cases, violence

must be used to resist evil. A man's life is in danger, and can be saved only by my telling a lie—therefore, in certain cases, one must lie. A man is starving, and I can only save him by stealing—therefore, in certain cases, one must steal. I lately read a story by Coppee, in which an orderly kills his officer, whose life was insured, and thereby saves the honor and the family of the officer, the moral being that, in certain cases, one must kill. Such devices, and the deductions from them, only prove that there are men who know that it is not well to steal, to lie, or to kill, but who are still so unwilling that people should cease to do these things that they use all their mental powers to invent excuses for such conduct. There is no moral law concerning which one might not devise a case in which it is difficult to decide which is more moral, to disobey the law or to obey it? But all such devices fail to prove that the laws, "Thou shalt not lie, steal, or kill," are invalid.

It is thus with the law of non-resistance. People know it is wrong to use violence, but they are so anxious to continue to live a life secured by "the strong arm of the law," that, instead of devoting their intellects to the elucidation of the evils which have flowed, and are still flowing, from admitting that man has a right to use violence to his fellow-men, they prefer to exert their mental powers in defense of that error. *"Fais ce que dois, advienne que pourra"*—"Do what's right, come what may"—is an expression of profound wisdom. We each can know indubitably what we ought to do, but what results will follow from our actions we none of us either do or can know. Therefore it follows that, besides feeling the call of duty, we are further driven to act as duty bids us by the consideration that we have no other guidance, but are totally ignorant of what will result from our action.

Christian teaching indicates what a man should do to perform the will of Him who sent him into life; and discussion as to what results we anticipate from such or such human actions have nothing to do with Christianity, but are just an example of the error which Christianity eliminates. None of us has ever yet met the imaginary criminal with the imaginary child, but all the horrors which fill the annals of history and of our own times came, and come, from this one thing, namely, that people will believe they really foresee speculative future results of actions.

The case is this. People once lived an animal life, and violated or killed whom they thought well to violate or to kill. They even ate one another, and public opinion approved of it. Thousands of years ago, as far back as the times of Moses, a day came when people had realized that to violate or kill one another is bad. But there were people for whom the reign of force was advantageous, and these did not approve of the change, but assured themselves and others that to do deeds of violence and to kill people is not always bad, but that there are circumstances when it is necessary and even moral. And violence and slaughter, though not so frequent or so cruel as before, continued, only with this difference, that those who committed or commended such acts excused themselves by pleading that they did it for the benefit of humanity.

It was just this sophistical justification of violence that Christ denounced. When two enemies fight, each may think his own conduct justified by the circumstances. Excuses can be made for every use of violence, and no infallible standard has ever been discovered by which to measure the worth of these excuses. Therefore Christ taught us to disbelieve in any excuse for violence, and (contrary to what had been taught by them of old times) never to use violence. One would have thought that those who have professed Christianity would be indefatigable in exposing deception in this matter; for in such exposure lay one of the chief manifestations of Christianity. What really happened was just the reverse. People who profited by violence, and who did not wish to give up their advantages, took on themselves a monopoly of Christian preaching, and declared that, as cases can be found in which non-resistance causes more harm than the use of violence (the imaginary criminal killing the imaginary child), therefore Christ's doctrine of non-resistance need not always be followed; and that one may deviate from His teaching to defend one's life or the life of others; or to defend one's country, to save society from lunatics or criminals, and in many other cases.

The decision of the question in what cases Christ's teaching should be set aside was left to the very people who employed violence. So that it ended by Christ's teaching on the subject of not resisting evil by violence being completely annulled. And what was worst of all was that the very people Christ denounced came to consider themselves the sole preachers and expositors of His doctrines. But the light shines through the darkness, and Christ's teaching is again exposing the pseudoteachers of Christianity. We may think about rearranging the world to suit our own taste—no one can prevent that; and we may try to do what seems to us pleasant or profitable, and with that object treat our fellow creatures with violence on the pretext that we are doing good. But so acting we cannot pretend that we follow Christ's teaching, for Christ denounced just this deception. Truth sooner or later reappears, and the false teachers are shown up, which is just what is happening today.

Only let the question of man's life be rightly put, as Christ put it, and not as it has been perversely put by the Church, and the whole structure of falsehood which the Church has built over Christ's teaching will collapse of itself. The real question is not whether it will be good or bad for a certain human society that people should follow the law of love and the consequent law of non-resistance. But it is this: Do you, who today live and tomorrow will die, you who are indeed tending deathward every moment, do you wish now, immediately and entirely, to obey the law of Him who sent you into life, and who clearly showed you His will, alike in tradition and in your mind and heart; or do you prefer to resist His will? And as soon as the question is put thus, only one reply is possible: I wish now, this moment, without delay or hesitation, to the very utmost of my strength, neither waiting for one or counting the cost, to do that which alone is clearly demanded by Him who sent me into the world; and on no account, and under no conditions, do I wish to, or can I, act otherwise—for herein lies my only possibility of a rational and unharassed life.

NIKOLAÏ PALKIN

E were spending the night at the house of a soldier ninety-five years old, who had served under Alexander I and Nicholas I.

"Tell me, are you ready to die?"

"Ready to die? How should I be yet? I used to be afraid of dying, but now I pray God for only one thing; that God would be pleased to let me make my confession and partake of the communion; I have so many sins on my conscience."

"What sins?"

"How can you ask? Let us see, when was it I served? Under Nicholas. Was the service then such as it is now? How was it then? Uh! it fills me with horror even to remember it. Then Alexander came. The soldiers used to praise this Alexander. They said he was gracious."

I remembered the last days of Alexander, when twenty men out of every hundred were beaten to death. Nicholas must have been a terror, if in comparison with him Alexander was called gracious.

"I happened to serve under Nicholas," said the old man, and he immediately began to grow animated and to give me his recollections.

"How was it then? At that time fifty blows with the

rod was thought nothing. . . . one hundred and fifty, two hundred, three hundred. . . . they used to whip men to death, and with cudgels too. . . . Never a week went by that they did not beat one or two men to death from each regiment. Today people don't know what a cudgel is, but then the word 'palka' was never out of men's mouths. 'Palka'! 'Palka!'

"Among us soldiers he was called Nikolaï Palkin.— Nicholas the cudgeler. He was really Nikolaï Palkin. That was his universal nickname. That's what I remember of that time," continued the old man. "Yes, when one has lived out a century, it is time for one to die, and when you think of it, it becomes hard.

"I have so many sins on my soul! It was a subordinate's work. One had to apply one hundred and fifty blows to a soldier"—the old man had been non-commissioned officer and sergeant major, but was now "kandidat"—"and you give him two hundred. And the man died on your hands, and you tortured him to death . . . that was a sin.

"The non-commissioned officers used to beat the young soldiers to death. They would strike them anywhere with the butt-end of the gun or with the fist, over the heart or on the head, and the man would die. And there was never any redress. If a man died, murdered that way, the authorities would write, 'Died by the will of God,' and thus it was covered up. And at that time did I realize what it meant? One thought only of oneself. But now when you crawl up on top of the stove and can't sleep o' nights, you keep thinking about it and living it over again. Good as it is to take the holy communion in accordance with the Christian law and be absolved, still horror seizes you.

Note by the Editor of this edition: The Russian word "palka" means in English: *cane* or *stick*.

When you remember all that you have been through, yes, and what others have suffered on your account, then no other hell is necessary; it is worse than any hell."

I vividly imagined what must have been the recollections of this solitary old man there, face to face with death, and a pang went through my heart. I remembered other horrors besides the cudgels, which he must have witnessed: men killed in running the gauntlet, put to death by shooting, the slaughter and pillage of cities in war—he had taken part in the Polish war—and I thought I would question him particularly in regard to all this: I asked him about running the gauntlet. He gave full particulars about this horrible punishment: how they drove the man, with his arms tied, between two rows of soldiers provided with sharpened sticks, how all struck at him, while behind the soldiers marched the officers shouting "Strike harder." When he told about this the old man gave the order in a commanding tone, evidently well satisfied with his memory and the commanding tone with which he spoke.

He told all the particulars without manifesting the slightest remorse, as if he were telling how they killed oxen and prepared fresh meat. He related how they drove the unhappy victims back and forth between the lines, how the tortured man would at last stumble and fall on the bayonets, how at first the bloody wheals began to appear, how they would cross one another, how gradually the wheals would blend together and swell and the blood would spurt out, how the blood-stained flesh would hang in clots, how the bones would be laid bare; how the wretch at first would scream, then only dully groan at every step and at every blow; how at length no sound would be heard, and the doctor, who was in attendance for this very purpose, would come up, feel the man's pulse, examine and decide whether the punishment could go on, whether he was already beaten to death, or whether it should be postponed till another occasion; and then they would bring him to, so that his wounds might be dressed, and he might be made ready to receive the full sum of blows which certain wild beasts, with Nikolaï Palkin at their head, had decided ought to be administered to him.

The doctor employed his science to keep the man from dying before he had endured all the tortures which his body could be made to endure. And the man, when he could no longer walk a step, was laid flat on the ground in his cloak, and with that bloody swelling over his whole back was carried to the hospital to be treated, so that when he was well again they might give him the thousand or two blows which he had not yet received, and could not bear all at one time.

He told how the victims implored death to come to their relief, and how the officers would not grant it to them, but would heal them for a second and third time, and at last beat them to death.

And all this because a man had either deserted from his regiment, or had the courage or the audacity and the self-confidence to complain in behalf of his comrades because they were ill fed, and those in command pilfered their rations.

He told all this; and when I tried to draw from him some expression of remorse for these things, he was at first amazed and afterward alarmed.

"No," said he, "that was all right; it was the judgment of the court. Was it my fault? It was by order of the court and according to law."

He displayed the same serenity and lack of remorse regarding the horrors of war, in which he had taken part, and of which he had seen so much in Turkey and Poland.

He told about children murdered, about prisoners dying of cold and starvation, about a young boy—a Polyak—run through by a bayonet and impaled on a tree. And when I asked him if his conscience did not torment him on account of these deeds, he utterly failed to understand me.

"This is all a part of war, according to law; for the Tsar and the fatherland. These deeds are not only not wrong, but are such as are honorable and brave, and atone for many sins." The only things that troubled him were his private actions, the fact that he, when an officer, had beaten and punished men. These actions tormented his conscience. But in order to be pardoned for them he had a resource: this was the holy communion, which he hoped he should be enabled to partake of before he died, and for which he was beseeching his niece. His niece promised that he should have it, because she recognized the importance of it; and he was content.

The fact that he had helped to ruin and destroy innocent women and children, that he had killed men with bullet and bayonet, that he had stood in line and whipped men to death and dragged them off to the hospital and back to torture again—all this did not trouble him at all; all this was none of his business, all this was done, not by him, but as it were, by some one else.

How was it possible that this old man, if he had understood what ought to have been clear to him, as he stood on the very threshold of eternity, did not realize that between him and his conscience and God, as now on the eve of death, there was and could be no mediator, so there was and could be none even at that moment when they compelled him to torture and beat men? How is it that he did not understand that now there was nothing that could atone for the evil he had done to men when he might have refrained from doing it? that he did not understand that there is an eternal law which he always knew and could not help knowing—a law which demands love and tenderness for man; and what he called law was a wicked and godless deception to which he should not give credence?

It was terrible to think of what must have arisen before his imagination during his sleepless nights on the oven, and his despair, if he had realized that when he had the possibility of doing good and evil to men, he had done nothing but evil; that when he had learned the distinctions of good and evil nothing else was now in his power than uselessly to torment himself and repent. His sufferings would have been awful!

But why should one desire to trouble him? Why torment the conscience of an old man on the very verge of death? Better give it comfort. Why annoy the people in recalling what is already past?

Past? What is past? Can a severe disease be past only because we say that it is past? It does not pass away, and never will pass away, and cannot pass away as long as we do not acknowledge ourselves sick. To be cured of a disease, one must first recognize it. And this we do not do. Not only do we fail to do it, but we employ all our powers not to see it, not to recognize it

Meantime, the disease, instead of passing away, changes its form, sinks deeper into the flesh, the blood, the bones. The disease is this: that men born good and gentle, men with love and mercy rooted in their hearts, perpetrate such atrocities on one another, themselves not knowing why or wherefore.

Our native Russians, men naturally sweet-tempered, good, and kind, permeated with the spirit of Christ's teaching, men who confess in their souls that they would be insulted at the suggestion of their not sharing their last crust with the poor, or pitying those in prison—these same men spend the best years of their lives in murdering and torturing their brethren, and not only are not remorseful for such deeds, but consider them honorable, or at least indispensable, and just as unavoidable as eating or breathing.

Is not this a horrible disease? Is it not the moral duty of every one to do all in his power to cure it, and first and foremost to point it out, to call it by name?

The old soldier had spent all his life in torturing and murdering other men. We ask, Why talk about it? The soldier did not consider himself to blame; and those dreadful deeds—the cudgel, the running of the gauntlet, and the other things—are all past; why then recall that which is already ancient history? This is done away with.

Nikolaï Palkin is no more. Why recall his régime? Only the old soldier remembered it before his death. Why stir the people up about it?

Thus in the time of Nicholas they spoke of Alexander. In the same way in the time of Alexander they recalled the deeds of Paul. Thus in the time of Paul they spoke of Catharine and all her profligacies, and all the follies of her lovers. Thus in the time of Catharine they spoke of Peter, and so on and so on. Why recall it?

Yes, why?

If I have a severe or dangerous disease difficult to cure, and I am relieved of it, I shall always be glad to be reminded of it. I shall not mention it only when I am suffering, and my suffering continues and grows worse all the time, and I wish to deceive myself; only then I shall not mention it! And we do not mention it because we know that we are still suffering. Why disturb the old man and stir up the people? The cudgels and the running of the gauntlet—all that is long past!

Past? It has changed its form, but it is not past. In every foregoing period there have been things which we remember not only with horror, but with indignation.

We read the descriptions of distraining for debt, burning for heresy, military colonization, whippings and running of the gauntlet, and are not only horror-struck at the cruelty of man, but we fail to imagine the mental state of those who did such things. What was in the soul of the man who could get up in the morning, wash his face and hands, put on the dress of a boyar, say his prayers to God, then go to the torture-chamber to stretch the joints and whip with the knout old men and women, and spend in this business his ordinary five hours, like the modern functionary in the senate; then return to his family and calmly sit down to dinner and finish the day reading the Holy Scripture? What was in the souls of those regimental and company commanders?

I knew such a man, who one evening danced the mazurka with a beautiful girl at a ball, and retired earlier than usual so as to be awake early in the morning to make arrangements to compel a runaway soldier—a Tartar—to be killed in running the gauntlet; and after he had seen this man whipped to death, he returned to his family and ate his dinner! You see all this took place in the time of Peter, and in the time of Alexander, and in the time of Nicholas. There has not been a time when terrible things of this kind have not taken place, which we in reading about them cannot understand. We cannot understand how men could look on such horrors as they perpetrated, and not see the senselessness of them, even if they did not recognize the bestial inhumanity of them. This has been so in all times. Is our day so peculiar, so fortunate, that we have no such horrors, no such doings, which will seem just as ridiculous and incomprehensible to our descendants? There are just such deeds, just such horrors, only we don't see them, as our predecessors did not see those in their day.

To us now, it is clear that the burning of heretics, the application of torture for eliciting the truth, is not only cruel, but also ridiculous. A child sees the absurdity of it. But the men of those times did not see it so. Sensible, educated men were persuaded that torture was one of the indispensable conditions of the life of man, that it was hard, nay, impossible, to get along without it. So also with corporal punishment, with slavery. And time passed; and now it is hard for us to comprehend the mental state of men in which such a mistake was possible. But this has been in all times because so it had to be, and also in our time, and we must be just as reasonable in regard to the horrors of our day.

Where are our tortures, our slavery, our whippings? It seems to us that we no longer have such things, that they used to be, but have disappeared. This seems to us so because we do not wish to comprehend the old, and we strenuously shut our eyes to it.

But if we look at the past, then our present position is revealed to us and its causes. If we only called bonfires, branding irons, tortures, the scaffold, recruiting stations, by their real names, then we should find also the right name for dungeons, jails, wars, and the general military obligation, and policemen. If we do not say, "Why mention it?" and if we look attentively at what was done in old times, then we should take notice of what is doing now.

If it became clear to us that it was stupid and cruel to cut men's heads off on the scaffold, and to elicit the truth from their lips by means of tearing their joints asunder, then likewise it would be also equally clear to us—if not even more so—that it is stupid and cruel to hang men, or put them into a state of solitary confinement, even worse than death, and to elicit the truth through hired lawyers and judges.

If it becomes clear to us that it is stupid and cruel to kill a man who has made a mistake, then also it will be clear that it is still more stupid to confine such a man in a jail, in order to finish corrupting him; if it is clear that it is stupid and cruel to compel muzhiks into being soldiers and to brand them like cattle, then it will seem equally stupid and cruel to make every man who has reached the age of twenty-one become a soldier. If it is clear that stupidity and cruelty are the cause of crime, then still clearer will be the stupidity of guards and police.

If we only cease to shut our eyes to the past, saying: "Why recall the past?" it will become clear to us that we have the same horrors, only under new forms.

We say that all this is past—now we have no tortures, no adulterous Catharines with their powerful lovers, no more slavery, no more whippings to death, and so on—but how is it in reality? Nine hundred thousand men in prison and under arrest, shut up in narrow, ill-smelling cells, and dying by a slow physical and moral death. Women and children are left without subsistence, and these men are maintained in caverns of corruption, in prisons, and in squads; and only inspectors, having full control of these slaves, get any advantage from this senseless, cruel confinement of them.

Tens of thousands of men with dangerous ideas go into exile, and carry these ideas into the farthest corners of Russia, go out of their minds, and hang themselves. Thousands sit in prisons, and either kill themselves with the connivance of the prison officers, or go mad in solitary confinement. Millions of the people go to rack and ruin physically and morally in the slavery of the factories. Hundreds of thousands of men every autumn leave their families, their young wives, and take lessons in murder, and systematically go to destruction. The Russian Tsar cannot go anywhere without being surrounded by a visible cordon of a hundred thousand soldiers, stationed ninety steps apart all along the road, and a secret cordon following him everywhere.

A king collects tribute and builds a castle, and in the castle he constructs a pond, and on the pond dyed with blue, with a machine which raises a wind, he sails around in a boat; but his people are perishing in factories: this happens in Ireland and in France and in Belgium.

It does not require great penetration to see that in our day it is just the same, and that our day is just as fecund with horrors—with the same horrors, with the same tortures—and that these, in the eyes of succeeding generations, will seem just as marvelous in their cruelty and stupidity. The disease is the same, and the disease is not felt by those that profit by these horrors.

Let them profit for a hundred, for a thousand times more. Let them build their castles, set up their tents, give their balls, let them swindle the people. Let the Nikolaï

Palkins whip the people to death, let them shut up hundreds of men secretly in fortresses; only let them do this themselves, so as not to corrupt the people, so as not to deceive them by compelling them to take part in this, as the old soldier was.

This horrible disease lies in the deception: in this fact that for a man there can be any sanctity and any law higher than the sanctity and the law of love to one's neighbor; in the deception, which conceals the fact, that, though a man in carrying out the demands of men may do many bad things, only one kind of thing he ought not to do. He ought never at any one's instigation to go against God, to kill and to torture his brethren.

Eighteen hundred years ago, to the question of the Pharisees, it was said: *"Render unto Cæsar the things that are Cæsar's, and to God the things that are God's."*

If there was any faith among men and they recognized any duty to God, then above all they would recognize it as their duty before God to do what God Himself taught man when He said: *"Thou shalt not kill"*; when He said, *"Do not unto others what you would not have others do to you"*; when He said, *"Love thy neighbor as thyself,"* saying it not in words only, but writing in ineradicable marks on the heart of every man—love to one's neighbor; mercy, horror of murder and of torture of one's brethren.

If men only believed in God, then they could not help acknowledging this first obligation to Him, not to torture, not to kill, and then the words, *"Render unto Cæsar the things that are Cæsar's, and to God the things that are God's,"* would have for them a clear, definite significance.

"To the Tsar or to any one all he wishes," the believing man would say, "but not what is contrary to God."

Cæsar needs my money—take it; my house, my labors—

take them; my wife, my children, my life—take them; all these things are not God's. But when Cæsar requires that I apply the rods to my neighbor's back, that is God's affair. My behavior—that is my life for which I must give an account to God; and what God has forbidden me to do that I cannot give to Cæsar. I cannot bind, imprison, whip, kill my fellowmen; all that is my life, and it belongs to God alone, and I may not give it to any one except God.

The words, *"To God the things that are God's,"* for us signify whatever they give to God—kopeks, candles, prayers, in general everything that is unnecessary to any one, much less to God; but everything else; all one's life, all one's soul which belongs to God, they give to Cæsar; in other words, according to the significance of the word *Cæsar* as understood by the Jews—to some entire stranger. This is horrible! Let the people remember this.

CHURCH AND STATE

HAT an extraordinary thing it is! There are people who seem ready to climb out of their skins for the sake of making others accept this, and not that, form of revelation. They cannot rest till others have accepted their form of revelation, and no other. They anathematize, persecute, and kill whom they can of the dissentients. Other groups of people do the same—anathematize, persecute, and kill whom they can of the dissentients. And others again do the same. So that they are all anathematizing, persecuting, and killing—demanding that every one should believe as they do. And it results that there are hundreds of sects all anathematizing, persecuting, and killing one another.

At first I was astonished that such an obvious absurdity—such an evident contradiction—did not destroy religion itself. How can religious people remain so deluded? And really, viewed from the general, external point of view it is incomprehensible, and proves irrefragably that every religion is a fraud, and that the whole thing is superstition, as the dominant philosophy of today declares. And looking at things from this general point of view, I inevitably came to acknowledge that all religion is a human fraud. But I could not help pausing at the reflection that the very absurdity and obviousness of the fraud, and the fact that nevertheless all humanity yields to it, indicates that this fraud must rest on some basis that is not fraudulent. Otherwise we could not let it deceive us—it is too stupid. The very fact that all of mankind that really lives a human life yields to this fraud, obliged me to acknowledge the importance of the phenomena on which the fraud is based. And in consequence of this reflection, I began to analyze the Christian teaching, which, for all Christendom, supplies the basis of this fraud.

That is what was apparent from the general point of view. But from the individual point of view—which shows us that each man (and I myself) must, in order to live, always have a religion show him the meaning of life—the fact that violence is employed in questions of religion is yet more amazing in its absurdity.

Indeed how can it, and why should it, concern any one to make somebody else, not merely have the same religion as himself, but also profess it in the same way as he does? A man lives, and must, therefore, know why he lives. He has established his relation to God; he knows the very truth of truths, and I know the very truth of truths. Our expression may differ; the essence must be the same—we are both of us men.

Then why should I—what can induce me to—oblige any one or demand of any one absolutely to express his truth as I express it?

I cannot compel a man to alter his religion either by violence or by cunning or by fraud—false miracles.

His religion is his life. How can I take from him his

religion and give him another? It is like taking out his heart and putting another in its place. I can only do that if his religion and mine are words, and are not what gives him life; if it is a wart and not a heart. Such a thing is impossible also, because no man can deceive or compel another to believe what he does not believe; for if a man has adjusted his relation toward God and knows that religion is the relation in which man stands toward God he cannot desire to define another man's relation to God by means of force or fraud. That is impossible, but yet it is being done, and has been done everywhere and always. That is to say, it can never really be done, because it is in itself impossible; but something has been done, and is being done, that looks very much like it. What has been, and is being done, is that some people impose on others a counterfeit of religion and others accept this counterfeit—this sham religion.

Religion cannot be forced and cannot be accepted for the sake of anything, force, fraud, or profit. Therefore what is so accepted is not religion but a fraud. And this religious fraud is a long-established condition of man's life.

In what does this fraud consist, and on what is it based? What induces the deceivers to produce it? and what makes it plausible to the deceived? I will not discuss the same phenomena in Brahminism, Buddhism, Confucianism, and Mohammedanism, though any one who has read about those religions may see that the case has been the same in them as in Christianity; but I will speak only of the latter—it being the religion known, necessary, and dear to us. In Christianity, the whole fraud is built up on the fantastic conception of a Church; a conception founded on nothing, and which as soon as we begin to study Christianity amazes us by its unexpected and use-less absurdity.

Of all the godless ideas and words there is none more godless than that of a Church. There is no idea which has produced more evil, none more inimical to Christ's teaching, than the idea of a Church.

In reality the word *ekklesia* means an assembly and nothing more, and it is so used in the Gospels. In the language of all modern nations the word *ekklesia* (or the equivalent word "church") means a house for prayer. Beyond that, the word has not progressed in any lan-guage—notwithstanding the fifteen hundred years' exist-ence of the Church-fraud. According to the definition given to the word by priests (to whom the Church-fraud is necessary) it amounts to nothing else than a preface which says: "All that I am going to say is true, and if you disbelieve I shall burn you, or denounce you, and do you all manner of harm." This conception is a sophistry, needed for certain dialectical purposes, and it has re-mained the possession of those to whom it is necessary. Among the people, and not only among common people, but also in society among educated people, no such con-ception is held at all, even though it is taught in the catechisms. Strange as it seems to examine this definition, one has to do so because so many people proclaim it seri-ously as something important, though it is absolutely false. When people say that the Church is an assembly of the true believers, nothing is really said (leaving aside the fantastic inclusion of the dead); for if I assert that the choir is an assembly of all true musicians, I have elu-cidated nothing unless I say what I mean by true musi-cians. In theology we learn that true believers are those who follow the teaching of the Church, *i.e.* belong to the Church.

Not to dwell on the fact that there are hundreds of such true Churches, this definition tells us nothing, and at first seems as useless as the definition of "choir" as the assembly of true musicians. But then we catch sight of the fox's tail. The Church is true, and it is one, and in it are pastors and flocks, and the pastors, ordained by God, teach this true and only religion. So that it amounts to saying: "By God, all that we are going to say, is all real truth." That is all. The whole fraud lies in that—in the word and idea of a Church. And the meaning of the fraud is merely that there are people who are beside themselves with desire to teach their religion to other people.

And why are they so anxious to teach their religion to other people? If they had a real religion they would know that religion is the understanding of life, the relation each man establishes to God, and that consequently you cannot teach a religion, but only a counterfeit of religion. But they want to teach. What for? The simplest reply would be that the priest wants rolls and eggs, and the archbishop wants a palace, fishpies, and a silk cassock. But this reply is insufficient. Such is no doubt the inner, psychological motive for the deception—that which maintains the fraud. But as it would be insufficient, when asking why one man (an executioner) consents to kill another against whom he feels no anger—to say that the executioner kills because he thereby gets bread and brandy and a red shirt, so it is insufficient to say that the metropolitan of Kief with his monks stuffs sacks with straw*

* The celebrated Catacombs of the Kief Monastery draw crowds

and calls them relics of the saints, merely to get thirty thousand rubles a year income. The one act and the other is too terrible and too revolting to human nature for so simple and rude an explanation to be sufficient. Both the executioner and the metropolitan explaining their actions would have a whole series of arguments based chiefly on historical tradition. Men must be executed; executions have gone on since the world commenced. If I don't do it another will. I hope, by God's grace, to do it better than another would. So also the metropolitan would say: External worship is necessary; since the commencement of the world the relics of the saints have been worshiped. People respect the relics in the Kief Catacombs and pilgrims come here; I, by God's grace, hope to make the most pious use of the money thus blasphemously obtained.

To understand the religious fraud it is necessary to go to its source and origin.

We are speaking about what we know of Christianity. Turn to the commencement of Christian doctrine in the Gospels and we find a teaching which plainly excludes the external worship of God, condemning it; and which, with special clearness, positively repudiates mastership. But from the time of Christ onward we find a deviation from these principles laid down by Christ. This deviation begins from the times of the Apostles and especially from that hankerer after mastership—Paul. And the farther

---

of pilgrims to worship the relics of the saints. It is said that a fire once broke out in one of the chapels, and that those who hastened to save the "incorruptible body" of one of the saints discovered that the precious relic was merely a bag stuffed with straw. This is only a specimen of many similar tales, some of which are true and others invented.—Tr.

to continue to be the chieftain of the robbers—to kill,
fight, lust, execute, and live in luxury? That can
e arranged."

d they arranged a Christianity for him, and arranged
ry smoothly, better even than could have been ex-
ed. They foresaw that, reading the Gospels, it might
r to him that all this (*i.e.* a Christian life) is de-
ded—and not the building of temples or worshiping
em. This they foresaw, and they carefully devised
a Christianity for him as would let him continue to
his old heathen life unembarrassed. On the one hand
st, God's Son, only came to bring salvation to him
to everybody. Christ having died, Constantine can
as he likes. More even than that—one may repent and
low a little bit of bread and some wine, and that will
g salvation, and all will be forgiven.

it more even than that: they sanctify his robber-
ftainship, and say that it proceeds from God, and they
nt him with holy oil. And he, on his side, arranges for
1 the congress of priests that they wish for, and orders
1 to say what each man's relation to God should be,
orders every one to repeat what they say.

nd they all started repeating it, and were contented,
now this same religion has existed for fifteen hundred
s, and other robber-chiefs have adopted it, and they
all been lubricated with holy oil, and they were all,
rdained by God. If any scoundrel robs every one and
s many people, they will oil him, and he will then be
God. In Russia, Catharine II, the adulteress who
d her husband, was from God; so, in France, was
oleon.

o balance matters the priests are not only from God,
are almost gods, because the Holy Ghost sits inside

Christianity goes the more it deviates, and the more it
adopts the methods of external worship and mastership
which Christ had so definitely condemned. But in the
early times of Christianity the conception of a Church was
only employed to refer to all those who shared the beliefs
which I consider true. That conception of the Church is
quite correct if it does not include those that make a
verbal expression of religion instead of its expression in
the whole of life—for religion cannot be expressed in
words.

The idea of a true Church was also used as an argument against dissenters. But till the time of the Emperor
Constantine and the Council of Nicæa, the Church was
only an idea.

Since the Emperor Constantine and the Council of
Nicæa the Church becomes a reality, and a fraudulent
reality—that fraud of metropolitans with relics, and priests
with the eucharist, Iberian Mothers of God,* synods, etc.,
which so astonish and horrify us, and which are so odious
that they cannot be explained merely by the avarice of
those that perpetuate them. The fraud is ancient, and was
not begun merely for the profit of private individuals. No
one would be such a monster of iniquity as to be the first
to perpetrate it, if that were the only reason. The reasons
which caused the thing to be done were evil: "By their
fruits ye shall know them." The root was evil—hatred,
pride, enmity against Arius and others; and another yet
greater evil, the alliance of Christianity with power.
Power, personified in the Emperor Constantine, who, in
the heathen conception of things, stood at the summit

---

* The Iberian Mother of God is the most celebrated of the. mirac-
ulous *ikons* in Moscow.—Tr.

of human greatness (he was enrolled among the gods), accepts Christianity, gives an example to all the people, converts the people, lends a helping hand against the heretics, and by means of the Ecumenical Council establishes the one true Christian religion.

The Catholic Christian religion was established for all time. It was so natural to yield to this deception that, to the present day, there are people who believe in the saving efficacy of that assembly. Yet that was the moment when a majority of Christians abandoned their religion. At that turning the great majority of Christians entered the heathen path, which they have followed ever since. Charlemagne and Vladimir* continued in the same direction.

And the Church fraud continues till now. The fraud consists in this: that the conversion of the powers-that-be to Christianity is necessary for those that understand the letter, but not the spirit, of Christianity; but the acceptance of Christianity without the abandonment of power is a satire on, and a perversion of, Christianity.

The sanctification of political power by Christianity is blasphemy; it is the negation of Christianity.

After fifteen hundred years of this blasphemous alliance of pseudo-Christianity with the State, it needs a strong effort to free oneself from all the complex sophistries by which, always and everywhere (to please the authorities),

---

* Vladimir adopted Christianity A.D. 988. Many inhabitants of his capital city, Kief, were disinclined to follow his example, so he "acted vigorously" (as a Russian historian remarks), *i.e.* he had the people driven into the Dniepr to be baptized. In other parts of his dominions Christianity was spread among the unwilling heathen population "by fire and sword."—TR.

the sanctity and righteousness of State-｜ possibility of its being Christian, has been

In truth, the words a "Christian State words "hot ice." The thing is either not violence, or it is not Christian.

In order to understand this clearly we those fantastic notions in which we have brought up, and must ask plainly, what is such historical and juridical science as h₂ us? Such sciences have no sound basis; tʰ merely to supply a vindication for the use

Omitting the history of the Persians, th let us take the history of that governme formed an alliance with Christianity.

A robbers' nest existed at Rome. It gre violence, murders, and it subdued nations. and their descendants, led by their chieftain sometimes called Cæsar, sometimes Augu and tormented nations to satisfy their de the descendants of these robber-chiefs, C reader of books and a man satiated by an ɛ ferred certain Christian dogmas to those of t instead of offering human sacrifices he prefeɪ instead of the worship of Apollo, Venus, preferred that of a single God with a son— decreed that this religion should be introc those that were under his power.

No one said to him: "The kings exerc among the nations, but among you it shall ɪ not murder, do not commit adultery, do not ｜ judge not, condemn not, resist not him that

But they said to him: "You wish to be callɛ

them as well as inside the Pope, and in our Synod with its commandant-officials.

And as soon as one of the anointed robber-chiefs wishes his own and another folk to begin slaying each other, the priest immediately prepare some holy water, sprinkle a cross (which Christ bore and on which he died because he repudiated such robbers), take the cross and bless the robber-chief in his work of slaughtering, hanging, and destroying.*

And it all might have been well if only they had been able to agree about it, and the anointed had not begun to call each other robbers, which is what they really are, and the people had not begun to listen to them and to cease to believe either in anointed people or in depositaries of the Holy Ghost, and had not learned from them to call them as they call each other, by their right names, *i.e.* robbers and deceivers.

But we have only spoken of the robbers incidentally, because it was they who led the deceivers astray. It is the deceivers, the pseudo-Christians, that we have to consider. They became such by their alliance with the robbers. It could not be otherwise. They turned from the road when they consecrated the first ruler and assured him that he, by his power, could help religion—the religion of humility, self-sacrifice, and the endurance of evil. All the history, not of the imaginary, but of the real, Church, *i.e.* of the priests under the sway of kings, is a series of useless efforts of these unfortunate priests to preserve the truth

---

* In England the holy water is not used, but an archbishop draws up a form of prayer for the success of the queen's army, and a chaplain is appointed to each regiment to teach the men Christianity.—TR.

of the teaching while preaching it by falsehood, and while abandoning it in practice. The importance of the priest-hood depends entirely on the teaching it wishes to spread; that teaching speaks of humility, self-sacrifice, love, poverty; but it is preached by violence and wrong-doing.

In order that the priesthood should have something to teach and that they should have disciples, they cannot get rid of the teaching. But in order to whitewash them-selves and justify their immoral alliance with power, they have, by all the cunningest devices possible, to conceal the essence of the teaching, and for this purpose they have to shift the center of gravity from what is essential in the teaching to what is external. And this is what is done by the priesthood—this is the source of the sham religion taught by the Church. The source is the alliance of the priests (calling themselves the Church) with the powers-that-be, *i.e.* with violence. The source of their desire to teach a religion to others lies in the fact that true religion exposes them, and they want to replace true religion by a fictitious religion arranged to justify their deeds.

True religion may exist anywhere except where it is evidently false, *i.e.* violent; it cannot be a State religion.

True religion may exist in all the so-called sects and heresies, only it surely cannot exist where it is joined to a State using violence. Curiously enough the names "Orthodox-Greek," "Catholic," or "Protestant" religion, as those words are commonly used, mean nothing but "reli-gion allied to power,"—State religion and therefore false religion.

The idea of a Church as a union of many—of the ma-jority—in one belief and in nearness to the source of the teaching, was in the first two centuries of Christianity merely one feeble external argument in favor of the correctness of certain views. Paul said, "I know from Christ Himself." Another said, "I know from Luke." And all said, "We think rightly, and the proof that we are right is that we are a big assembly, *ekklesia,* the Church." But only beginning with the Council of Nicæa, organized by an emperor, does the Church become a plain and tangible fraud practised by some of the people who professed this religion.

They began to say, "It has pleased us and the Holy Ghost." The "Church" no longer meant merely a part of a weak argument, it meant *power* in the hands of certain people. It allied itself with the rulers, and began to act like the rulers. And all that united itself with power and submitted to power, ceased to be a religion and became a fraud.

What does Christianity teach, understanding it as the teaching of any or of all the churches?

Examine it as you will, compound it or divide it—the Christian teaching always falls with two sharply separated parts. There is the teaching of dogmas: from the divine Son, the Holy Ghost, and the relationship of these persons—to the eucharist with or without wine, and with leavened or with unleavened bread; and there is the moral teaching: of humility, freedom from covetousness, purity of mind and body, forgiveness, freedom from bondage, peacefulness. Much as the doctors of the Church have labored to mix these two sides of the teachings, they have never mingled, but like oil and water have always remained apart in larger or smaller circles.

The difference of the two sides of the teaching is clear to every one, and all can see the fruits of the one and of the other in the life of men, and by these fruits can conclude which side is the more important, and (if one may use the comparative form) more true. One looks at the history of Christendom from this aspect, and one is horror-struck. Without exception, from the very beginning and to the very end, till today, look where one will, examine what dogma you like—from the dogma of the divinity of Christ, to the manner of making the sign of the cross,* and to the question of serving the communion with or without wine—the fruit of mental labors to explain the dogmas has always been envy, hatred, executions, banishments, slaughter of women and children, burnings and tortures. Look on the other side, the moral teaching from the going into the wilderness to commune with God, to the practice of supplying food to those who are in prison; the fruits of it are all our conceptions of goodness, all that is joyful, comforting, and that serves as a beacon to us in history. . . .

People before whose eyes the fruits of the one and other side of Christianity were not yet evident, might be misled and could hardly help being misled. And people might be misled who were sincerely drawn into disputes about dogmas, not noticing that by such disputes they were serving not God but the devil, not noticing that Christ said plainly that He came to destroy all dogmas; those also might be led astray who had inherited a traditional belief in the importance of these dogmas, and had received such a perverse mental training that they could not see their mistake; and again, those ignorant people might be led astray to whom these dogmas seemed nothing but words or fantastic notions. But we to whom

* One of the main points of divergence between the "Old-believers" and the "Orthodox" Russian church was whether in making the sign of the cross two fingers or three should be extended.—TR.

the simple meaning of the Gospels—repudiating all dogmas—is evident, we before whose eyes are the fruits of these dogmas in history, cannot be so misled. History is for us a means—even a mechanical means—of verifying the teaching.

Is the dogma of the Immaculate Conception necessary or not? What has come of it? Hatred, abuse, irony. And did it bring any benefit? None at all.

Was the teaching that the adulteress should not be sentenced necessary or not? What has come of it? Thousands of times people have been softened by that recollection.

Again, does everybody agree about any one of the dogmas? No. Do people agree that it is good to give to him that has need? Yes, all agree.

But the one side, the dogmas—about which every one disagrees, and which no one requires—is what the priesthood gave out, and still give out, under the name of religion while the other side, about which all can agree, and which is necessary to all, and which saves people, is the side which the priesthood, though they have not dared to reject it, have also not dared to set forth as a teaching, for that teaching repudiates them.

Religion is the meaning we give to our lives, it is that which gives strength and direction to our life. Every one that lives finds such a meaning, and lives on the basis of that meaning. If man finds no meaning in life, he dies. In this search man uses all that the previous efforts of humanity have supplied. And what humanity has reached we call revelation. Revelation is what helps man to understand the meaning of life.

Such is the relation in which man stands toward religion.

FROM THE KINGDOM OF GOD

MONG the early responses called forth by my book ["My Religion"] were letters from American Quakers. In these letters, while expressing their sympathy with my ideas in regard to the unlawfulness of violence and war where Christians are concerned, the Quakers made known to me many details in relation to their sect, which for more than two hundred years has professed the doctrine of Christ in the matter of non-resistance, and which never has, nor does it now use weapons for self-defense. Together with the letters, the Quakers sent me many of their pamphlets, periodicals, and books. From these publications I learned that already, many years ago, they had demonstrated the Christian's duty of keeping the commandment of non-resistance to evil by violence, and the error of the church which countenances wars and executions.

Having shown by a succession of arguments and texts that war—the slaughter and mutilation of men—is inconsistent with a religion founded on peace and good-will to men, the Quakers go on to assert that nothing is so conducive to the defamation of Christ's truth in the eyes of the heathen, or so successful in arresting the spread of Christianity throughout the world, as the refusal to obey this commandment, made by men who call themselves Christians, and by the sanction thus given to war and violence. The doctrine of Christ, which has entered into the consciousness of men, not by force or by the sword, as they say, but by non-resistance to evil, by humility, meekness, and the love of peace, can only be propagated among men by the example of peace, love, and concord given by its followers.

A Christian, according to the teaching of the Lord, should be guided in his relations toward men only by the love of peace, and therefore there should be no authority having power to compel a Christian to act in a manner contrary to God's law, and contrary to his chief duty toward his fellow-men.

The requirements of the civil law, they say, may oblige men, who, to win some worldly advantages, seek to conciliate that which is irreconcilable, to violate the law of God; but for a Christian, who firmly believes that his salvation depends upon following the teaching of Christ, this law can have no meaning.

My acquaintance with the activity of the Quakers and with their publications, with Fox, Paine, and particularly with a work published by Dymond in 1827, proved to me not only that men have long since recognized the impossibility of harmonizing Christianity and war, but that this incompatibility has been proved so clearly and irrefragably, that one can only wonder how it is possible for this incongruous union of Christianity with violence—a doctrine which is still taught by the church—to remain in force.

Besides the information obtained from the Quakers, I

also received from America about the same time advices
on the subject from another and hitherto unknown source.
The son of William Lloyd Garrison, the famous anti-
slavery champion, wrote to me that, having read my book,
wherein he had found ideas similar to those expressed by
his father in 1838, and taking it for granted that I should
be interested to know that fact, he sent me a book written
by Mr. Garrison some fifty years ago, entitled "Non-
resistance."

This avowal of principle took place under the following
circumstances:—In 1838, on the occasion of a meeting of
the Society for the Promotion of Peace, William Lloyd
Garrison, while discussing means for the suppression of
war, arrived at the conclusion that the establishment
of universal peace can have no solid foundation save in
the literal obedience to the commandment of non-resistance to violence (Matthew v. 39), as understood by the
Quakers, with whom Garrison was on friendly terms. Having arrived at this conclusion, he wrote, offering to the
Society the following proclamation, which at that time,
in 1838, was signed by many of its members:—

"*Declaration of Sentiments adopted by the Peace Convention, held in Boston, September 18, 19, and 20,
1838:—*

"Assembled in Convention, from various sections of the
American Union, for the promotion of Peace on earth and
Good-will among men, We, the undersigned, regard it as
due to ourselves, to the cause which we love, to the
country in which we live, and to the world, to publish a
Declaration, expressive of the principles we cherish, the
purpose we aim to accomplish, and the measures we shall

adopt to carry forward the work of peaceful, universal reformation.

"We cannot acknowledge allegiance to any human government; neither can we oppose any such government by a resort to physical force. We recognize but one King and Lawgiver, one Judge and Ruler of mankind. We are bound by the laws of a Kingdom which is not of this world; the subjects of which are forbidden to fight; in which Mercy and Truth are met together, and Righteousness and Peace have kissed each other; which has no state lines, no national partitions, no geographical boundaries; in which there is no distinction of rank or division of caste, or inequality of sex; the officers of which are Peace, its exactors Righteousness, its walls Salvation, and its gates Praise; and which is destined to break in pieces and consume all other kingdoms. Our country is the world, our countrymen are all mankind. We love the land of our nativity only as we love all other lands. The interests, rights, liberties of American citizens are no more dear to us than are those of the whole human race. Hence, we can allow no appeal to patriotism to revenge any national insult or injury; the Prince of Peace, under whose stainless banner we rally, came not to destroy, but to save, even the worst of enemies. He has left us an example, that we should follow His steps. God commendeth his love toward us, in that while we were yet sinners, Christ died for us.

"We conceive that if a nation has no right to defend itself against foreign enemies, or to punish its invaders, no individual possesses that right in his own case. The unit cannot be of greater importance than the aggregate. If one man may take life, to obtain or defend his rights, the same license must necessarily be granted to communities, states, and nations. If *he* may use a dagger or a pistol, *they* may employ cannon, bombshells, land and naval forces. The means of self-preservation must be in proportion to the magnitude of interests at stake, and the number of lives exposed to destruction. But if a rapacious and bloodthirsty soldiery, thronging these shores from abroad, with intent to commit rapine and destroy life, may not be resisted by the people or magistracy, then ought no resistance to be offered to domestic troubles of the public peace or of private security. No obligation can rest upon Americans to regard foreigners as more sacred in their persons than themselves, or to give them a monopoly of wrong-doing with impunity.

"The dogma, that all the governments of the world are approvingly ordained of God, and that the powers that be in the United States, in Russia, in Turkey, are in accordance with His will, is not less absurd than impious. It makes the impartial Author of human freedom and equality unequal and tyrannical. It cannot be affirmed that the powers that be, in any nation, are actuated by the spirit or guided by the example of Christ, in the treatment of enemies; therefore, they cannot be agreeable to the will of God; and therefore their overthrow, by a spiritual regeneration of their subjects, is inevitable.

"We register our testimony not only against all wars, whether offensive or defensive, but all preparations for war; against every naval ship, every arsenal, every fortification; against the militia system and a standing army; against all military chieftains and soldiers; against all monuments commemorative of victory over a fallen foe, all trophies won in battle, all celebrations in honor of military or naval exploits; against all appropriations for the defense of a nation by force and army, on the part of any legislative body; against every edict of government requiring of its subjects military service. Hence we deem it unlawful to bear arms, or to hold a military office.

"As every human government is upheld by physical strength, and its laws are enforced virtually at the point of the bayonet, we cannot hold any office which imposes upon its incumbent the obligation to compel men to do right, on pain of imprisonment or death. We therefore voluntarily exclude ourselves from every legislative and judicial body, and repudiate all human politics, worldly honors, and stations of authority. If *we* cannot occupy a seat in the legislature or on the bench, neither can we elect *others* to act as our substitutes in any such capacity.

"It follows that we cannot sue any man at law, to compel him by force to restore anything which he may have wrongfully taken from us or others; but if he has seized our coat, we shall surrender up our cloak, rather than subject him to punishment.

"We believe that the penal code of the old covenant, 'An eye for an eye, and a tooth for a tooth,' has been abrogated by Jesus Christ; and that under the new covenant, the forgiveness instead of the punishment of enemies has been enjoined upon all His disciples, in all cases whatsoever. To extort money from enemies, or set them upon a pillory, or cast them into prison, or hang them upon gallows, is obviously not to forgive, but to take retribution. 'Vengeance is mine, I will repay, saith the Lord.'

"The history of mankind is crowded with evidences proving that physical coercion is not adapted to moral regeneration; that the sinful disposition of men can be subdued only by love; that evil can be exterminated from

the earth only by goodness; that it is not safe to rely upon
an arm of flesh, upon man whose breath is in his nostrils,
to preserve us from harm; that there is great security in
being gentle, harmless, long-suffering, and abundant in
mercy; that it is only the meek who shall inherit the earth,
for the violent who resort to the sword are destined to
perish with the sword. Hence, as a measure of sound
policy—of safety to property, life, and liberty—of public
quietude and private enjoyment—as well as on the ground
of allegiance to Him who is King of kings and Lord of
lords, we cordially adopt the non-resistance principle;
being confident that it provides for all possible consequences, will insure all things needful to us, is armed with
omnipotent power, and must ultimately triumph over
every assailing force.

"We advocate no jacobinical doctrine. The spirit of
jacobinism is the spirit of retaliation, violence, and murder. It neither fears God nor regards man. We would be
filled with the spirit of Jesus Christ. If we abide by our
principles, it is impossible for us to be disorderly, or plot
treason, or participate in any evil work; we shall submit
to every ordinance of man, for the Lord's sake; obey all
the requirements of government, except such as we deem
contrary to the commands of the gospel; and in no case
resist the operation of law, except by meekly submitting
to the penalty of disobedience.

"But while we shall adhere to the doctrine of non-
resistance and passive submission, we purpose, in a moral
and spiritual sense, to speak and act boldly in the cause
of God; to assail iniquity in high places and in low places;
to apply our principles to all existing civil, political, legal,
and ecclesiastical institutions; and to hasten the time

when the kingdoms of this world will have become the kingdoms of our Lord and of His Christ, and He shall reign forever.

"It appears to us a self-evident truth, that, whatever the gospel is designed to destroy at any period of the world, being contrary to it, ought now to be abandoned. If, then, the time is predicted when swords shall be beaten into plowshares, and spears into pruning-hooks, and men shall not learn the art of war any more, it follows that all who manufacture, sell, or wield those deadly weapons do thus array themselves against the peaceful dominion of the Son of God on earth.

"Having thus briefly stated our principles and purposes, we proceed to specify the measures we propose to adopt in carrying our object into effect.

"We expect to prevail through the foolishness of preaching—striving to commend ourselves unto every man's conscience, in the sight of God. From the press we shall promulgate our sentiments as widely as practicable. We shall endeavor to secure the coöperation of all persons, of whatever name or sect. The triumphant progress of the cause of Temperance and of Abolition in our land, through the instrumentality of benevolent and voluntary associations, encourages us to combine our own means and efforts for the promotion of a still greater cause. Hence, we shall employ lecturers, circulate tracts and publications, form societies, and petition our state and national governments, in relation to the subject of Universal Peace. It will be our leading object to devise ways and means for effecting a radical change in the views, feelings, and practices of society, respecting the sinfulness of war and the treatment of enemies.

"In entering upon the great work before us, we are not

unmindful that, in its prosecution, we may be called to test our sincerity even as in a fiery ordeal. It may subject us to insult, outrage, suffering, yea, even death itself. We anticipate no small amount of misconception, misrepresentation, calumny. Tumults may arise against us. The ungodly and violent, the proud and pharisaical, the ambitious and tyrannical, principalities and powers, and spiritual wickedness in high places, may contrive to crush us. So they treated the Messiah, whose example we are humbly striving to imitate. If we suffer with Him we know that we shall reign with Him. We shall not be afraid of their terror, neither be troubled. Our confidence is in the Lord Almighty, not in man. Having withdrawn from human protection, what can sustain us but that faith which overcomes the world? We shall not think it strange concerning the fiery trial which is to try us, as though some strange thing had happened unto us; but rejoice, inasmuch as we are partakers of Christ's sufferings. Wherefore, we commit the keeping of our souls to God, in well-doing, as unto a faithful Creator. For every one that forsakes house, or brethren, or sisters, or father, or mother, or wife, or children, or lands, for Christ's sake, shall receive a hundredfold, and shall inherit everlasting life.

"Firmly relying upon the certain and universal triumph of the sentiments contained in this declaration, however formidable may be the opposition arrayed against them—in solemn testimony of our faith in their divine origin—we hereby affix our signatures to it, commending it to the reason and conscience of mankind, giving ourselves no anxiety as to what may befall us, and resolving in the strength of the Lord God calmly and meekly to abide the issue."

Later on, Garrison founded a Non-resistance Society and started a periodical entitled *The Non-resistant,* wherein the full significance and consequences of the doctrine were plainly set forth, as has been stated in the proclamation. I gained, subsequently, further information concerning the fate of this society and the periodical from a biography of William Lloyd Garrison, written by his sons.

Neither the periodical nor the society enjoyed a long life. The majority of Garrison's associates in the work of liberating the slaves, apprehensive lest the too radical views expressed in the *The Non-resistant* might alienate men from the practical business of the abolition of slavery, renounced the doctrine of non-resistance as expressed in the declaration, and both periodical and society passed out of existence.

One would suppose that this declaration of Garrison, formulating, as it did, an important profession of faith in terms both energetic and eloquent, would have made a deeper impression on men, and have become a subject for universal consideration. On the contrary, not only is it unknown in Europe, but even among those Americans who honor the memory of Garrison there are but few who are familiar with this.

A similar fate befell another American champion of the same doctrine, Adin Ballou, who died recently, and who for fifty years had preached in favor of non-resistance to evil. How little is known in regard to the question of non-resistance may be gathered from the fact that the younger Garrison (who has written an excellent biography of his father in four large volumes), in answer to my inquiry whether any society for the defense of the principles of non-resistance was yet alive and possessed adherents,

wrote me that, so far as he knew, the society has dissolved
and its members were no longer interested, while at this
very time Adin Ballou, who had shared Garrison's labors,
and who had devoted fifty years of his life to the teaching
of the doctrine of non-resistance, both by pen and by
tongue, was still living in Hopedale, Massachusetts. Afterward I received a letter from Wilson, a disciple and co-
worker of Ballou, and subsequently I entered into corre-
spondence with Ballou himself. I wrote to him, and he
sent me his works, from one of which I made the following extract:—"Jesus Christ is my Lord and Master," says
Ballou in one of his articles, written to show the inconsistency of Christians who believe in the right of
defensive and offensive warfare. "I have covenanted to
forsake all and follow Him, through good and evil report,
until death. But I am nevertheless a Democratic Repub-
lican citizen of the United States, implicity sworn to bear
true allegiance to my country, and to support its Constitution, if need be, with my life. Jesus Christ requires me
to do unto others as I would that others should do unto
me. The Constitution of the United States requires me to
do unto twenty-seven hundred thousand slaves" (they
had slaves then; now they could easily be replaced by
workmen) "the very contrary of what I would have them
do unto me—viz., assist to keep in a grievous bondage. . . .
But I am quite easy. I vote on. I help govern on. I am
willing to hold any office I may be elected to under the
Constitution. And I am still a Christian. I profess on.
I find difficulty in keeping covenant both with Christ and
the Constitution.

"Jesus Christ forbids me to resist evil-doers by taking
'eye for eye, tooth for tooth, blood and life for life.' My
government requires the very reverse, and depends, for

its own self-preservation, on the halter, the musket, and the sword, seasonably employed against its domestic and foreign enemies.

"In the maintenance and use of this expensive life-destroying apparatus we can exemplify the virtues *of forgiving our injuries, loving our enemies, blessing them that curse us, and doing good to those that hate us.* For this reason we have regular Christian chaplains to pray for us and call down the smiles of God on our holy murders.

"I see it all" (that is, the contradiction between profession and life), "and yet I insist that I am as good a Christian as ever. I fellowship all; I vote on; I help govern on; I profess on; *and I glory in being at once a devoted Christian and a no less devoted adherent to the existing government.* I will not give in to those miserable non-resistant notions. I will not throw away my political influence, and leave unprincipled men to carry on government alone.

"The Constitution says—'Congress shall have power to declare war, grant letters of marque and reprisal,' and I agree to this, I indorse it. I swear to help carry it through. I vote for men to hold office who are sworn to support all this. What, then, am I less a Christian? Is not war a Christian service? Is it not perfectly Christian to murder hundreds of thousands of fellow human beings; to ravish defenseless females, sack and burn cities, and enact all the other cruelties of war? Out upon these new-fangled scruples! This is the very way to forgive injuries, and love our enemies! If we only do it all in true love nothing can be more Christian than wholesale murder!"

In another pamphlet, entitled "How many does it take?" he says—"One man must not kill. If he does, it is murder;

two, ten, one hundred men, acting on their responsibility, must not kill. If they do, it is still murder. But a state or nation may kill as many as they please, and it is no murder. It is just, necessary, commendable, and right. Only get people enough to agree to it, and the butchery of myriads of human beings is perfectly innocent. But how many does it take? This is the question. Just so with theft, robbery, burglary, and all other crimes. Man-stealing is a great crime in one man, or a very few men only. But a whole nation can commit it, and the act becomes not only innocent, but highly honorable."

The following is, in substance, a catechism of Ballou, compiled for the use of his congregation:—

THE CATECHISM OF NON-RESISTANCE

Q. Whence comes the word non-resistance?

A. From the utterance: "But I say unto you, That ye resist not evil."—Matthew v. 39.

Q. What does this word denote?

A. It denotes a lofty Christian virtue, commanded by Christ.

Q. Are we to understand the word non-resistance in its broad sense, that is, as meaning that one should offer no resistance to evil whatsoever?

A. No; it should be understood literally as Christ taught it—that is, not to return evil for evil. Evil should be resisted by all lawful means, but not by evil.

Q. From what does it appear that Christ gave that meaning to non-resistance?

A. From the words which he used on that occasion. He said: "Ye have heard that it hath been said, An eye

for an eye, and a tooth for a tooth. But I say unto you,
That ye resist not evil: but whosoever shall smite thee on
thy right cheek, turn to him the other also. And if any
man will sue thee at the law, and take away thy coat, let
him have thy cloke also."

Q. Whom did he mean by the words: "Ye have heard
that it hath been said"?

A. The patriarchs and the prophets, and that which
they spoke and which is contained in the Old Testament,
that the Jews generally call the Law and Prophets.

Q. To what laws did Christ allude in the words: "Ye
have heard"?

A. To those in which Noah, Moses, and other prophets
grant the use of personal violence against those who commit it, for the purpose of punishing and destroying evil
deeds.

Q. Mention such commandments.

A. "Whoso sheddeth man's blood, by man shall his
blood be shed."—Genesis ix. 6.

"He that smiteth a man, so that he die, shall be surely
put to death. And if any mischief follow, then thou shalt
give life for life, eye for eye, tooth for tooth, hand for
hand, foot for foot, burning for burning, wound for
wound, stripe for stripe."—Exodus xxi. 12, 23, 24, 25.

"And he that killeth any man shall surely be put to
death. And if a man cause a blemish in his neighbor; as
he hath done, so shall it be done to him; breach for
breach, eye for eye, tooth for tooth."—Leviticus xxiv. 17,
19, 20.

"And the judges shall make diligent inquisition: and,
behold, if the witness be a false witness, and hath testified
falsely against his brother; then shall ye do unto him, as
he had thought to have done unto his brother. And thine

eye shall not pity: but life shall go for life, eye for eye, tooth for tooth, hand for hand, foot for foot."—Deuteronomy xix. 18, 19, 21.

These are the injunctions of which Jesus speaks.

Noah, Moses, and the prophets taught that he who murders, mutilates, or tortures his neighbor doeth evil. In order to combat and destroy this evil, the evil-doer must be chastised by death, mutilation, or some personal torture. Transgressions are to be avenged by transgressions, murder by murder, torture by torture, evil by evil. Thus taught Noah, Moses, and the prophets. But Christ forbids all this. The gospel says: "I say unto you, resist ye not evil, avenge not one transgression by another, but rather bear a repetition of the offense from the evildoer." That which has been allowed is now forbidden. Having understood what resistance we have been taught, we know exactly what Christ meant by non-resistance.

Q. Did the teaching of the Ancients admit of resisting transgression by transgression?

A. Yes; but Christ forbade it. A Christian has no right in any case to take the life of, or to offend against, the evildoer.

Q. May he not kill or wound another in self-defense?

A. No.

Q. May he enter a complaint to the magistrates for the purpose of chastising the offender?

A. No. For that which he does through others, he practically does himself.

Q. May he fight in the army against foreign or domestic enemies?

A. Certainly not. He can take no part in war, or in the preparation therefor. He cannot make use of weapons. He cannot resist one transgression by another, whether he is alone or in company, either personally or through other agents.

Q. May he voluntarily select or drill soldiers for the government?

A. He cannot do this, if he wishes to be *faithful* to the law of Christ.

Q. May he voluntarily contribute money to assist a government which is supported by military power, executions, and violence in general?

A. No; unless the money is to be used for some special purpose, justifiable in itself, where the object and the means employed are good.

Q. May he pay taxes to such a government?

A. No; he should not pay taxes on his own accord, but he should not resist the levying of a tax. A tax imposed by the government is levied independently of the will of the citizens. It may not be resisted without recourse to violence, and a Christian should not use violence; therefore he must deliver his property to the forced damage caused by authorities.

Q. May a Christian vote at elections and take part in courts of law or in the government?

A. No. To take a part in elections, courts of law, or in the administration of government is the same thing as a participation in the violence of the government.

Q. What is the chief significance of the doctrine of non-resistance?

A. To show that it is possible to extirpate evil from one's own heart, as well as from that of one's neighbor. This doctrine forbids men to do that which perpetuates and multiplies evil in this world. He who attacks another, and does him an injury, excites a feeling of hatred, the worst of all evil. To offend our neighbor because he has offended us, with ostensible motive of self-defense, means but to repeat the evil act against him as well as against ourselves—it means to beget, or ar least to let loose, or to encourage the Evil Spirit whom we wish to expel. Satan cannot be driven out by Satan, falsehood cannot be purged by falsehood, nor can evil be conquered by evil. True non-resistance is the only real method of resisting evil. It crushes the serpent's head. It destroys and exterminates all evil feeling.

Q.   But admitting that the idea of the doctrine is correct, is it practicable?

A.   As practicable as any virtue commanded by the law of God. Good deeds cannot be performed under all circumstances without self-sacrifice, privations, suffering, and, in extreme cases, without the loss of life itself. But he who prizes life more than the fulfilment of God's will is already dead to the only true life. Such a man, in trying to save his life, will lose it. Furthermore, wherever non-resistance costs the sacrifice of one's life, or of some essential advantage of life, resistance costs thousands of such sacrifices.

Non-resistance preserves; resistance destroys.

It is much safer to act justly than injustly; to endure an offense rather than resist it by violence; safer even in regard to the present life. If all men refused to resist evil, the world would be a happy one.

Q. But if only a few were to act thus, what would become of them?

A. Even if but one man were to act thus, and the others should agree to crucify him, would it not be more glorious for him to die in the glory of non-resisting love, praying for his enemies, than live wearing the crown of Cæsar, besprinkled with the blood of the murdered? But whether it be one man or thousands of men who are firmly determined not to resist evil by evil, still, whether in the midst of civilized or uncivilized neighbors, men who do not rely on violence are safer than those who do. A robber, a murderer, a villain, will be less likely to harm them if he finds them offering no armed resistance. "All they that take the sword shall perish with the sword," and he who seeks peace, who acts like a friend, who is inoffensive, who forgives and forgets injuries, generally enjoys peace, or if he dies, he dies a blessed death.

Hence, if all were to follow the commandment of non-resistance, there would manifestly be neither offense nor evil-doing. If even the majority were composed of such men they would establish the rule of love and good-will even toward the offenders, by not resisting evil by evil nor using violence. Even if such men formed a numerous minority, they would have such an improving moral influence over society that every severe punishment would be revoked, and violence and enmity would be replaced by peace and good-will. If they formed but a small minority, they would rarely experience anything worse than the contempt of the world, while the world, without preserving it or feeling grateful therefor, would become better and wiser from its latent influence. And if, in the most extreme cases, certain members of the minority might be persecuted unto death, these men, thus dying for the truth, would have left their doctrine already sanctified by the blood of martyrdom.

Peace be with all ye who seek peace; and may the all-conquering love be the imperishable inheritance of every soul who submits of its own accord to the law of Christ.

Resist not evil by violence.—ADIN BALLOU.

For fifty years Ballou wrote and published books chiefly on the subject of non-resistance. In these writings, remarkable for their eloquence and simplicity of style, the question is considered in all its aspects. He proved it to be the duty of every Christian who professes to believe that the Bible is a revelation from God, to obey this commandment. He enumerates the arguments against the commandment of non-resistance, drawn from the Old as well as the New Testament, the expulsion from the Temple, among others, and answers each one in turn. Setting the Bible aside, he points out the practical good sense on which this principle is founded, sums up the arguments against it, and refutes them. For instance, in one chapter of his work he treats of non-resistance to evil in exceptional cases, and affirms that granting the truth of the supposition that there are cases to which the rule of non-resistance cannot be applied, that would prove that the rule in general is inconsistent. Citing such exceptional cases, he proves that these are they very occasions when the application of this rule is both wise and necessary. The question has been viewed from every side, and no argument, whether of opponent or sympathizer, has been neglected or left unanswered. I mention this in order to call attention to the deep interest which works of this class ought to excite in men who profess Christianity; and it would seem therefore that Ballou's zeal should have been recognized, and the ideas he expressed either accepted or disproved. But such was not the case.

The life-work of Garrison, the father, his founding the society of the Non-resistant, and his declaration, convinced me, more even than my intercourse with the Quakers, that the divergence of the Christianity of the State from Christ's law of non-resistance by violence has been long since noticed and pointed out, and men have labored and still do labor to counteract it. Thus Ballou's earnestness has fortified my opinion. But the fate of Garrison, and particularly that of Ballou, almost unknown, notwithstanding fifty years of active and persistent work in one direction, has confirmed me in the belief that there exists a certain inexpressed but fixed determination to oppose all such attempts by a wall of silence.

In August of 1890 Ballou died, and his obituary appeared in the American *Religio-Philosophical Journal* of August 23d.

From this obituary we learn that Ballou was the spiritual leader of a community, that he had preached from 8000 to 9000 sermons, married 1000 couples, and written 500 articles, but in regard to the object of his life's devotion not a word is said; the word "non-resistance" is never mentioned.

All the exhortations of the Quakers for 200 year, all the efforts of Garrison, the father, the foundation of his society, his periodical, and his declarations, as well as the life-work of Ballou, are the same as if they had never existed.

Slavery conflicted with all the moral principles taught by Plato and Aristotle, and vet neither of them perceived this, because the disavowal of slavery must have destroyed that life by which they lived. And the same thing is repeated in our times.

The division of mankind into two classes, the existence of political and military injustice, is opposed to all those moral principles which our society professes, and yet the most progressive and cultivated men of the age seem not to perceive this.

Almost every educated man at the present day is striving unconsciously to preserve the old-time conception of society, which justifies his attitude, and to conceal from others and from himself its inconsistencies, chief among which is the necessity of adopting the Christian ideal, which is subversive of the very structure of our social existence. It is this antiquated social system, in which they no longer believe, because it is really a thing of the past, that men are trying to uphold.

Contemporary literature, philosophical, political, and artistic—all contemporary literature affords a striking proof of the truth of my statement. What wealth of imagination, what form and color, what erudition and art, but what a lack of 'serious purpose, what reluctance to face any exact thought! Ambiguity of expression, indirect allusion, witticisms, vague reflection, but no straightforward or candid dealing with the subject they treat of, namely, life.

Indeed, our writers treat of obscenities and improprieties; in the guise of refined paradox they convey suggestions which thrust men back to primeval savagery, to the lowest dregs, not only of pagan life, but animal life, which we outlived 5000 year ago. Delivering themselves from the Christian life-conception, which for some simply interferes with the accustomed current of their lives, while for others it interferes with certain advantages, men must of necessity return to the pagan life-conception and to the doctrines to which it gave rise. Not only are patriotism and the rights of the aristocracy preached at the present time as they used to be 2000 years ago, but also the coarsest epicureanism and sensuality, with this difference only—that the teachers of old believed in the doctrines they taught, whereas those of the present day neither do nor can possess any faith in what they utter, because there is no longer any sense in it. When the ground is shifting under our feet, we cannot stand still, we must either recede or advance. It sounds exaggerated to say that the enlightened men of our time, the advanced thinkers, are speciously degrading society, plunging it into a condition worse than pagan—into a state of primeval barbarism.

In no other matter has this tendency of the leading men of our time been so plainly shown as in their attitude toward that phenomenon in which at present all the inconsistency of social life is concentrated—toward war, universal armament, and military conscription.

The equivocal, if not unscrupulous, attitude of the educated men of our time toward this question is a striking one. It may be stated from three points of view. Some regard this phenomenon as an accidental state of affairs, which has sprung from the peculiar political situation of Europe, and believe it to be susceptible of adjustment by diplomatic and international mediation, without injury to the structure of nations. Others look upon it as something appalling and cruel, fatal yet unavoidable—like disease or death. Still others, in cold blood, calmly pronounce war to be an indispensable, salutary, and therefore desirable event.

Men may differ in their views in regard to this matter, but all discuss it as something with which the will of the individuals who are to take part in it has nothing whatever to do; therefore they do not even admit the natural question which presents itself to most men; viz., "Is it my duty to take part in it?" In the opinion of these judges there is no reason in such a question, and every man, whatever may be his personal prejudices in regard to war, must submit in this matter to the demands of the ruling powers.

The attitude of those in the first category, who expect

deliverance from war by means of diplomatic and international mediation, is well defined in the results of the London Peace Congress, and in an article together with letters concerning war from prominent writers, which may be found in the *Revue des Revues* (No. 8, 1891).

These are the results of the Congress.

Having collected from all parts of the globe the opinions of scientists, both written and oral, the Congress, opening with a *Te Deum* in the cathedral, and closing with a dinner and speeches, listened for five days to numerous addresses, and arrived at the following conclusions:—

Resolution I. The Congress affirms its belief that the brotherhood of man involves as a necessary consequence a brotherhood of nations, in which the true interests of all are acknowledged to be identical. The Congress is convinced that the true basis for an enduring peace will be found in the application by nations of this great principle in all their relations one to another.

II. The Congress recognizes the important influence which Christianity exercises upon the moral and political progress of mankind, and earnestly urges upon ministers of the gospel and other teachers of religion and morality the duty of setting forth these principles of Peace and Goodwill, which occupy such a central place in the teaching of Jesus Christ, of philosophers and of moralists, and *it recommends that the third Sunday in December in each year be set apart for that purpose.*

III. The Congress expresses its opinion that all teachers of history should call the attention of the young to the grave evils inflicted on mankind in all ages by war, and to the fact that such war has been waged, as a rule, for most inadequate causes.

IV The Congress protests against the use of military drill in connection with the physical exercises of schools, and suggests the formation of brigades for saving life rather than any of quasi-military character; and it urges the desirability of impressing on the Board of Examiners, who formulate the questions for examination, the propriety of guiding the minds of children into the principles of Peace.

V. The Congress holds that the doctrine of the universal rights of man requires that aboriginal and weaker races shall be guarded from injustice and fraud when brought into contact with civilized peoples, alike as to their territories, their liberties, and their property, and that they shall be shielded from the vices which are so prevalent among the so-called advanced races of men. It further expresses its conviction that there should be concert of action among the nations for the accomplishment of these ends. The Congress desires to express its hearty appreciation of the conclusions arrived at by the late Anti-Slavery Conference, held in Brussels, for the amelioration of the condition of the peoples of Africa.

VI. The Congress believes that the warlike prejudices and traditions which are still fostered in the various nationalities, and the misrepresentations by leaders of public opinion in legislative assemblies, or through the press, are not infrequently indirect causes of war. The Congress is therefore of opinion that these ends should be counteracted by the publication of accurate statements and information that would tend to the removal of misunderstanding amongst nations, and recommends to the Inter-Parliamentary Committee the importance of considering the question of starting an international newspaper, which should have such a purpose as one of its primary objects.

VII. The Congress proposes to the Inter-Parliamentary Conference that the utmost support should be given to every project for the unification of weights and measures, of coinage, tariffs, postal and telegraphic arrangements, means of transport, etc., which would assist in constituting a commercial, industrial, and scientific union of the peoples.

VIII. In view of the vast moral and social influence of woman, the Congress urges upon every woman throughout the world to sustain, as wife, mother, sister, or citizen, the things that make for peace; as otherwise she incurs grave responsibilities for the continuance of the systems of war and militarism, which not only desolate but corrupt the home-life of the nation. To concentrate and to practically apply this influence, the Congress recommends that women should unite themselves with societies for the promotion of international peace.

IX. This Congress expresses the hope that the Financial Reform Association and other similar societies in Europe and America should unite in convoking at an early date a conference to consider the best means of establishing equitable commercial relations between States by the reduction of import duties as a step toward Free Trade. The Congress feels that it can affirm that the whole of Europe desires Peace, and is impatiently waiting for the moment when it shall see the end of those crushing armaments which, under the plea of defense, become in their turn a danger, by keeping alive mutual distrust, and are, at the same time, the cause of the general economic disturbance which stands in the way of settling in a satisfactory manner the problems of labor and poverty, which should take precedence of all others.

X. This Congress, recognizing that a general disarmament would be the best guarantee of *Peace*, and would lead to the solution, in the general interest, of those questions which now must divide States, expresses the wish that a Congress of Representatives of all the States of Europe may be assembled as soon as possible to consider the means of effecting a gradual general disarmament, which already seems feasible.

XI. This Congress, considering that the timidity of a single Power or other cause might delay indefinitely the convocation of the above-mentioned Congress, is of the opinion that the Government which should first dismiss any considerable number of soldiers would confer a signal benefit on Europe and mankind, because it would oblige other Governments, urged on by public opinion, to follow its example, and by the moral force of this accomplished fact would have increased rather than diminished the conditions of its national defense.

XII. This Congress, considering the question of disarmament, as well as the Peace question generally, depends upon public opinion, recommends the Peace Societies here represented, and all friends of Peace, to carry on an active propaganda among the people, especially at the time of Parliamentary elections, in order that the electors should give their votes to those candidates who have included in their programme Peace, Disarmament, and Arbitration.

XIII. This Congress congratulates the friends of Peace on the resolution adopted by the International American Conference (with the exception of the representatives of Chili and Mexico) at Washington in April last, by which it was recommended that arbitration should be obligatory in all controversies concerning diplomatic and consular privileges, boundaries, territories, indemnities, right of navigation, and the validity, construction, and enforcement of treaties, and in all other causes, whatever their origin, nature, or occasion, except only those which, in the judgment of any of the nations involved in the controversy, may imperil its independence.

XIV. This Congress respectfully recommends this resolution to the statesmen of Europe, and expresses the ardent desire that treaties in similar terms be speedily entered into between the other nations of the world.

XV. This Congress expresses its satisfaction at the adoption by the Spanish Senate, on June 18th last, of a project of law authorizing the Government to negotiate general or special treaties of arbitration for the settlement of all disputes, except those relating to the independence and internal government of the States affected; also at the adoption of resolutions to a like effect by the Norwegian Storthing on March 6th last, and by the Italian Chamber on July 11th.

XVI. That a committee of five be appointed to prepare and address communications, in the name of the Congress to the principal religious, political, economical, labor, and peace organizations in civilized countries, requesting them to send petitions to the governmental authorities of their respective countries, praying that measures be taken for the formation of suitable tribunals for the adjudication of international questions, so as to avoid the resort to war.

XVII. Seeing (1) that the object pursued by all Peace Societies is the establishment of juridical order between nations:

(2) That neutralization by international treaties constitutes a step toward this juridical state, and lessens the number of districts in which war can be carried on:

This Congress recommends a larger extension of the rule of neutralization, and expresses the wish:—

(1) That all treaties which at present assure to certain States the benefit of neutrality remain in force, or, if necessary, be amended in a manner to render the neutrality more effective, either by extending neutralization to the whole of the State, of which a part only may be neutralized, or by ordering the demolition of fortresses, which constitute rather a peril than a guarantee for neutrality.

(2) That new treaties, provided that they are in harmony with the wishes of the populations concerned, be concluded for establishing the neutralization of other States.

XVIII. The Committee Section proposes:—

(1) That the next Congress be held immediately before or immediately after the next session of the Inter-Parliamentary Conference, and at the same places.

(2) That the question of an international Peace Emblem be postponed *sine die*.

(3) The adoption of the following resolutions:—

(*a*) Resolved, that we express our satisfaction at the formal and official overtures of the Presbyterian Church in the United States of America, addressed to the highest representatives of each church organization in Christendom, inviting the same to unite with itself in a general conference, the object of which shall be to promote the substitution of international arbitration for war.

(*b*) That this Congress, assembled in London from the 14th to the 19th July, desires to express its profound reverence for the memory of Aurelio Salfi, the great Italian jurist, a member of the Committee of the International League of Peace and Liberty.

(4) That the memorial to the various heads of the civilized States adopted by this Congress, and signed by the President, should, so far as practicable, be presented to each Power by an influential deputation.

(5) That the Organization Committee be empowered to make the needful verbal emendations in the papers and resolutions presented.

(6) That the following resolutions be adopted:—

(*a*) A resolution of thanks to the Presidents of the various sittings of the Congress.

(*b*) A resolution of thanks to the chairman, the secretary, and the members of the Bureau of this Congress.

(*c*) A resolution of thanks to the conveners and members of the sectional committees.

(*d*) A resolution of thanks to Rev. Canon Scott Holland, Rev. Dr. Reuan Thomas, and Rev. J. Morgan Gibbon, for their pulpit addresses before the Congress, and that they be requested to furnish copies of the same for publication; and also Stamford Hall Congregational Church for the use of those buildings for public services.

(*e*) A letter of thanks to Her Majesty for permission to visit Windsor Castle.

(*f*) And also a resolution of thanks to the Lord Mayor and Lady Mayoress, to Mr. Passmore Edwards, and other friends who have extended their hospitality to the members of the Congress.

XIX. This Congress places on record a heartfelt expression of gratitude to Almighty God for the remarkable harmony and concord which have characterized the meetings of the Assembly, in which so many men and women of varied nations, creeds, tongues, and races have gathered in closest coöperation; and in the conclusion of the labors of this Congress, it expresses its firm and unshaken belief in the ultimate triumph of the cause of *Peace,* and of the principles which have been advocated at these meetings.

The fundamental idea of the Congress is—firstly, that it is necessary to disseminate by all means among all men the belief that war is not advantageous for mankind, and that peace is a great benefit; and secondly, to influence governments, impressing upon them the advantages and necessity of disarmament.

To accomplish the first end, the Congress advises teachers of history, women, and ministers of the gospel, to teach people, every third Sunday of December, the evils of war and the benefits of peace; to accomplish the second, the Congress addresses itself to governments, suggesting to them disarmament and arbitration.

To preach the evils of war and the benefits of peace! But the evils of war are so well known to men, that from the earliest ages the most welcome greeting was always: "Peace be unto you!"

Not only Christians but all pagans were fully aware of the benefits of peace and of the evils of war thousands of years ago, so that the advice to the ministers of the gospel to preach against the evils of war and to advocate the benefits of peace every third Sunday in December is quite superfluous.

A real Christian cannot do otherwise than preach thus, constantly, as long as he lives. But if there are those who are called Christians, or Christian preachers, who do not do this, there must be a cause for it, and so long as this cause exists no advice will avail. Still less effective will be the advice to governments to disband armies and have recourse to International Courts of Arbitration. Governments know very well all the difficulties and burdens of conscription and of maintaining armies, and if in the face of such difficulties and burdens they still continue to do so, it is evident that they have no means of doing otherwise, and the advice of a Congress could in no way bring about a change. But scientists will not admit this, and still hope to find some combination of influences by means of which those governments which make war may be induced to restrain themselves.

"Is it possible to avoid war?" writes a scientist in the *Revue des Revues* (No. 8 of 1891). "All agree in recognizing the fact that if war should ever break out in Europe, its consequences would be similar to those of the great invasions. It would imperil the very existence of nations; it would be bloody, atrocious, desperate. This consideration, and the consideration of the terrible nature of the engines of destruction at the command of modern science, retards its declaration and temporarily maintains the present system—a system which might be continued indefinitely, if it were not for the enormous expenses that burden the European nations and threaten to culminate in disasters fully equal to those occasioned by war.

"Impressed with these thoughts, men of all nationalities have sought for means to arrest, or at least to diminish, the shocking consequences of the carnage that threatens us.

"Such are the questions which are to be debated by the next Congress of Universal Peace to be held in Rome, which have already been discussed in a recently published pamphlet on Disarmament.

"Unfortunately, it is quite certain that with the present organization of the greater number of the European states, isolated one from the other and controlled by different interests, the absolute cessation of war is an illusion which it would be folly to cherish. Still, the adoption of somewhat wiser rules and regulations in regard to these international duels would at least tend to limit these horrors. It is equally Utopian to build one's hope on projects of disarmament, whose execution, owing to considerations of a national character, which exist in the minds of all our readers, is practically impossible." (This probably means that France cannot disarm until she has retaliated.) "Public opinion is not prepared to accept them, and, furthermore, the international relations make it impossible to adopt them. Disarmament demanded by one nation of another, under conditions imperiling its security, would be equivalent to a declaration of war.

"Still, we must admit that an exchange of opinions between the nations interested may to a certain extent aid in establishing an international understanding, and also contribute to lessen the military expenses that now crush European nations, to the great detriment of the solution of social questions, the necessity of the solution of which is realized by each nation individually, under the penalty of being confronted by a civil war, due to the efforts made to prevent a foreign one.

"One may at least hope for a decrease of the enormous expenses necessary for the present military organization, which is maintained for the purpose of invading a foreign territory in twenty-four hours, or of a decisive battle a week after the declaration of war."

It ought not to be possible for one nation to attack another and take possession of its territory within twenty-four hours. This practical sentiment was expressed by

Maxime du Camp, and is the conclusion of his study of the subject.

Maxime du Camp offers the following propositions:—

"1st. A Diplomatic Congress, to assemble every year.

"2d. No war to be declared until two months after the incident which gave rise to it." (Here the difficulty lies in determining the nature of the incident that kindled the war—that is, every declaration of war is caused by several circumstances, and it would be necessary to determine from which one the two months are to be reckoned.)

"3d. No war shall be declared until the vote of the people shall have been taken.

"4th. Hostilities must not begin until a month after the declaration of war."

"No war shall be declared . . ." etc. But who is to *prevent* hostilities *beginning?* Who will compel men to do this or that? Who will compel governments to wait a certain stated time? Other nations. But all the other nations are in the very same position, requiring to be restrained and kept within bounds, in other words, *coerced.* And who will *coerce* them? And how is it to be done? By public opinion. But if public opinion has sufficient influence to force a nation to postpone its action until a stated time, this public opinion can prevent it from waging war at any time.

But, it is said, there might be a balance of power, which would oblige nations to restrain themselves. This very experiment has been and is still being tried; this was the object of the Holy Alliance, the League of Peace, etc.

But all would agree to this, it is said. If all would agree

to this, then wars would cease, and there would be no need of Courts of Appeal or of Arbitration.

"A Court of Arbitration would take the place of war. Disputes would be decided by a Board of Arbitrators, like that which pronounced on the Alabama claims. The Pope has been requested to decide the question concerning the Caroline Islands: Switzerland, Belgium, Denmark, and Holland have declared that they prefer the decision of a Court of Arbitration to war."

I believe Monaco has expressed a similar wish. It is a pity that Germany, Russia, Austria, and France have thus far shown no sign of imitating their example.

It is astonishing how easily men can deceive themselves when they feel inclined.

The governments will agree to allow their disputes to be decided by a Board of Arbitration and to dismiss their armies. The trouble between Russia and Poland, England and Ireland, Austria and the Czechs, Turkey and the Slavs, France and Germany, will be settled by mutual consent. This is very much like suggesting to merchants and bankers that they shall sell at cost price, and devote their services gratuitously to the distribution of property.

Of course the essence of commerce and banking consists in buying cheap and selling dear, and therefore the suggestion to sell at cost price and the consequent overthrow of money amounts to a proposal of self-destruction.

The same is true in regard to governments.

The suggestion to governments to desist from violence, and to adjust all differences by arbitration, would be to recommended a suicidal policy, and no government would ever agree to that. Learned men found societies (there are more than one hundred of them), they assemble in Congresses (like those held in London and Paris, and the one which is to be held in Rome), they read essays, hold banquets, make speeches, edit journals devoted to the subject, and by all these means they endeavor to prove that the strain upon nations who are obliged to support millions of soldiers has become so severe that something must be done about it; that this armament is opposed to the character, the aims, and the wishes of the populations; but they seem to think that if they consume a good deal of paper, and devote a good deal of eloquence to the subject, that they may succeed in conciliating opposing parties and conflicting interests, and at last effect the suppression of war.

When I was a child I was told that if I wished to catch a bird I must put salt on its tail. I took a handful and went in pursuit of the birds, but I saw at once that if I could sprinkle salt on their tails I could catch them, and that what I had been told was only a joke. Those who read essays and works on Courts of Arbitration and the disarmament of nations must feel very much the same.

If it were possible to sprinkle salt on a bird's tail it would be tantamount to saying that the bird could not fly, and therefore it would be no effort to catch it. If a bird has wings and does not wish to be caught, it will not allow any salt to be put on its tail, for it is the nature of a bird to fly. Likewise it is the nature of a government not to be ruled, but to rule its subjects. And a government rightly is named such only when it is able to rule its subjects, and not be ruled by them. This, therefore, is its constant aim, and it will never voluntarily resign its power. And as it derives its power from the army it will never give up the army, nor will it ever renounce that for which the army is designed—war.

The misapprehension springs from the fact that the

learned jurists, deceiving themselves as well as others, depict in their books an ideal of government—not as it really is, an assembly of men who oppress their fellow-citizens, but in accordance with the scientific postulate, as a body of men who act as the representatives of the rest of the nation. They have gone on repeating this to others so long that they have ended by believing it themselves, and they really seem to think that justice is one of the duties of governments. History, however, shows us that governments, as seen from the reign of Cæsar to those of the two Napoleons and Prince Bismarck, are in their very essence a violation of justice; a man or a body of men having at command an army of trained soldiers, deluded creatures who are ready for any violence, and through whose agency they govern the State, will have no keen sense of the obligation of justice. Therefore governments will never consent to diminish the number of those well-trained and submissive servants, who constitute their power and influence.

Such is the attitude of certain scientists toward that self-contradiction under which the world groans, and such are their expedients for its relief. Tell these scientists that the question deals only with the personal relations of each individual toward the moral and religious question, and then ask them what they think of the lawfulness or unlawfulness of taking part in the general conscription, and their sole reply will be a shrug of the shoulders; they will not even deign to give a thought to your question. Their way of solving the difficulty is to make speeches, write books, choose their presidents, vice-presidents, and secretaries; assembled in a body, to hold forth in one city or another. They think that the result of their efforts will be to induce governments to cease to recruit soldiers, on whom all their power depends; they expect that their appeals will be heard, and that armies will be disbanded, leaving governments defenseless, not only in the presence of neighbors, but of their subjects; that they, like highwaymen who, having bound their defenseless victims in order to rob them, no sooner hear the outcries of pain than they loosen the rope that causes it, and let their prisoners go free.

And there really are men who believe in this, who spend their time in promoting Leagues of Peace, in delivering addresses, and in writing books; and of course the governments sympathize with it all, pretending that they approve of it; just as they pretend to support temperance, while they actually derive the larger part of their income from intemperance; just as they pretend to maintain liberty of the constitution, when it is the absence of liberty to which they owe their power; just as they pretend to care for the improvement of the laboring classes, while on oppression of the workman rest the very foundations of the State; just as they pretend to uphold Christianity, when Christianity is subversive of every government.

In order to accomplish these ends they have long since instituted laws in regard to intemperance that can never avail to destroy it; educational projects that not only do not prevent the spread of ignorance, but do everything to increase it; decrees in the name of liberty that are no restraint upon despotism; measures for the benefit of the working-man which will never liberate him from slavery; they have established a Christianity which serves to prop the government rather than destroy it. And now another interest is added to their cares—the promotion of peace. Governments, or rather those rulers who are going about at present with their ministers of state, making up their minds on such radical questions as, for instance, whether the slaughter of millions shall begin this year or next—they are quite well assured that discussions on peace are not going to prevent them from sending millions of men to slaughter whenever they see fit to do so. They like to hear these discussions, they encourage them, and even take part themselves.

It does no harm to the government; on the contrary, it is useful, by way of diverting observation from that radical question: When a man is drafted, ought he or ought he not to fulfil his military duty?

Thanks to all these unions and congresses, peace will presently be established; meanwhile put on your uniforms, and be prepared to worry and harass each other for our benefit, say the governments. And the scientists, the essayists, and the promoters of congresses take the same view.

This is one way of looking at it, and so advantageous for the State that all prudent governments encourage it.

The way another class has of regarding it is more tragic. They declare that although it is the fate of humanity to be forever striving after love and peace, it is nevertheless abnormal and inconsistent. Those who affirm this are mostly the sensitive men of genius, who see and realize all the horror, folly, and cruelty of war, but by some strange turn of mind never look about them for any means of escape, but who seem to take a morbid delight in realizing to the utmost the desperate condition of mankind. The view of the famous French writer, Maupassant, on the subject of war, affords a noteworthy example of this kind. Gazing from his yacht upon a drill and target-practice of French soldiers, the following thoughts arise in his mind:—

"I have but to think of the word 'war' and a paralyzing sense of horror creeps over me, as though I were listening to stories of witchcraft, or tales of the Inquisition, or of things abominable, monstrous, unnatural, of ages past.

"When people talk of cannibals we smile contemptuously with a sense of superiority to such savages. But who are the savages, the true savages? Those who fight that they may drive off the conquered, or those who fight for the pure pleasure of killing? Those sharp-shooters running over yonder are destined to be killed like a flock of sheep who are driven by the butcher to the slaughter-house. Those men will fall on some battlefield with a sabre-cut in the head, or with a ball through the heart. Yet they are young men, who might have done useful work. Their fathers are old and poor; their mothers, who have idolized them for twenty years as only mothers can idolize, will learn after six months, or perhaps a year, that the son, the baby, the grown-up child on whom so much love and pains were lavished, who was reared at such an expense, has been torn by a bullet, trampled under foot, or crushed by a cavalry charge, and finally flung like a dead dog into some ditch. Why must her boy, her beautiful, her only boy, the hope and pride of her life, why must he be killed? She knows not; she can but ask why.

"War! . . . The fighting! . . . The murdering! . . . The slaughter of men! . . . And today, with all our wisdom, civilization, with the advancement of science, the degree of philosophy to which the human spirit has attained, we have schools where the art of murder, of aiming with deadly accuracy and killing large numbers of men at a distance, is actually taught, killing poor, harmless devils who have families to support, killing them without even the pretext of the law.

"*It is stupefying that the people do not rise up in arms against the governments. What difference is there between monarchies and republics? It is stupefying that society does not revolt as a unit at the very sound of the word war.*

"Alas! we shall never be free from oppression of the hateful, hideous customs, the criminal prejudices, and the ferocious impulses of our barbarous ancestors, for we are beasts; and beasts we shall remain, moved by our instincts and susceptible of no improvement.

"Any one but Victor Hugo would have been banished when he uttered his sublime cry of freedom and truth:—

" 'Today force is called violence, and the nations condemn it; they inveigh against war. Civilization, listening to the appeal of humanity, undertakes the case and prepares the accusation against the victors and the generals. The nations begin to understand that the magnitude of a crime cannot lessen its wickedness; that if it be criminal to kill one man, the killing of numbers cannot be regarded in the light of extenuation; that if it be shameful to steal, it cannot be glorious to lead an invading army.

" 'Let us proclaim these absolute truths, let us dishonor the name of war!'

"But the wrath and indignation of the poet are all in vain," continues Maupassant. "War is more honored than ever.

"A clever expert in this business, a genius in the art of murder, Von Moltke, once made to a peace-delegate the following astonishing reply:—

" 'War is sacred; it is a divine institution; it fosters every lofty and noble sentiment in the human heart: honor, self-sacrifice, virtue, courage, and saves men, so to speak, from settling into the most shocking materialism.'

"Assembling in herds by the hundred thousand, marching night and day without rest, with no time for thought of for study, never to read, learning nothing, of no use whatsoever to any living being, rotting with filth, sleeping in the mud, living like a wild beast in a perennial state of stupidity, plundering cities, burning villages, ruining whole nations; then to encounter another mountain of human flesh, rush upon it, cause rivers of blood to flow, and strew the fields with the dead and the dying, all stained with the muddy and reddened soil, to have one's limbs severed, one's brain scattered as wanton waste, and to perish in the corner of a field while one's aged parents, one's wife and children, are dying of hunger at home—this is what it means to be saved from falling into the grossest materialism!

"Soldiers are the scourge of the world. We struggle against nature, ignorance, all kinds of obstacles, in the effort to make our wretched lives more endurable. There are men, scientists and philanthropists, who devote their whole lives to benefit their fellow-men, seeking to improve their condition. They pursue their efforts tirelessly, adding discovery to discovery, expanding the human intelligence, enriching science, opening new fields of knowledge, day by day increasing the well-being, comfort, and vigor of their country.

"Then war comes upon the scene, and in six months all the results of twenty years of patient labor and of human genius are gone forever, crushed by victorious generals.

"And this is what they mean when they speak of man's rescue from materialism!

"We have seen war. We have seen men maddened; returned to the condition of the brutes, we have seen them kill in wanton sport, out of terror, or for mere bravado and show. Where right exists no longer, and law is dead, where all sense of justice has been lost, we have seen innocent men shot down on the highway. We have seen dogs chained to their master's doors killed by way of target-practice, we have seen cows lying in a field fired at by the mitrailleuses, just for the fun of shooting at something.

"And this is what they call saving men from the most shocking materialism!

"To invade a country, to kill the man who defends his home because he wears a blouse and does not wear a *kepi,* to burn the dwellings of starving wretches, to ruin or plunder a man's household goods, to drink the wine found in the cellars, to violate the women found in the streets, consume millions of francs in powder, and to leave misery and cholera in their track.

"This is what they mean by saving men from the most shocking materialism!

"What have military men ever done to prove that they possess the smallest degree of intelligence? Nothing whatever. What have they invented? The cannon and the musket; nothing more.

"Has not the inventor of the wheelbarrow, by the simple and practical contrivance of a wheel and a couple of boards, accomplished more than the inventor of modern fortification?

"What has Greece bequeathed to the world? Its literature and its marbles. Was she great because she conquered, or because she produced? Was it the Persian invasion that saved Greece from succumbing to the most shocking materialism?

"Did the invasions of the Barbarians save and regenerate Rome?

"Did Napoleon I continue the great intellectual movement started by the philosophers at the end of the last century?

"Very well, then; can it be a matter of surprise, since governments usurp the rights of life and death over the people, that the people from time to time assume the right of life and death over their governments?

"They defend themselves, and they have the right. No man has an inalienable right to govern others. It is allowable only when it promotes the welfare of the governed. It is as much the duty of those who govern to avoid war as it is that of a captain of a ship to avoid shipwreck.

"When a captain has lost his ship he is indicted, and if he is found to have been careless or even incompetent, he is convicted. As soon as war has been declared why should not the people sit in judgment upon the act of the government?

"If they could once be made to understand the power that would be theirs, *if they were the judges of the rulers who lead them on to slay their fellow-men, if they refused to allow themselves to be needlessly slaughtered, if they were to turn their weapons against the very men who have put them into their hands—that day would see the last of war . . . But never will that day arrive."*—"Sur l'Eau."

The author perceives the full horror of war, realizes that the government is its author, that government forces men to go slay, or be slain, when there is no need for it; he realizes that the men who make up the armies might turn their weapons against the government and demand a reckoning. Still the author does not believe that this will ever happen, or that there is any possible deliverance from the existing condition of affairs.

He grants that the result of war is shocking, but he believes it to be inevitable; assuming that the never ceasing requisition of soldiers on the part of government is as inevitable as death, then wars must follow as a matter of course.

These are the words of a writer of talent, endowed with a faculty of vividly realizing his subject, which is the essence of the poetic gift. He shows us all the cruel contradictions between creed and deed; but since he fails to offer a solution, it is evident that he feels that such a contradiction must exist, and regards it as a contribution to the romantic tragedy of life. Another and an equally gifted writer, Edouard Rod, paints with colors still more vivid the cruelty and folly of the present situation, but he, like Maupassant, feels the influence of the dramatic element, and neither suggests a remedy nor anticipates any change.

"Why do we toil? Why do we plan and hope to execute? And how can one even love one's neighbor in these troublous times, when the morrow is nothing but a menace? ... Everything that we have begun, our ripening schemes, our plans for work, the little good that we might accomplish, will it not all be swept away by the storm that is gathering?　Everywhere the soil quakes beneath our feet, and threatening clouds hang low in the horizon. Ah! if we had nothing more to fear than the bugbear of the Revolution! . . . Unable to conceive a society worse than our own, I am more inclined to distrust than to fear the one that may replace it, and if I should suffer in consequence of the change, I should console myself with the reflection that the executioners of the present were victims of the past, and the hope of a change for the better would make me endure the worst. But it is not this remote danger which alarms me. I see another close at hand and far more cruel, since it is both unjustifiable and irrational, and nothing good can come out of it. Day by day the chances of war are weighed, and day by day they become more pitiless.

"The human mind refuses to believe in the catastrophe which even now looms up before us, and which the close of this century must surely witness, a catastrophe which will put an end to all the progress of our age, and yet we must try to realize it. Science has devoted all her energy these twenty years to the invention of destructive weapons, and soon a few cannon-balls will suffice to destroy an army; not the few thousands of wretched mercenaries, whose life-blood has been bought and paid for, but whole nations are about to exterminate each other; during conscription their time is stolen from them in order to steal their lives with more certainty. By way of stimulating a thirst for blood mutual animosities are excited, and gentle, kind-hearted men allow themselves to be deluded, and it will not be long before they attack each other with all the ferocity of wild beasts; multitudes of peace-loving citizens will obey a foolish command, God only knows on what pretext—some stupid frontier quarrel, perhaps, or it may be some colonial mercantile interest. . . . They will go like a flock of sheep to the slaughter, yet knowing where they go, conscious that they are leaving their wives and their children to suffer hunger; anxious, but unable to resist the enticement of those plausible and treacherous words that have been trumpeted into their ears. *Unresistingly they go; although they form a mass and a force, they fail to realize the extent of their power, and that if they were all agreed they might establish the reign of reason and fraternity,* instead of lending themselves to the barbarous trickeries of diplomacy.

"So self-deceived are they that bloodshed takes on the aspect of duty, and they implore the blessing of God upon their sanguinary hopes. As they march, they trample underfoot the harvests which they themselves have planted, burning the cities which they have helped to build, with songs, shouts of enthusiasm, and music. And their sons will raise a statue to those who have slain them by the most approved methods. . . . The fate of a whole generation hangs on the hour when some saturnine politician shall make the sign, and the nations will rush upon each other. We know that the noblest among us will be cut down, and that our affairs will go to destruction. *We know this, we tremble in anger, yet are powerless.* We have been caught in a snare of bureaucracy and waste paper from which we can only escape by measures too energetic for us. We belong to the laws which we have made for our protection, and which oppress us. *We are nothing more than the creatures of that antinomic abstraction, the State, which makes of each individual a slave in the name of all, each individual of which all, taken separately, would desire the exact contrary of what he will be made to do.*

"And if it were but the sacrifice of a single generation! But many other interests are involved.

"Paid orators, demagogues, taking advantage of the

passions of the masses and of the simple-minded who are dazzled by high-sounding phrases, have so embittered national hatreds that tomorrow's war will decide the fate of a race: one of the component parts of the modern world is threatened; the vanquished nation will morally disappear; it matters not which chances to be the victim, a power will disappear (as though there had ever been one too many for the good). A new Europe will then be established on a basis so unjust, so brutal, so bloodstained, that it cannot fail to be worse than that of today—more iniquitous, more barbarous, and more agressive....

"Thus a fearful depression hangs over us. We are like men dashing up and down a narrow passageway, with muskets pointed at us from all the roofs. We work like sailors executing their last manœver after the ship has begun to sink. Our pleasures are those of the prisoner to whom a choice dish is offered a quarter of an hour before his execution. Anxiety paralyzes our thought, and the utmost we can do is to wonder, as we con the vague utterances of ministers, or construe the meaning of the words of monarchs, or turn over those ascribed to the diplomatists, retailed at random by the newspapers, never sure of their information, whether all this is to happen tomorrow or the day after, whether it is this year or next that we are all to be killed. In truth, one might seek in vain throughout the pages of history for an epoch more unsettled or more pregnant with anxiety."—"Le Sens de la Vie."

He shows us that the power is really in the hands of those who allow themselves to be destroyed, in the hands of separate individuals who compose the mass; that the root of all evil is the State. It would seem as if the contradiction between one's faith and one's actual life had reached its utmost limit, and that the solution could not be far to seek.

But the author is of a different opinion. All that he sees in this is the tragedy of human life, and having given us a detailed description of the horror of this state of things, he perceives no reason why human life should not be spent in the midst of this horror Such are the views of the second class of writers, who consider only the fatalistic and tragic side of war.

There is still another view, and this is the one held by men who have lost all conscience, and are consequently dead to common sense and human feeling.

To this class belong Moltke, whose opinions are quoted by Maupassant, and nearly all military men who have been taught to believe this cruel superstition, who are supported by it, and who naturally regard war not only as an inevitable evil, but as a necessary and even profitable occupation. And there are civilians too, scientists, men of refinement and education, who hold very much the same views.

The famous academician Doucet, in reply to a query of the editor of the *Revue des Revues* in regard to his opinions on war, replies as follows in the number containing letters concerning war:—

"DEAR SIR—When you ask of the least belligerent of all the academicians if he is a partizan of war, his reply is already given. Unfortunately you yourself classify the peaceful contemplations which inspire your fellow-countrymen at the present hour as idle visions.

"Ever since I was born I have always heard good men protesting against this shocking custom of international carnage. All recognize this evil and lament it. But where is its remedy?

"The effort to suppress duelling has often been made. It seems to be so easy. Far from it. All that has been accomplished toward achieving this noble purpose amounts to nothing, nor will it ever amount to more. Against war and duelling the congresses of the two hemispheres vote in vain. Superior to all arbitrations, conventions. and legislations will ever remain human honor, which has always demanded the duel, and national interests, which have always called for war. Nevertheless, I wish with all my heart that the Universal Peace Congress may succeed at last in its difficult and honorable task.—Accept the assurance, etc.

"CAMILE DOUCET."

It amounts to this, that honor obliges men to fight, that it is for the interest of nations that they should attack and destroy one another, and that all endeavors to abolish war can but excite a smile.

Jules Claretie expresses himself in similar terms:—

DEAR SIR,—A sensible man can have but one opinion on the question of war and peace. Humanity was created to live—to live for the purpose of perfecting its existence by peaceful labor. The mutual relations of cordiality which are promoted and preached by the Universal Congress of Peace may be but a dream perhaps, yet certainly is the most delightful of dreams. The vision of the land of promise is ever before the eyes, and upon the soil of the future the harvest will ripen, secure from the plowing of the projectile, or the crushing of cannon-wheels. But, alas! . . . Since philosophers and philanthropists are not the rulers of mankind, it is fit that our soldiers should guard our frontiers and our homes, and their weapons, skilfully wielded, are perhaps the surest guarantees of the peace we love so well. Peace is given only to the strong and the courageous.—Accept the assurances of, etc.,

"JULES CLARETIE."

The substance of this is, that there is no harm in talking about what no one intends to do, and what ought not in any event to be done. When fighting is in order, there is no alternative but to fight.

Émile Zola, the most popular novelist in Europe, gives utterance to his views on the subject of war in the following terms:—

"I look upon war as a fatal necessity which seems to us indispensable because of its close connection with human nature and all creation. Would that it might be postponed as long as possible! Nevertheless a time will come when we shall be forced to fight. At this moment I am regarding the subject from the universal standpoint, and am not hinting at our unfriendly relations with Germany, which are but a trifling incident in the world's history. I affirm that war is useful and necessary, since it is one of the conditions of human existence. The fighting instinct is to be found not only among the different tribes and peoples, but in domestic and private life as well. It is one of the chief elements of progress, and every advancing step taken by mankind up to the present time has been accompanied by bloodshed.

"Men have talked, and still do talk, of disarmament; and yet disarmament is utterly impossible, for even though it were possible, we should be compelled to renounce it. It is only an armed nation that can be powerful and great. I believe that a general disarmament would be followed by a moral degradation, assuming the form of a widespread effeminacy which would impede the progress of humanity. Warlike nations have always been vigorous. The military art has contributed to the development of other arts. History shows us this. In Athens and Rome, for instance, commerce, industry, and literature reached their highest development when these cities ruled the world by the force of arms. And nearer to our own time we found an example in the reign of Louis XIV. The wars of the great king, so far from impeding the advance of arts and sciences, seemed rather to promote and to favor their progress."

War is useful!

But chief among the advocates of these views, and the most talented of all the writers of this tendency, is the academician Vogüé, who in an article on the military section of the Exhibition of 1889, writes as follows:—

"On the Esplanade des Invalides, the center of exotic and colonial structures, a building of a more severe order stands out from the midst of the picturesque bazaar; these various fragments of our terrestrial globe adjoin the palace of war. A magnificent theme and antithesis for humanitarian rhetoric which never loses a chance to lament a juxtaposition of this kind, and to utter its 'this will kill that' [*ceci tuera cela**]; that the confederacy of

* Words taken from Victor Hugo's "Notre Dame," where he says that printing will kill architecture.—AUTHOR.

nations brought about by science and labor will overpower the military instinct. Let it cherish this vision of a golden age, caressing it with fond hopes. We have no objection; but should it ever be realized, it would very soon become an age of corruption. History teaches us that the former has been accomplished by the means of the latter, that blood is necessary to hasten and to seal the confederacy of nations. In our own time the natural sciences have strengthened the mysterious law which revealed itself to Joseph de Maistre through the inspiration of his genius and meditation on primordial dogmas; he saw how the world would redeem its hereditary fall by offering a sacrifice. Science shows us that the world is made better by struggle and violent selection; this affirmation of the same law, with varied utterance, comes from two sources. It is by no means a pleasant one. The laws of the world, however, are not established for our pleasure, but for our perfection. Let us then enter this necessary and indispensable palace of war, and we shall have the opportunity to observe how our most inveterate instinct, losing nothing of its power, is transformed in its adaptation to the various demands of historical moments."

This idea, namely, that the proof of the necessity of war may be found in the writings of De Maistre and of Darwin, two great thinkers, as he calls them, pleases Vogüé so much that he repeats it.

"Sir," he writes to the editor of the *Revue des Revues*, "you ask my opinion in regard to the possible success of the Universal Peace Congress. I believe, with Darwin, that vehement struggle is the law governing all being, and I believe, with Joseph de Maistre, that it is a divine law—two different modes of characterizing the same principle. If, contrary to all expectations, a certain fraction of humanity—for example, all the civilized West—should succeed in arresting the issue of this law, the more primitive races would execute it against us; in these races the voice of nature would prevail over human intellect. And they would succeed, because the certainty of *peace*—I do not say peace, but the absolute *certainty of peace*—would in less than half a century produce a corruption and a decadence in men more destructive than the worst of wars. I believe that one should act in regard to war—that criminal law of humanity—as in regard to all criminal laws: modify it, or endeavor to make its execution as rare as possible, and use every means in our power to render it superfluous. But experience of all history teaches us that it cannot be suppressed, so long as there shall be found on earth two men, bread, money, and a woman between them. I should be very glad if the Congress could prove to me the contrary; but I doubt if it can disprove history, and the law of God and of nature.—Accept my assurance, etc.,

"E. M. de Vogüé."

This may be summed up as follows: History and nature, God and man, show us that so long as there are two men left on earth, and the stakes are bread, money, and woman, just so long there will be war. That is, that no amount of civilization will ever destroy that abnormal concept of life which makes it impossible for men to divide bread, money (of all absurdities), and woman without a fight. It is odd that people meet in congresses and hold forth as to the best method of catching birds by putting salt on their tails, although they must know that this can never be done! It is astonishing that men like Rod, Maupassant, and others, clearly realizing all the horrors of war, and all the contradictions that ensue from men not doing what they ought to do, and what it would be to their advantage to do, who bemoan the tragedy of life, and yet fail to see that this tragic element would vanish as soon as men ceased to discuss a subject which should not be discussed, and ceased to do that which is both painful and repulsive for them to do!

One may wonder at them; but men who, like Vogüé and others, believe in the law of evolution, and look upon war as not only unavoidable, but even useful, and therefore desirable—such men are fairly shocking, horrible in their moral aberration. The former at least declare that they hate evil and love good, but the latter believe there is neither good nor evil.

All this discussion of the possibility of establishing peace instead of continual warfare is but the mischievous sentimentalism of idle talkers. There is a law of evolution which seems to prove that I must live and do wrong. What, then, can I do? I am an educated man—I am familiar with the doctrine of evolution; hence it follows that I shall work evil. "Entrons au palais de la guerre." There is a law of evolution, and therefore there can be no real evil; and one must live one's life and leave the rest to the law of evolution. This is the last expression of refined civilization; it is with this idea that the educated classes at the present day deaden their conscience.

The desire of these classes to preserve their favorite theories and the life that they have built up on them can go no further. They lie, and by their specious arguments deceive themselves as well as others, obscuring and deadening their intuitive perceptions.

Rather than adapt their lives to their consciousness, they try by every means to befog and to silence it. But the light shines in the darkness, and even now it begins to dawn.

*   *   *

Strange and contradictory as it may seem, modern men hate the very order of things which they themselves support.

I believe it is Max Müller who describes the astonishment of an Indian converted to Christianity, who, having apprehended the essence of the Christian doctrine, came to Europe and beheld the life of Christians. He could not recover from his astonishment in the presence of the reality, so different from the state of things he had expected to find among Christian nations.

If we are not surprised at the contradiction between our convictions and our actions, it is only because the influences which obscure this contradiction act upon us. We have but to look at our life from the standpoint of the Indian, who understood Christianity in its true significance, without any concessions or adaptations, and to behold the barbarous cruelties with which our life is filled, in order to be horrified at the contradictions in the midst of which we live, without noticing them.

One has but to remember the preparations for war, the cartridge-boxes, the silver-plated bullets, the torpedoes, and—the Red Cross; the establishment of prisons for solitary confirment, experiments with *electrocution,* and—the care for the welfare of the prisoners; the philanthropic activity of the rich, and—their daily life, which brings about the existence of the poor, whom they seek to benefit. And these contradictions arise, not, as it might seem, because men pretend to be Christians while they are actually heathens, but because they lack something, or because there is some power which prevents them from being what they really desire to be, and what they even conscientiously believe themselves to be. It is not that modern men merely pretend to hate oppression, the inequality of class distinctions, and all kinds of cruelty, whether practised against their fellow-men or against animals. They *are* sincere in their hatred of these abuses; but they do not know how to abolish them, or they lack the courage to alter their own mode of life, which depends upon all this, and which seems to them so important.

Ask, indeed, any individual if he considers it praiseworthy or even honorable for a man to fill a position for which he receives a salary so high as to be out of all proportion to the amount of his labor, as, for instance, that of collecting from the people, often from beggars, taxes which are to be devoted to the purchase of cannon, torpedoes, and other instruments for murdering the men with whom we wish to live in peace, and who wish to live in peace with us; or, to receive a salary for spending his life either in perfecting these instruments of murder, or in the military exercises by which men are trained for slaughter? Ask whether it be praiseworthy or compatible with the dignity of man, or becoming to a Christian, to undertake, also for money, to arrest some unfortunate man, some illiterate drunkard, for some petty theft not to be compared with the magnitude of our own appropriation, or for manslaughter not conducted by our advanced methods; and for such offenses to throw people into prison, or put them to death? Ask whether it be laudable and becoming in a man and a Christian, also for money, to teach the people foolish and injurious superstitions instead of the doctrine of Christ? Whether, again, it be laudable and worthy of a man to wrench from his neighbor, in order to gratify his own caprice, the very necessa-

ries of life, as the great landowners do; or to exact from
his fellow-man an excessive and exhausting toil for the
purpose of increasing his own wealth, as the mill-owners
and manufacturers do; or to take advantage of human
necessities to build up colossal fortunes, as the merchants do?

Every individual would reply not, especially if the
question regarded his neighbor. And at the same time
the very man who acknowledges all the ignominy of such
deeds, when the case is presented to him, will often, of
his own accord, and for no advantage of a salary, but
moved by childish vanity, the desire to possess a trinket
of enamel, a decoration, a stripe, voluntarily enter the
military service, or become an examining magistrate, a
justice of the peace, a minister of state, a bishop, accept-
ing an office whose duties will oblige him to do things,
the shame and ignominy of which he cannot help realizing.

Many of these men will, I am sure, defend themselves
on the ground of the lawfulness and necessity of their
position; they will argue that the authorities are of God,
that the functions of State are indispensable for the good
of mankind, that Christianity is not opposed to wealth,
that the rich youth was bidden to give up his goods only
if he wished to be perfect, that the present distribution
of wealth and commerce is beneficial to all men, and that
it is right and lawful. But however much they may try to
deceive themselves and others, they all know that what
they do is opposed to the highest interests of life, and at
the bottom of their hearts, when they listen only to their
consciences, they are ashamed and pained to think of
what they are doing, especially when the baseness of their
deeds has been pointed out to them. A man in modern life,

whether he does or does not profess to believe in the
divinity of Christ, must know that to be instrumental
either as a Czar, minister, governor, or policeman, as in
selling a poor family's last cow to pay taxes to the treasury,
the money of which is devoted to the purchase of cannon
or to pay the salaries or pensions of idle and luxurious
officials, is to do more harm than good; or to be a party
to the imprisonment of the father of a family, for whose
demoralization we are ourselves responsible, and to bring
his family to beggary; or to take part in piratical and
murderous warfare; or to teach absurd superstitions of
idol-worship instead of the doctrine of Christ; or to im-
pound a stray cow belonging to a man who has no land;
or to deduct the value of an accidentally injured article
from the wages of a mechanic; or to sell something to a
poor man for double its value, only because he is in dire
necessity;—the men of our modern life cannot but know
that all such deeds are wrong, shameful, and that they
ought not to commit them. They do all know it. They
know that they are doing wrong, and would abstain from
it, had they but the strength to oppose those forces which
blind them to the criminality of their actions while drawing them on to do wrong.

But there is nothing that demonstrates so vividly the
degree of contradiction to which human life has attained
as the system that embodies both the method and the
expression of violence—the general conscription system.
It is only because a general armament and military conscription have come imperceptibly and by slow degrees,
and that governments employ for their support all the
means of intimidation at their disposal—bribery, bewilderment, and violence—that we do not realize the glaring
contradiction between this state of affairs and those

Christian feelings and ideas with which all modern men are penetrated.

This contradiction has become so common that we fail to see the shocking imbecility and immorality of the actions, not only of those men who, of their own accord choose the profession of murder as something honorable, but of those unfortunates who consent to serve in the army, and of those who, in countries where military conscription has not yet been introduced, give of their own free will the fruits of their labor to be used for the payment of mercenaries and for the organization for murder. All these men are either Christians or men professing humanitarianism and liberalism, who know that they participate in the most imbecile, aimless, and cruel murders; yet still they go on committing them. But this is not all. In Germany, where the system of general military conscription originated, Caprivi has revealed something that has always been carefully hidden: that the men who run the risk of being killed are not only foreigners, but are quite as likely to be fellow-countrymen—workingmen—from which class most of the soldiers are obtained. Nevertheless, this admission neither opened men's eyes nor shocked their sensibilities. They continue just as they did before, to go like sheep, and submit to anything that is demanded of them. And this is not all. The German Emperor has recently explained with minute precision the character and vocation of a soldier, having distinguished, thanked, and rewarded a private for killing a defenseless prisoner who attempted to escape. In thanking and rewarding a man for an act which is looked upon even by men of the lowest type of morality as base and cowardly, Wilhelm pointed out that the principal duty of a soldier, and one most highly prized by the authorities, is that of an executioner—not like the professional executioners who put to death condemned prisoners only, but an executioner of the innocent men whom his superiors order him to kill.

Yet more. In 1891 this same Wilhelm, the *enfant terrible* of State authority, who expresses what other men only venture to think, in a talk with certain soldiers, uttered publicly the following words, which were repeated the next day in thousands of papers:—

"Recruits! You have given *me* the oath of allegiance before the altar and the servant of the Lord. You are still too young to comprehend the true meaning of what has been said here, but first of all take care ever to follow the orders and instructions that are given to you. You have taken the oath of allegiance to *me;* this means, children of my guards, that you are now *my* soldiers, that you have given yourselves up to me, body and soul.

"But one enemy exists for you—*my* enemy. With the present socialistic intrigues *it may happen that I shall command you to shoot your own relatives, your brothers, even your parents* (from which may God preserve us!), *and then you are in duty bound to obey my orders un-hesitatingly.*"

This man expresses what is known, but carefully concealed, by all wise rulers. He says outright that the men who serve in the army serve *him* and *his* advantage, and should be ready for that purpose to kill their brothers and fathers.

Roughly but distinctly he lays bare all the horror of the crime for which men who become soldiers prepare themselves—all that abyss of self-abasement into which they fling themselves when they promise obedience. Like a bold hypnotizer, he tests the depth of the slumber; he applies red-hot iron to the sleeper's body; it smokes and shrivels, but the sleeper does not awaken.

Poor, sick, miserable man, intoxicated with power, who by these words insults all that is sacred to men of modern civilization! And we, Christians, liberals, men of culture, so far from feeling indignant at this insult, pass it over in silence. Men are put to the final test in its rudest form; but they hardly observe that a test is in question, that a choice is put before them. It seems to them as if there were no choice, but only the one necessity of slavish submission. It would seem as if these insane words, offensive to all that a civilized human being holds sacred, ought to rouse indignation—but nothing of the kind happens. Year after year every young man in Europe is subjected to the same test, and with very few exceptions they all forswear what is and should be sacred to every man; all manifest a readiness to kill their brothers and even their fathers, at the order of the first misguided man who wears a red and gold livery, asking only when and whom they are to be ordered to kill—for they are ready to do it.

Even by savages certain objects are held sacred, for whose sake they are ready to suffer rather than submit. But what is sacred for the man of the modern world? He is told: Be my slave, in a bondage where you may have to murder your own father; and he, oftentimes a man of learning, who has studied all the sciences in the university, submissively offers his neck to the halter. He is dressed in a clown's garments, ordered to leap, to make contortions, to salute, to kill—and he submissively obeys; and when at last allowed to return to his former life, he continues to hold forth on the dignity of man, freedom, equality, and brotherhood.

"But what is to be done?" we often hear men ask in

perplexity. "If every man were to refuse, it would be a different matter; but, as it is, I should suffer alone without benefiting any one." And they are right; for a man who holds the social life-conception cannot refuse. Life has no significance for him except as it concerns his personal welfare; it is for his advantage to submit, therefore he does so.

To whatever torture or injury he may be subjected he will submit, because he can do nothing alone; he lacks the foundation which alone would enable him to resist violence, and those who are in authority over him will never give him the chance of uniting with others.

It has often been said that the invention of the terrible military instruments of murder will put an end to war, and that war will exhaust itself. This is not true. As it is possible to increase the means for killing men, so it is possible to increase the means for subjecting those who hold the social life-conception. Let them be exterminated by thousands and millions, let them be torn to pieces, men will still continue like stupid cattle to go to the slaughter, some because they are driven thither under the lash, others that they may win the decorations and ribbons which fill their hearts with pride.

And it is with material like this that the public leaders—conservatives, liberals, socialist, anarchist—discuss the ways and means of organizing an intelligent and moral society, with men who have been so thoroughly confused and bewildered that they will promise to murder their own parents. What kind of intelligence and morality can there be in a society organized from material like this? Just as it is impossible to build a house from bent and rotten timber, however manipulated, so also is it impossible with such materials to organize an intelligent and moral society. They can only be governed like a drove of cattle, by the shouts and lash of the herdsman. And so, indeed, they are governed.

Again, while on the one hand we find men, Christians in name, professing the principles of liberty, equality, and fraternity, on the other hand we see these same men ready, in the name of liberty, to yield the most abject and slavish obedience; in the name of equality, to approve of the most rigid and senseless subdivision of men into classes; and in the name of fraternity, ready to slay their own brothers.

The contradiction of the moral consciousness, and hence the misery of life, has reached its utmost limit, beyond which it can go no further. Life, based on prin ciples of violence, has culminated in the negation of the basis on which it was founded. The organization, on principles of violence, of a society whose object was to insure the happiness of the individual and the family, and the social welfare of humanity, has brought men to such a pass that these benefits are practically annulled.

POSTSCRIPT

"LIFE AND DEATH OF DROZHIN"*

OSES, in his commandments given to mankind five thousand years ago, laid down the law: *Thou shalt not kill.* The same command has been preached by all the prophets; the same law has been preached by the sages and teachers of the whole world; the same law was preached by Christ, who forbade not only murder, but everything that might lead to it, all provocation and anger against one's brother. And the same is written in the heart of every man so clearly that no action is more opposed to the whole being of every unperverted man than the murder of his own kind—of

---

* Yevdokim Nikititch Drozhin, or Drozhzhin, was born August 11, 1866, at Tolstui Lug in the Government of Kursk, Russia. His parents were peasants. He early displayed great love for learning, and before he was seventeen he was an assistant in a local parochial school. Afterward he received instruction in the Teacher's Seminary at Byelgorod. Through the influence of a young peasant from his own locality—Nikolaï Trofimovitch Izyumchenko—he became imbued with socialistic and revolutionary views, and on this account

a human being. And here, notwithstanding the fact that this law of God was clearly revealed to us by Moses, by the prophets, and by Christ, and is written so ineradicably in our hearts that there can be no doubt of its obligation upon us, not only this law is not recognized in our world, but a law absolutely opposed to this is recognized—the law of the obligation for every man of our time to be enrolled in the military service; in other words, to stand in the ranks of murderers, to take an oath of readiness to commit murder, to learn the trade of killing, and actually to kill one's fellow-men whenever this is required.*

---

was not allowed to graduate, but afterward he qualified as a teacher and accepted a position as village teacher at Chernitcheva, where he remained two years. In 1899 he made the acquaintance of D. A. Hilkof, and fell under the influence of Count Tolstoï's writings. His literary activities and his exchange of letters with Izyumchenko and others brought upon him the attention of the police and he was arrested. Nearly all the rest of his life is the story of his resistance of the military conscription in accordance with Tolstoï's explanation of Christ's doctrine of non-resistance. He was enrolled in the so-called Disciplinary Battalion, where he was treated with the greatest harshness as if he had been a criminal instead of a Christian. Owing to his hardships his health was broken, and he died of consumption in prison at Voronezh, February 7, 1895. His friend, C. I. Popof, wrote his life, which was published by Vladimir Tchertkof in 1898, together with the present postscript of Count Tolstoï.—ED.

* In countries where there is no obligation of military obedience, God's law, and that of conscience concerning murder, although not so evidently, is nevertheless broken by all citizens because the service, the enlistment and the maintenance of armies, put on the basis of money consciously paid by all the citizens for the business of murder, considered necessary by all, is exactly the same kind of consent to murder and coöperation in it as a personal participation in military service.—AUTHOR'S NOTE.

In the time of heathendom, the Christians were commanded to express in words their recantation of belief in Christ and God, and as a sign of their recantation to offer sacrifices to the heathen gods.

Now, in our time, Christians are compelled to renounce Christ and God, not only by the offer of sacrifice to the heathen gods—to offer sacrifices to the heathen gods is possible even while remaining a Christian at heart—but also by doing an action which is most indubitably opposed to Christ and God and forbidden by Christ and God—to take an oath of readiness to commit murder, and very frequently to commit murder itself.

And as formerly men were found who would not consent to worship the heathen gods, and for their faith in Christ and God sacrificed their lives, so also now there have been and are men who will not renounce Christ and God, who will not consent to take oaths of their readiness to commit murder, who will not enter the ranks of murderers, and who, in behalf of their faith, perish in the most horrible sufferings, as was the case with Drozhin whose life is told in this book.

And as in days gone by those who were accounted half foolish, strange people, the martyrs of Christianity who perished because they did not wish to renounce Christ, merely by their faith in Christ destroyed the heathen world, and cleared the way for Christianity, so now also, men like Drozhin, who are accounted half foolish and fanatical for preferring tortures and death to disobeying God's law, by their very faith in this law are destroying the existent cruel order of things more effectually than a revolution, and are revealing to men a new and joyous state of universal brotherhood, the coming of the kingdom of God which the prophets foretold and the foundations of which were laid by Christ eighteen hundred years ago.

But besides the fact that men like Drozhin, who refuse to renounce God and Christ, by their action help to bring about the coming of that kingdom of God predicted by the prophets, they show by their example the only undoubted route whereby that kingdom of God may be attained, and all that stands in the way of its establishment may be destroyed.

The distinction between the martyrdoms of Christianity and those of the present day consists only in the fact that then the heathen demanded heathen deeds from the Christians; while now men who are not heathen but Christians, or at least call themselves so, demand of Christians heathen and most horribly heathen deeds, such as murder, which the heathen never demanded: and in this, that then the power of heathendom rested on its ignorance, on the fact that it did not know, did not understand Christianity; while now the cruelty of so-called Christianity rests on deception, on conscious deception.

Then, in order to free Christianity from violence, it was necessary to persuade the heathen of the truth of Christianity; but this in large measure it was impossible to do. Julian the Apostate and many better men of that time were truly persuaded that the heathen religion was an enlightenment and a blessing, while Christianity was darkness, ignorance, and evil. But now, in order to free Christianity from violence and cruelty, it is necessary only to lay bare the deception of a false Christianity. But this deception is laid bare by one simple, inflexible law of truth, which inevitably invites the false Christian powers to use violence by the torture and murder of Christians for the observation of the very thing which they preach.

Formerly the Christian who refused to worship the heathen gods would say to the heathen:—

"I renounce your faith, I am a Christian, and I cannot and will not serve your gods, but I will serve the only true God and His Son, Jesus Christ."

And the heathen authorities punished him because he preached a religion which they considered false and dangerous, and his punishment did not contain any contradiction, and brought no reproach on that heathen religion in the name of which he was punished.

But now the Christian who renounces murder preaches his doctrine, not to heathen any longer, but to men who call themselves Christians. And if he says, "I am a Christian, and I cannot and will not carry out the demand to murder, which is opposed to the Christian law," then they cannot say to him, as the heathen used to say, "You are practising a false and dangerous religion, and therefore we punish you;" but they say to him: "We also are Christians, but you do not properly understand Christianity when you· declare that the Christian cannot kill. The Christian may and must kill when he is commanded to do so by any one who, at a certain moment, considers himself his superior. And for the reason, that you do not agree with the doctrine that the Christian ought not to love his enemies, but ought to kill them all when he is bidden, we Christians who are preaching the law of humility, love, and forgiveness, punish you."

It has come about that the powers calling themselves Christian at every such collision with the men that renounce murder are compelled in the most palpable and triumphant way to be apostates to that Christian and moral law on which alone their power is based.

Moreover, unhappily for the false powers and happily

for all humanity, the conditions of military service have become of late entirely different from what they used to be, and consequently the demands of the powers have become still more evidently unchristian, and the refusals to fulfil these demands have become convincing.

Formerly, scarcely a hundredth of all the population was called to the military service, and the authorities might have well supposed that men of a low order of morality would enter the service, such as would find nothing contrary to their Christian consciences in doing so, as used to be the case to a certain degree when men were sent off as soldiers for a punishment. Then, if they summoned to the military service a man who, by his moral qualities, could not be a murderer, this was an unfortunate accident and an exception.

But now, when all men are compelled to undergo military obligations, the best of them, those that are most Christianly disposed and farthest from the possibility of taking part in murder, all have to confess themselves as murderers and apostates from God.

Formerly, the army raised by the authorities was composed of ragged, coarse, unchristian, and ignorant men or volunteers and mercenaries; formerly no one or almost no one read the Gospels, and men did not know its spirit, but believed what the priests told them; and formerly only a few, especially fanatically inclined people, sectaries, considered it a sin to serve in the army, and refused to do so.

But now there is not a single man in Christian countries who would not be consciously under obligations, with his money, and in a large part of Europe personally, to take part in preparations for murder or in murder itself; now almost all men know the Gospels and the spirit of

Christ's teachings, all know that the priests are bribed impostors, and no one but the most clownish of men believe in them; and now already not only sectaries, but men who do not preach any special dogma, men of cultivation, free-thinkers, renounce military service, and not only renounce it for themselves, but openly declare to every one that murder is not compatible with the profession of Christianity.

And, therefore, one such refusal of military service like Drozhin's, a refusal maintained in spite of tortures and death—one such refusal shakes the whole colossal fabric of violence based on falsehood, and threatens it with destruction.

Terrible force is lodged in the hands of the authorities, and not merely a material force—a vast amount of money, institutions, riches, submissive functionaries of the clergy and the army—the mighty spiritual forces of influence are lodged in the hands of the government. It can, unless it is bribed, suppress, annihilate, all those that are opposed to it. The suborned clergy preaches to the soldiers in the churches; suborned writers write books justifying the army; in the schools, those of higher and those of lower grade, false catechisms are made obligatory, and the children are taught in accordance with them that to kill in war and in executing justice is not only possible, but mandatory. All those that enter the army take the oath of allegiance; everything that might reveal the deception is sternly repressed and punished—the most terrible punishments are inflicted on men that refuse to carry out the demands of service in the army, that is, of murder.

And wonderful to relate, all this vast potential mass of men, armed with all the powers of human authority, trembles, and hides itself, feeling its fault, and shakes in its very being, and is ready at any minute to crumble and fly into powder, at the appearance of a single man like Drozhin who would not yield to human demands, but obeyed the law of God and was faithful to it.*

And in our day men like Drozhin are not unique; there are thousands, tens of thousands, and their number, and what is better their significance, increases every year and every hour. In Russia we know tens of thousands of men who refused to take the oath of allegiance to the new Tsar, and who regarded military service as murder, inconsistent not merely with Christianity, but with the commonest demands of honor, justice, and morality. We know such men in all the countries of Europe; we know about the Nazarenes who appeared more than fifty years ago in Austria and Servia, and who, from a few hundreds, have now increased to more than thirty thousand, refusing participation in military service in spite of all persecution.

We knew, not long ago, a very highly educated man of perfect independence of thought, an army surgeon, who refused military service because he considered contrary to his conscience service of such an institution as the army, meant only to inflict violence on men and murder

---

* Mr. E. I. Popof in a note says: "In September I sent to one of the newspapers a brief obituary of Drozhin, relating the cause of his imprisonment, sickness, and death, and this obituary was soon reprinted in other periodicals: *Nedyelya* (The Week), No. 36; *Russkiya Vyedomosti*, No. 250; *Saratovsky Listok*, No. 193; and strangely enough, the government, it would seem, was obliged to be satisfied with the promulgation, though unofficial, of the severity with which it punished disobedience to military demands, but at the same time, a few days after the obituary was published, it sent a secret circular to all the newspaper offices, forbidding any mention of this man and his work to be made."

them. But, however important it is that there are many
of these men, and that they are all the time increasing,
it is still more important that the only true way has been
found on which humanity undoubtedly proceeds toward
its emancipation from the chains of evil that bind it,
and that no one and nothing can any longer hinder it,
since no violent efforts for the annihilation of evil are
required for deliverance along this route; it disappears of
itself and melts away as wax in the fire, and all it requires
is only not to take part in it. And in order not to take part
in this evil from which we suffer, we need no especial
intellectual or physical exertions; all it requires is to yield
to our nature, to be good and upright before God and in
our own eyes.

"You wish me to be a murderer and I cannot do this;
both God and my own conscience forbid it. And therefore
do with me what you wish, but I will not kill or prepare
for murder, or assist in it."

Now this simple reply, which every man ought infallibly to make because it proceeds out of the very consciousness of the men of our day, is destroying all the
evils of violence which have so long weighed down the
world. The statement is made that it says this in the
sacred Scriptures: (Rom. xiii. I-7.)—

Let every soul be in subjection to the higher powers:
for there is no power but of God; and the powers that be
are ordained of God. Therefore he that resists the power
withstands the ordinance of God, and they that withstand
shall receive to themselves judgement. For rulers are not
a terror to the good work, but to the evil. And wouldst
thou have no fear of the power? do that which is good,
and thou shall have praise from the same: for he is a
minister of God to thee for good. But if thou do that

which is evil, be afraid; for he bears not the sword in vain: for he is a minister of God, an avenger for wrath to him that does evil. Wherefore you must be in subjection not only because of the wrath, but also for conscience' sake. For for this cause ye pay tribute also; for they are ministers of God's service, attending continually upon this very thing. Render to all their dues: tribute to whom tribute is due; custom to whom custom; fear to whom fear; honor to whom honor.

And therefore it is necessary to be obedient to the authorities. .

But now, this most politic Paul, who was telling the Romans that they must be obedient to the authorities, says quite another thing to the Ephesians:—

Finally, be strong in the Lord, and in the strength of his might. Put on the whole armor of God, that you may be able to stand against the wiles of the devil. For our wrestling is not against flesh and blood, but against the principalities, against the powers, against the worldrulers of the darkness of this age, against the terrestrial spirits of wickedness. (Eph. vi. 10–12).

Paul's advice to the Romans in regard to subjection to the existing authorities can in no wise be reconciled with Christ's words, the whole meaning of which consists in emancipating men from the powers of the world and subjecting them to the power of God alone:—

If the world hates you, you know that it hated me before it hated you (John xv. 18).

If they persecuted me, they will also persecute you (John xv. 20).

If you were of the world, the world would love its own, but because you are not of the world, but I chose you out of the world, therefore the world hates you (John xv. 19).

They will deliver you up to the councils, and in their synagogues they will scourge you, and before governors and kings shall you stand for my sake for a testimony unto them (Matt. x. 18; Mark xiii. 9).

And you shall be hated of all men for my name's sake (Matt. x. 22).

They shall lay their hands on you and shall persecute you, delivering you up to the synagogues and prisons, bringing you before kings and governors for my name's sake (Luke xxi. 12).

Whoever kills you shall think he is offering service unto God. And these things will they do, because they have not known the Father nor me. But these things have I spoken unto you, that when their hour is come, you may remember them, how I told you (John xvi. 2–4).

Fear them not therefore; for there is nothing covered that shall not be revealed; and hid that shall not be known (Matt. x. 26).

And be not afraid of them who kill the body, but are not able to kill the soul, but rather fear him who is able to destroy both soul and body (Matt. x. 28).

The prince of this world has been judged (John xvi. II).

Be of good cheer, I have overcome the world (John xvi. 33).

Christ's whole teaching is a pointing out of the way of emancipation from the power of the world, and Christ, even while He Himself was persecuted, predicted to His disciples that, if they put their faith in His teachings, the world would persecute them. And He advised them to be of good cheer, and not fear their persecutors. But not only did He teach them this by His words; He, by His whole life and His relations to the authorities, gave them an example of how they ought to treat those that wanted to persecute them. Christ not only did not submit to the authorities, but He kept accusing them: He accused the Pharisees of destroying God's law by their human traditions; He accused them of a false observance of the Sabbath, of a false way of sacrificing in the temples; He accused them for all their hypocrisy and cruelty; He accused the cities of Chorazin, Bethsaida, and Capernaum, and He predicted their destruction.

To the question whether He would pay the tribute imposed at His entrance into Capernaum, He said pointedly that His children, that is, His disciples, were free from all tribute, and were not obliged to pay it; and only that He might not offend the tax-collectors, that He might not tempt them to the sin of committing violence, did He command that the stater which was found by chance in the fish, and which did not belong to any one and had not been taken from any one, should be handed over.

To the crafty question whether tribute should be paid to Cæsar, He said:—

"*Render unto Cæsar the things that are Cæsar's, and unto God the things that are God's.*"

In other words, give to Cæsar that which belongs to him and was made by him—money; but God's property, that which God has made and has lodged in you—your soul, your conscience—render up to no one except to God, and therefore do not do for Cæsar anything that God has forbidden. And this answer astonished them all by its boldness. and at the same time by its inevitableness.*

---

* Not merely utter misconception of Christ's teaching, but complete unwillingness to comprehend it, can permit the astonishing misinterpretation whereby the words *to Cæsar the things that are*

When Christ was brought before Pilate as a conspira-
tor who was stirring up the people and commanding them
not to pay tribute to Caesar (Luke xxiii. 2), He, saying
what He found it necessary to say, astonished and disturbed all the functionaries by paying no attention to
their questions, refusing to answer them. And for this
accusing of the authorities and disobedience to them He
was condemned and put to death.

The whole history of the suffering and death of Christ
is nothing else than the history of those calamities to
which every man must be subjected who follows Christ's
example in obedience to God, and disobedience to the
powers of the world. And now they would persuade us
that all Christ's teaching must not only be amended, but
changed, in consequence of inconsiderate and crafty
words written by Paul to the Romans.

But above and beyond the fact that Paul's words are
contrary to Christ's life and teachings, with every desire
to be subject to the authorities, as Paul commands, not
out of fear but in accordance with conscience, this has
become in our time utterly impossible. Passing by the
inner contradiction between Christianity and subjection
to the authorities—subjection to the authorities, not out
of fear, but in accordance with conscience, has become

Cæsar's, are taken to mean the unavoidability of subjection to
Cæsar. In the first place, there is no question of subjection; in the
second place, if Christ had recognized the obligation of a money
tribute and therefore of subjection, He would have said frankly,
"Yes, it must be paid," but He said *render unto Cæsar what is
his*—that is to say, money—but your life to God; and by these last
words He not only did not encourage subjection to the authorities,
but on the contrary He showed that in everything that belongs to
God one ought not to be subject to Cæsar.—AUTHOR'S NOTE.

impossible in our time, because, in consequence of
the universal spread of knowledge, power as something
worthy of respect, something lofty, and above all something definite and complete, has been utterly annihilated,
and there is no possibility of rehabilitating it. Now it
was a good thing, not from fear but from conscience, to
be subject to authority when men saw in authority what
the Romans saw, an emperor-God; or as the Chinese see
in the God-inspired son of heaven; or as in the Middle
Ages, yes, up to the very Revolution, in kings or emperors,
God-anointed sovereigns; or as not long since here in
Russia the common people saw in the Tsar a terrestrial
god; when men did not imagine tsars, kings, and emperors
as anything else than gods in supreme positions performing wise and glorious actions: but, as it is now, when,
notwithstanding all the endeavors of the authorities and
all their partizans, and even of their subjects, to restore
the fascination of power, education, history, experience,
the common intercourse of men, have destroyed this
glamour so that it is as impossible ever to restore it as to
restore the ice melted in the spring, and just as impossible
to build anything substantial on it as it is to go in a sledge
on melting ice and an opening river.

What is to be done now when all, with the exception
of the most boorish and uncultivated, who, all the time
decreasing in numbers, know very well what kind of
depraved people were Louis XI of France, Elizabeth of
England, John IV of Russia, Catherine, Napoleon, Nicholas I, who reigned and disposed of the fates of millions;
and who reigned, not in consequence of any holy, inevitable law, as it used to be thought, but simply because
these people were able by various deceptions, tricks,
crimes, so to strengthen their power that they could not

be cast down, punished, or expelled, as afterward Charles I, Louis XVI, Maximilian of Mexico, Louis Philippe, and others have been.

What is to be done now, when all know that the kings and emperors reigning at the present time not only are not extraordinary, saintly, great, wise men engaged in advancing the interests of their peoples, but on the contrary are for the most part badly educated, ill informed, boastful, depraved, often very stupid and wicked men, occupied not at all with the well-being of their subjects, but with their personal interests, and especially with the desperate task of bolstering up their tottering power, maintained only by chicanery and fraud.

But over and above the fact that men now see the stuff which make the sovereigns who used to seem to them exceptional beings, that men now have looked behind the scenes of this theatrical representation and find it impossible ever to re-create the illusion they used to have, they see and know this also, that these sovereigns do not really reign themselves, but in constitutional monarchies the power is wielded by members of chambers and ministers who have obtained their positions by intrigues and bribes, and in non-constitutional monarchies by wives, ministries, flatterers, and all kinds of assistants, who manage to attach themselves to their courts.

How can a man feel any respect for power and submit himself to it, not out of fear, but in accordance with his conscience, when he knows that this power is nothing existent apart from himself, but is the outcome of the intrigue, the chicanery of men, and is constantly passing from one person to another. A man who knows this not only cannot conscientiously submit to the power, but he cannot help striving to destroy the existent power and get into possession of it himself; that is to say, having crept into power, he grasps as much as he can. This is what happens in reality.

The power of which Paul spoke, the power to which one may submit conscientiously, has already outlived its time. It no longer exists. Like the ice, it has melted and can no longer support anything. The formerly firm and solid surface of the river has become a liquid, and in order to go on it the sledge and horses are no longer available, you must have a boat and oars. Just exactly in the same way the scale of life in consequence of enlightenment has changed to such a degree that power, in the sense in which it was formerly understood, has no longer any place in our world, but remains a coarse expression of violence and deception. But it is impossible to submit to violence and deception "not because of the wrath but for conscience' sake."

"But how not submit to the authorities? If one does not submit to the authorities, there will be terrible misfortunes; evil men will torment, oppress, and kill the righteous."

I also say, "How avoid submitting to the authorities, how make up our minds not to submit to the authorities, to any undoubted power, that from which we cannot escape, under which we always find ourselves, and the demands of which we know unquestionably, unmistakably?"

It is said, "How make up our minds not to submit to the authorities?"

What powers? In Catherine's time, when Pugatchof*

---

* Sophia of Anhalt, married under the name of Catherine to

was in revolt, half of the people clung to him and were under his power. Which power, then, should one have submitted to—Catherine's or Pugatchof's? Yes, and in the reign of that same Catherine who robbed her husband of his power though they had taken an oath to obey him as Tsar, which should we have felt obliged to obey? Peter III, as before, or Catherine?

Not one Russian Tsar, from Peter I till Nicholas I inclusively, mounted the throne in such a way as to leave it evident whose power one must submit to. To whom should one have submitted—Peter I or Sophia, or Ioann, Peter's elder brother? Sophia had equal rights to the throne, and the proof of it is found in the fact that after her women reigned who had less claims to the throne— the two Catherines, Anna, Elizabeth. Whose power should one have submitted to after Peter, when courtiers alone placed on the throne a soldier's wife, the mistress of the minister—Menshikof, Sheremetief—Peter—Catherine I? And how about Peter II, then Anna and Elizabeth, and finally Catherine II, who had no more right to the throne than Pugatchof, while in the time of her reign one legitimate heir—Ioann—was kept in prison and was killed by her orders, while another legitimate heir was Paul, a youth who had attained his majority? And whose authority should one have submitted to, the authority of

---

Peter III, found his brutality unendurable, and is believed to have caused his death. In 1774, a Cossack, Emilian Pugatchof, raised an army of runaway serfs, robbers, and pirates, and proclaimed that he was the Tsar Peter III. The troops sent against him joined him, and people were inclined to believe his claim. Catherine sent Alexander Bibikof to conquer him. The impostor fled to the southern Volga, but was at last hemmed in and surrendered by his own troops, and was cruelly executed at Moscow.—ED.

Paul or of Alexander at the time when the conspirators who killed Paul were as yet only planning to kill him? And whose power should one have submitted to, Constantine or Nicholas, when Nicholas accepted the power from Constantine?

All history is the history of one power balanced against another, as well in Russia as in all other countries. Moreover, even not in the time of civil war and the suppression of certain monarchs and the substitution of them by others, in the most peaceful times, it was necessary to submit to Arakcheyef who had usurped the power, or to strive to overturn him and persuade the Tsar of the inability of his ministers. Men do not dispose of supreme power, but of its servants; must one submit to these servants when their demands are evidently wicked and harmful?

So that, however much we might wish to submit to authority, it is impossible, since there is no one definite earthly power, and all earthly powers totter, change, and are at war with one another. How and where is any power genuine? And so what power shall one submit to?

But besides the fact that the power which demands submission to itself is doubtful, and we may not know whether it is genuine or not, this dubious power demands of us no equal, no harmless actions, such as the building of pyramids, temples, palaces, or even service of the powerful ones of this world and satisfying their whims and luxuries. It might be possible to do that.

But this questionable power demands of us the thing most terrible to man—murder, the preparation for it, the acknowledgment of our readiness for it; demands an action which is clearly contrary to the law of God and therefore destroys the soul. Can I, on account of submission to the accidental, vacillating, contradictory human power, forget the demands of the one power of God which is so clearly and unquestionably known to me, and thus destroy my soul?

"One must submit to the authorities."

"Yes, one most submit to the authorities," say I also, "only not to the authority of an emperor, a king, a president, a parliament, or their appointed chiefs, whom I don't know and whom I have nothing in common with, but to the authority of God, whom I do know, and with whom I live, from whom I received my soul, and to whom I shall render up my soul tomorrow."

It is said, "There will be misfortunes if we do not submit to the authorities."

And this is the truth if by "authority" is meant genuine authority, and not human deception, which is called power, authority. These misfortunes exist, and terrible, horrible misfortunes which we shall experience for the precise reason that we do not submit to the power of God—the one that is free from doubt, that has been revealed to us both in the Scriptures and in our hearts. We say: Our misfortunes consist in this, that the rich and the idler flourish, and the poor and industrious go to the wall; in this, that the people are deprived of land, and therefore must work like galley slaves in factories, making things which are of no use to them; in this, that the people get intoxicated on the vodka which the government sells to them; in this, that young men go as soldiers, become dissipated, carry diseases, and are separated from a simple life of labor; in this, that the rich sit on the judgment seat and the poor lie in prisons; in this, that the people are stupefied in schools and churches, and functionaries and the clergy are rewarded for it by money taken from the people; in this, that all the energies of the people—men and money—are expended in wars and on the army, and this army is put into the hands of leaders, who, by means of it, suppress everything that is not consonant with their advantage.

These misfortunes are terrible. But what is the source of them? And on what are they based?

Simply on the fact that men do not submit to the one true power and its law which is inscribed on their hearts, but submit to artificial human regulations which they call the law. If men submitted to the one true power of God and His law, they would not take upon themselves the obligation of killing their fellow-men, they would not go as soldiers, and they would not contribute money for the support and hire of the army.

And if there were no army, there would be none of those cruelties and injustices which it entails. Only by means of the army can one establish and support that order, whereby all the land is in the hands of those that do not work on it, while those that work on it are deprived of it; only by means of the army could they take away the labors of the poor and give them to the rich; only by means of the army could they intentionally stupefy the people, and deprive them of the possibility of true enlightenment.

The army consists of soldiers—we ourselves are the soldiers! If we refuse to be soldiers, there will be nothing of the sort.

The position of people is now such that nothing can change except obedience to a true, and not a false, authority.

"But this new state of things without an army, without government, will be many times worse than that in which we now are," is the reply to this.

"Worse for whom?" I ask. "For those that are now in authority, for one one-hundredth of the whole people? In truth, for this part of the people it will be worse. But not for the working population, deprived of land and the products of their labor, simply because for these nine-tenths of the people their position cannot be worse than what it is now."

But by what right do we suppose that the position of the people will be worse off from the fact that they become obedient to the law against murder, revealed to them by God, and put into their hearts? Why, to say that every thing in this world will become worse, if the men in it obey the law which was given to them by God for their guidance in this world, is equivalent to saying that it would be worse if men would use a given machine, not according to their fancy, but in accordance with the direction for its use given by the one who selected and set up the machine.

There was a time when humanity lived like the wild beasts, and every one took for his own life all he could, robbing any one else of what he wanted, slaying and slaughtering his neighbors.

Then came the time when men coalesced into societies, into kingdoms, and began to divide off into nations; defending themselves from other nations. Men became less beastlike, but nevertheless they considered it not only possible, but even indispensable, to kill their enemies external and internal.

But now the time is coming, indeed it has already come, when men, according to Christ's words, are entering into a new state of the brotherhood of all men, into that new state long ago foretold by the prophets when all men should be taught of God, should unlearn the art of war, beat their swords into plowshares and their spears into pruning-hooks, and enter into the kingdom of God, the kingdom of unity and peace.

This state was foretold by the prophets; but Christ's teaching showed how and by whom it could be realized, but especially by brotherly unity, one of the first phenomena of which was to be the annihilation of violence. And the importance of annihilating violence is already recognized by men, and therefore this condition becomes as unavoidable as formerly after the wild state came the monarchical state.

Humanity in our time is passing through the birth-pangs of this approaching kingdom of God, and this travail will infallibly end with birth. But the dawning of this new life does not come of itself; its approach depends on us. We must do it. The kingdom of God is within us.

And in order to bring about the kingdom of God within us, I repeat it, we need no special intellectual or physical powers; we need only to be what we are, what God made us—that is to say, reasonable and, above all, righteous beings, heeding the voice of our consciences.

"But that is the very difficulty—men are not reasonable and are not righteous beings," I hear said by those who, in order to have the right to be wicked, declare that the whole human race is bad, and that this is not only the true revealed religious truth, but that taught by experience. "Men are all wicked and unreasonable," they assert, "and therefore it is indispensable that the reasonable and righteous people maintain order."

Now, if all men are lacking in reason and are bad,

where are we to find the reasonable and the good? and if there are such, then how shall we know them? and if we know them, then by what means shall we—and who will be these *we?*—place them at the head of other men? But even if we succeed in placing these exceptionally reasonable and righteous men at the head of the others, then will not these reasonable and righteous men cease to be such if they began to use violence and punish the unreasonable and wicked? And what is most important, you say that in order to prevent certain robbers, thieves, and murderers from maltreating and killing men, you institute courts, the police, the army, which will certainly maltreat and kill men, whose obligation will consist wholly in doing this, and you will induce all men to these institutions. But, you see, by such a method you really exchange a small and suppositious evil for a great universal evil everywhere consummated. In order to resist certain imaginary murderers you compel all men to be really murderers. And so I repeat, that, for the establishment of a fraternal bond among men, there is no need of any special effort, either intellectual or physical, but only to be what God has made us, reasonable and righteous beings, and to act in accordance with these qualities.

It does not fall to each one of us to suffer the experience which Drozhin went through—and if it does befall us, God help us to endure it without changing to Him; but whether we wish it or not, to each one of us, even if we live in a country where there is no military obligation or if we are not accustomed to obey it, to each of us is given the chance, in one way or another, to submit, though it may be in lower and easier forms, to the experience, and of willy-nilly taking his stand on the side of the oppressors and even becoming one of them, or on the side of the oppressed and helping them to bear their trials or even sharing them. To every one of us, even if we do not take a direct part in the persecutions against the latter-day martyrs, such as emperors, ministers, governors, judges, who sign the decrees for the torture of these martyrs, or such a still more direct part in their tortures as is taken by the jailers, guards, and executioners—to each one of us, nevertheless, is offered the chance of taking the most active part in these deeds by the judgments which we pronounce upon them in print, in letters, and in conversations.

Often, simply because we are too lazy to think of the meaning of such a phenomenon, simply because we do not wish to disturb our comfort by a lively representation of what these men must experience who, for their justice, candor, and philanthropy, are suffering in jails and exile, we, not thinking of what we are saying repeat the criticism which we have heard or read: "What is to be done? They deserve it. These are dangerous fanatics; the government must put an end to such performances"—or words to that effect, which uphold the persecutors, and increase the sufferings of the victims. All of us think a dozen times of some action, of the spending of a certain sum of money, of the breaking up or building of a house; but to speak a word seems so unimportant that we speak for the most part without thinking. But meantime speech is the most significant of all the actions which we can do.

From words grows public opinion. And public opinion alone is higher than all the kings and rulers, directs all the acts of men. And therefore every one of our judgements on behavior like Drozhin's may be the act of God bringing about the coming of the kingdom of God, the brotherhood of men, helping those advanced men who give their lives to bring it about, and it may be an act hostile to God, opposing Him, and coöperating in the torture of those men who are giving themselves to His service.

Drozhin, in his diary, relates the cruel effect on him of such a frivolous and God-opposing word. He tells how in the first period of his imprisonment, when, notwithstanding all his physical sufferings and humiliations, he still continued to experience a joyous, calming consciousness that he was doing his duty, how at this time he was affected by a letter from another revolutionist who, out of *love for him,* urged him to take pity on himself, to recant and fulfil the demands of the authorities—take the oath of allegiance and serve in the army.

Evidently this young man, with revolutionary inclinations and according to the ordinary code of the revolutionists fully admitted to their ranks, according to the principle, *the end justifies the means*—all compromises with conscience—did not in the least comprehend the religious feelings which guided Drozhin, and therefore wrote him thoughtlessly, advising him not to destroy himself as a weapon useful for the revolution, and to fulfil all the demands of the authorities. These words, it would seem, ought not to have any special significance, but nevertheless Drozhin writes that they robbed him of his peace of mind and that they made him ill.

And this is comprehensible. All men who move humanity forward, and who are the first and only ones to enter upon that path whereby soon all will be traveling, find it no easy task to get started, but are always met with suffering and inward struggle. The inner voice invites them along the new way; all attachments, traditions, weaknesses—everything pulls them back. And at such moments of unstable equilibrium every word of encouragement or of discouragement has enormous influence. The most powerful man may be hindered by a child when this man is putting forth all his forces in order to move a weight beyond his strength. Drozhin experienced a terrible despair at these seemingly unimportant words of his friend, and he recovered his calmness only when he received a letter from his friend Izyumchenko, who was joyously bearing the same lot, and who expressed a firm conviction in the propriety of what they were doing.*

And, therefore, however far we personally may stand from any action of this kind, we always involuntarily participate in them, we have our influence on them by our relation to them, by our judgment of them.

If we take the standpoint of the revolutionary friend, if we reckon that, owing to the fact that maybe sometime, somewhere, we may be in a condition to act on the external conditions of life, we may and must decline the first demands of conscience. We not only do not moderate the sufferings and struggles of men who are rushing to the service of God, but we are also preparing these sufferings of the internal discord for all those that have to decide a dilemma in life. But to decide this comes to all.

And, therefore, all of us, however far we stand from such events, have a share in them through our opinions and judgments. And an inadvertent, frivolous-spoken word may be the cause of the keenest sufferings for the

---

* This friend, for the same kind of refusal to take part in military service, was incarcerated in Kursk, in the city jail. Now, while I am writing this, he is shut up, without permission to see any one whoever, in the strongest *sekret*, or dungeon, of the Moscow forwarding prison, on his way to the government of Tobolsk, where he has been exiled by the emperor's decision.—AUTHOR'S NOTE.

best people in the world. It is impossible to be too careful of the use of this weapon. *By thy words art thou justified and by thy words art thou condemned.*

But many of us are called to take part in such events, not by words alone, but also far more directly. I refer to the clerks who, in one way or another, take part in those hopeless persecutions which only strengthen the movement, such as the government institutes against men like Drozhin. I speak of the participants in these persecutions, beginning with the emperor, the ministers, the judges, the procurers, down to the jailers and guards who torture these martyrs. Here all of you, participants in these persecutions, know that this man whom you are torturing is not only no criminal, but an exceptionally good man, that he is tortured because he wishes with all the forces of his soul to be good; you know simply that he is young, that he has friends, a mother, that he loves you and pardons you. And him you may shut up in prison, strip to the skin, starve, deprive of food, drink, sleep, prevent from meeting his relations and friends.

How can you, O emperor, who signed such an ukase; O minister, procurer, prison nachalnik, jailer, sit down to your dinner, knowing that he is lying on a cold floor, that, full of torments, he is weeping over your wrath; how can you caress your child, how can you think of God, of death which will bring you to Him?

However you may pretend to be the executioners of unchangeable laws, you are simply men, and good men, and you are sorry, and we are sorry for you, and only in this pity and love to one another is our life.

You say need compels us to serve in this capacity. Now you know that is not true. You know that there is no poverty, that the word is conventional, that what is poverty for you is luxury for another; you know that you can find another service—one in which you will not have to persecute people, especially such people! You see just as the prophets were persecuted, then Christ, then His disciples, so always those that love men and lead them straight forward to their good have been, and are still, persecuted. Thus, how can you escape being participants in these persecutions?

It is horrible to torture a bird, an animal. How much more horrible to torture a young man, a good, pure youth, filled with love for his fellows, and wishing them well! It is horrible to be a participant in this deed, and above all to be a participant all vainly—to destroy his body, yourselves, your souls, and at the same time not only fail to stop the accomplishment of the work of bringing in the kingdom of God, but, on the other hand, against your will to assist in its triumph!

It is coming and is already at hand.

ON THE NEGRO QUESTION

(Letter to V. Tchertkoff)

THANK you very much for sending me your biography of Garrison.

Reading it, I lived again through the spring of my awakening to true life. While reading Garrison's speeches and articles I vividly recalled to mind the spiritual joy which I experienced twenty years ago, when I found out that the law of non-resistance—to which I had been inevitably brought by the recognition of the Christian teaching in its full meaning, and which revealed to me the great joyous ideal to be realised in Christian life—was even as far back as the forties not only recognised and proclaimed by Garrison (about Ballou I learnt later), but also placed by him at the foundation of his practical activity in the emancipation of the slaves.

My joy was at the time mingled with bewilderment as to how it was that this great Gospel truth, fifty years ago explained by Garrison, could have been so hushed up that I had now to express it as something new.

My bewilderment was especially increased by the circumstances that not only people antagonistic to the progress of mankind, but also the most advanced and progressive men, were either completely indifferent to this law, or actually opposed to the promulgation of that which lies at the foundation of all true progress.

But as time went on it became clearer and clearer to me that the general indifference and opposition which were then expressed, and still continue to be expressed— pre-eminently amongst political workers—towards this law of non-resistance are merely symptoms of the great significance of this law.

"The motto upon our banner," wrote Garrison in the midst of his activity, "has been from the commencement of our moral warfare 'OUR COUNTRY IS THE WORLD; OUR COUNTRYMEN ARE ALL MANKIND.' We trust that it will be our only epitaph. Another motto we have chosen is, 'UNIVERSAL EMANCIPATION.' Up to this time we have limited its application to those who in this country are held by Southern taskmasters as marketable commodities, goods and chattels, and implements of husbandry. Henceforth we shall use it in its widest latitude—the emancipation of our whole race from the dominion of man, from the thraldom of self, from the government of brute force, from the bondage of sin, and the bringing it under the dominion of God, the control of an inward spirit, the government of the law of love. . . ."

Garrison, as a men enlightened by the Christian teaching, having begun with the practical aim of strife against slavery, very soon understood that the cause of slavery was not the casual temporary seizure by the Southerners of a few millions of negroes, but the ancient and universal recognition, contrary to the Christian teaching, of the right of coercion on the part of certain people in regard to certain others. A pretext for recognising this right has always been that men regarded it as possible to eradicate or diminish evil by brute force, *i.e.*, also by evil. Having once realised this fallacy, Garrison put forward against slavery neither the suffering of slaves, nor the cruelty of slaveholders, nor the social equality ot men, but the eternal Christian law of refraining from opposing evil by violence; *i.e.*, of "non-resistance." Garrison understood that which the most advanced among the fighters against slavery did not understand: that the only irrefuatble argument against slavery is the denial of the right of any man over the liberty of another under any conditions whatsoever.

The Abolitionists endeavoured to prove that slavery was unlawful, disadvantageous, cruel: that it depraved men, and so on; but the defenders of slavery in their turn proved the untimeliness and danger of emancipation, and the evil results liable to follow it. Neither the one nor the other could convince his opponent. Whereas Garrison, understanding that the slavery of the negroes was only a particular instance of universal coercion, put forward a general principle with which it was impossible nót to agree—the principle that under no pretext has any man the right to dominate, *i.e.*, to use coercion over his fellows. Garrison did not so much insist on the right of negroes to be free as he denied the right of any man whatsoever, or of any body of men, forcibly to coerce another man in any way. For the purpose of combating slavery he advanced the principle of struggle against all the evil of the world.

This principle advanced by Garrison was irrefutable, but it affected and even overthrew all the foundations of established social order, and therefore those who valued their position in that existing order were frightened at its announcement, and still more at its application to life;

they endeavoured to ignore it, to elude it; they hoped to attain their object without the declaration of the principle of non-resistance to evil by violence, and that application of it to life which would destroy, as they thought, all orderly organisation of human life. The result of this evasion of the recognition of the unlawfulness of coercion was that fratricidal war which, having externally solved the slavery question, introduced into the life of the American people the new—perhaps still greater—evil of that corruption which accompanies every war.

Meanwhile the substance of the question remained unsolved, and the same problem, only in a new form, now stands before the people of the United States. Formerly the question was how to free the negroes from the violence of the slaveholders; now the question is how to free the negroes from the violence of all the whites, and the whites from the violence of all the blacks.

The solution of this problem in a new form is to be accomplished certainly not by the lynching of negroes, nor by any skilful and liberal measures of American politicians, but only by the application to life of that same principle which was proclaimed by Garrison half a century ago.

The other day in one of the most progressive periodicals I read the opinion of an educated and intelligent writer, expressed with complete assurance in its correctness, that the recognition by me of the principle of non-resistance to evil by violence is a lamentable and somewhat comic delusion which, taking into consideration my old age and certain merits, can only be passed over in indulgent silence.

Exactly the same attitude towards this question did I encounter in my conversation with the remarkably intelligent and progressive American Bryan. He also, with the evident intention of gently and courteously showing me my delusion, asked me how I explained my strange principle of non-resistance to evil by violence, and as usual he brought forward the argument, which seems to every-one irrefutable, of the brigand who kills or violates a child. I told him that I recognise non-resistance to evil by violence because, having lived seventy-five years, I have never, except in discussions, encountered that fantastic brigand, who, before my eyes desired to kill or violate a child, but that perpetually I did and do see not one but millions of brigands using violence towards children and women and men and old people and all the labourers in the name of the recognised right of violence over one's fellows. When I said this my kind interlocutor, with his naturally quick perception, not giving me time to finsh, laughed, and recognised that my argument was satisfactory.

No one has seen the fantastic brigand, but the world, groaning under violence, lies before everyone's eyes. Yet no one sees, nor desires to see, that the strife which can liberate man from violence is not a strife with the fantastic brigand, but with those actual brigands who practise violence over men.

Non-resistance to evil by violence really means only that the mutual interaction of rational beings upon each other should consist not in violence (which can be only admitted in relation to lower organisms deprived of reason) but in rational persuasion; and that, consequently, towards this substitution of rational persuasion for coercion all those should strive who desire to further the welfare of mankind.

It would seem quite clear that in the course of the last

century, fourteen million people were killed, and that now
the labour and lives of millions of men are spent on wars
necessary to no one, and that all the lands is in the hands
of those who do not work on it, and that all the produce
of human labour is swallowed up by those who do not
work, and that all the deceits which reign in the world
exist only because violence is allowed for the purpose of
suppressing that which appears evil to some people, and
that therefore one should endeavour to replace violence
by persuasion. That this may become possible it is necessary first of all to renounce the right of coercion.

Strange to say, the most progressive people of our circle
regard it as dangerous to repudiate the right of violence
and to endeavour to replace it by persuasion. These people, having decided that it is impossible to persuade a
brigand not to kill a child, think it also impossible to
persuade the working men not to take the land and the
produce of their labour from those, who do not work, and
therefore these people find it necessary to coerce the
labourers.

So that however sad it is to say so, the only explanation
of the non-understanding of the significance of the principle of non-resistance to evil by violence consists in this,
that the conditions of human life are so distorted that
those who examine the principle of non-resistance imagine
that its adaptation to life and the substitution of persuasion for coercion would destroy all possibility of that
social organisation and of those conveniences of life which
they enjoy.

But the change need not be feared; the principle of non-
resistance is not a principle of coercions but of concord
and love, and therefore it cannot be made coercively
binding upon men. The principle of non-resistance to evil

by violence, which consists in the substitution of persuasion for brute force, can be only accepted voluntarily, and in whatever measure it is freely accepted by men and applied to life—*i.e.*, according to the measure in which people renounce violence and establish their relations upon rational persuasion—only in that measure is true progress in the life of men accomplished.

Therefore, whether men desire it or not, it is only in the name of this principle that they can free themselves from the enslavement and oppression of each other Whether men desire it or not, this principle lies at the basis of all true improvement in the life of men which has taken place and is still to take place.

Garrison was the first to proclaim this principle as a rule for the organisation of the life of men. In this is his great merit. If at the time he did not attain the pacific liberation of the slaves in America, he indicated the way of liberating men in general from the power of brute force.

Therefore Garrison will for ever remain one of the greatest reformers and promoters of true human progress.

THE INEVITABLE REVOLUTION

FOREWORD

know that very many people, particularly among those who are called educated, will glance at this writing of mine and, understanding what the question is about, will simply shrug their shoulders, smile contemptuously and cease to read further. Still the old "non-resistance," they will say, how is it that he doesn't weary of it?

I know that this will be so, firstly, for people, called learned, who know that they are not in agreement with what I say; and secondly, for people who are to be found ardently pursuing governmental or revolutionary activities, for whom this writing of mine will present a dilemma: to acknowledge as nonsensical either all that they are doing and have been doing for years and for the sake of which they have sacrificed so much, or that which I say. This will be so for many so-called educated people, who in the most important questions of life are accustomed not to thinking for themselves and working out their own opinions, but to professing the creed of the surrounding majority, engaged in justifying their situation. But I know that all people who think for themselves and also the majority of working people, who have not been perverted

by the piling up of empty, false knowledge, which is called
in our time scientific, will be with me. I know this because
in our time for people of independent thought as for the vast
majority of working folk, the foolishness and immorality
productive of unnecessary suffering for them themselves
become more and more apparent with every day. These and
others, already in our time, cannot but acknowledge in the
end this truth, simple and now sharp clear to the eye, that
for the betterment of life one thing only is necessary, to stop
doing that which causes this suffering.

I

It would seem that those external conditions in which man
finds himself in our time ought to have led him to the highest
pitch of happiness. Land, suitable for cultivation and
accessible to people, is so plentiful that all men could, with
a surplus left over, use it for a prosperous life for everyone.
Means of communicating thought and means of transport
(printing, posts and telegraph, railways, steam and electric
engines, aeroplanes and so forth), these are the means to
what is most conducive to human well-being, the means to
unity, leading to a high degree of perfectibility. Means of
struggle with nature, lightening the burden of labour, have
been invented to such an extent that it would appear that
everybody would be able to satisfy their needs fully without
the hardship of labour depriving them of leisure and ruining
their health. Everything exists to increase the well-being of
people, but instead of this the people of our time suffer, are
tormented in body and soul as they have never in previous
times suffered and been tormented, and these sufferings and
torments grow with every year.

It will be said that suffering always characterises the life of men. Yes, suffering is characteristic, but not those forms of suffering which the people of our time are now suffering. External sufferings are characteristic of human life, every kind of illness, floods, fires, earthquakes, droughts are also characteristic, and the periodic sufferings from intermittent wars or the cruelties of some rulers, but not those sufferings which everyone now endures without cease. Everyone suffers now: both those who wield power by direct force or wealth, and those who with continuing hatred endure their dependence on the powerful and wealthy. And they all suffer now not from external causes, not from earthquakes and floods, not from Neros, Ivan IVs, Genghis Khans and so on, but suffer from one another, suffer as a result of everyone being divided into two hostile, mutually detesting camps: the ones suffer from dependence on and hatred of those who rule over them, the others suffer from fear and feelings of contempt and ill will towards those over whom they rule, and others again from consciousness of the precariousness of their situation, from those endless utmost cruelties which are engendered and erupt from time to time, but without ever stopping the smouldering conflict between the two mutually detesting camps.

They suffer especially cruelly mainly because both they and the others in the depth of their souls know that the cause of their suffering is in themselves, that it ought to have been possible to free themselves from those sufferings inflicted on them by themselves, but it appears to the one and the other that they cannot do this, that it is not they who are guilty but their enemies, and as they attack one another with great animosity so do they more and more aggravate their situation.

So the cause of the disastrous situation in which mankind now finds itself is a cause absolutely particular to, exclusive to, characteristic of our time alone.

II

From the earliest known times of men's collective life, we know that men have always united with one another, through their family, tribal, exchange, commercial ties, and still more by the subjection of the many to one or several rulers. Such subjection of the ones to the others, of the majority to the minority, was so common to all peoples and existed for such a long time that everyone, both those who ruled over the many and those who were in subjection to them, considered such an arrangement of life inevitable, natural and the only one possible for the collective life of men. The rulers considered that being destined by God himself to rule over the peoples, they had an obligation to try to the best of their abilities to use their power for a tranquil, peaceful and happy life for their subjects. And this was voiced many times in all the teachings of sages and also in the religious teachings of the most ancient and numerous sections of mankind: in Tao-Teh-King and the laws of Manu. The subjects too, considered such an arrangement of life foreordained of God, inevitable, and therefore obediently subjected themselves to the power, and supported it for the possibility of the maximum enjoyment of freedom in relation with those who like themselves were dependent subjects. In such wise was this arrangement of life based on violence. And so mankind lived for centuries. It was so in India and in China; it was so in Greece and Rome and in medieval Europe; and however repugnant to the consciousness of mankind in our time, so it continues to be for the majority of men now too. Both in

Europe and in the East, men have for centuries lived as subjects and rulers, and they continue to live now, not admitting for the majority any possibility of any means of unity whatever other than violence. Nevertheless, in all the religious teachings of the ancient world: in Brahminism, in Buddhism, in Taoism, in Confucianism, and also in the teachings of the Greek and Roman sages, side by side with the maintenance of the power of those ruling by violence, there was always expressed from different sides yet another teaching, namely that the love of men for one another is the best means of human intercourse because it provides for men their greatest well-being. This view has been expressed variously and with varying degrees of clarity in the different teachings of the East, but for nineteen hundred years down to our own time this view has been expressed with striking and definite clarity in Christianity. Christianity pointed out to men not only that love is the means of human intercourse giving them well-being, but also that love is the highest law of the life of men and that therefore, the law of love is incompatible with the previous arrangement of life based on violence.

The chief significance of Christianity and that which distinguishes it from all previous teachings is that it proclaimed the law of love as the highest law of life in such a way as to admit of no exceptions and *always* requiring the obligation to fulfill it; and so pointed to those common digressions from the law of love which side by side with the acknowledged blessings of love were permitted in the previous arrangement of life, founded on the power of rulers and maintained by violence. Under the previous arrangement of life, violence, including therein killing in self-defence or defence of one's kin or fatherland, to inflict punishment on criminals and so forth, was an inevitable

condition of social life. Christianity, however, putting love
as the highest law of life, acknowledging all men as equals,
advocating the forgiveness of all injuries, insults, violence,
and the returning of good for evil, could not permit in any
circumstances the violence of man against man, which always
in its ultimate development demanded even killing. Thus
Christianity in its true meaning, acknowledging love as the
fundamental law of life, directly and definitely repudiated
that very violence, which lay at the base of every previous
arrangement of life.

Such was and is the chief significance of Christianity. But
people, who adopted Christianity and for centuries lived in
the complex governmental arrangements founded on
violence, adopted Christianity partly not understanding its
significance at all, and partly understanding, but trying to
conceal it from themselves and other people; and took from
Christianity only that which was not repugnant to their
established mode of life. There thus sprang up on the original
Christianity the teaching of the church, which united the
teaching of Christ with the ancient Hebrew teaching,
and which by various dogmas and decrees absolutely alien
to Christianity so skillfully concealed the essence of
Christianity that violence, so obviously incompatible
with Christianity in its true meaning, came to be considered
both by those suffering coercion and those imposing it not
only not repugnant to the Christian teaching of love, but
completely lawful and in accordance with Christian teaching.

Men lived, submitting to acts of violence and performing
them, and side by side with this advocating the teaching of
love, in obvious contradiction to violence. This inner
contradiction has always dwelt in the Christian world and in
accordance with the intellectual development of men
became ever more and more obvious. In the other non-

Christian larger half of mankind—Egypt, India, China (I do not speak of the Mahometan world, which lived by a teaching proceeding out of Christianity) where there was also—in Brahmanism, in Buddhism, in Confucianism, and in Taoism—exactly proclaimed the teaching of love between men, living under the law of violence, the contradiction between these two incompatibles began to make its appearance but not so sharply and powerfully as in Christianity. But, although in the religious teachings of the East, in India, China this inner contradiction, the incompatibility of the law of violence and the law of love was not indicated with such clarity as it was in Christianity, in the non-Christian world, too, it was and is being worked out, it has grown ever more and more clear to men that change is inevitable from the old outlived principle of violence to the new law of love, entering from various sides the consciousness of men.

III

The recognition of the law of love entered more and more into the consciousness of men, obliging them to replace violence, but in the meantime life continued to proceed on the previous basis.

It continued thus for centuries. But there came a time when the truth that love is the highest law of man's life and that therefore violence, incompatible with love, cannot be the highest law of life, the truth, so characteristic of the spiritual nature of man and expressed more or less clearly in all religious teachings and particularly clearly in Christianity, notwithstanding all the efforts the rulers and their assistants, entered the consciousness of men ever more and more and in our time has already begun more or less consciously to reach the majority of men. As it is impossible to extinguish a fire by heaping it up with shavings, so too was it impossible to smother, once it had arisen in men's consciousness and had been so clearly expressed in all religious teachings and being so near to the heart of mankind, the truth that the unity characteristic of man's nature is a unity based on love, and not on violence, on fear. And this truth, not, it is true, in its direct expression, but in the various situations and demands arising out of this truth, more and more frequently makes itself felt in the world as a whole, seeking its application to life. Thus, among the Christian peoples this truth appeared earlier than in other countries in the demands for equality of civil rights, equality of men (albeit only from a single government), in the abolition of slavery, in the recognition of the rights of women, in the teachings of socialism, communism, anarchism; this truth was manifest in the great variety of societies and conferences for peace, is manifest too in the many so-called sects, both Christian and Mahometan, which directly repudiate the law of violence and seek to free themselves from subjection to it.

In the Christian world and in the Mahometan world close to it, this truth has entered more clearly into the consciousness of men, but also in the Far East this truth has not ceased to do its work. Thus even in India and in China, where violence is sanctioned by religious law, violence and castes in India are in our time now presented to men as something out of keeping with human nature.

Men all over the world, although still not acknowledging the law of love in all its significance, already feel the complete impossibility of continuing in a life according to the previous law of violence and seek another basis for mutual intercourse, compatible with the spiritual growth of mankind.

There is only one such basis and thousands of years ago it was already expressed by the world's best men.

IV

The previous basis of the unity of men, violence, does not in our time inspire in men, as it previously did, a blind faith, but appears on the contrary something that is already repugnant to their consciousness.

A majority of men already feel more or less vividly the inevitability of arranging life on bases other than that of power. But old habits, traditions, upbringing, customs, chiefly the arrangement of life itself are such that men, wishing to undertake the tasks arising from the law of love, bring them to completion by means of violence, that is, by means of that which is directly opposed to that law of love in the name of which they are acting and doing that which they are doing.

So in our time revolutionaries, communists, anarchists, in the name of love, the welfare of the people, bring about their destruction by assassination. In the very name of love, again for the welfare of the people, governments set up their prisons, fortresses, penal servitudes, executions. In the name of love, the supreme blessing not of one but of all peoples, the diplomats establish their alliances, congresses, resting upon ever increasing and ever greater and greater armed forces. In the name of love again rich men, gathering wealth which they retain thanks only to laws maintained by violence, establish all their sorts of philanthropic institutions, the immunity of which is again maintained by such violence.

This is done in this way everywhere. The great evil of

violence, unnoticed by men, is done in the name of the intention apparently to do good. And as it cannot be otherwise, this not only does not improve the situation, but on the contrary only makes it worse. And therefore the condition of the men of our time has become steadily worse and worse, has become far worse than the condition of men in the ancient world. It became worse due to the fact that in our time the means of violence increased a hundred times, but the increase in the means of violence increased as well the evil resulting from the violence. However cruel and brutal the Neros and Ivan IVs could be, they did not have at their disposal the means of influencing people which are now available to the Napoleons, Bismarcks with their wars, and the English parliaments with their suppressions of the Hindus, and our Russian Schlusselburgs, penal servitudes, exiles. There were in old Slavia robbers, Pugachevs, but there were not these instruments of killing, bombs, dynamite, making it possible for a single weak man to kill hundreds. In former times, there was the enslavement of some to others, but there was not that general seizure of land such as there now is, and those difficulties in acquiring the necessities of life; and therefore there was not that desperate situation, in which millions of unemployed now find themselves, a situation incomparably worse than the situation of earlier slaves: now the workers seek slavery, and suffer because they cannot find masters to own them. In our time, precisely in consequence of the non-recognition of the cause of evil lying in violence and the concealment of this evil behind good intentions, especially under the present means of social intercourse, armaments and the debauchery of peoples, the situation of the working masses has brought them to the most grievous straits, has raised to the highest pitch their resentment against the rulers and the rich in direct proportion to their reaching the highest degree of consciousness of the precariousness of the situation of the rulers and the rich and their fear of the working peoples and hostility to them.

V

It is becoming more and more impossible for the life of the people of our time, both rulers and those over whom the rulers exercise their power, to continue. And this is felt keenly by the ones and the others. Life was possible for mankind with its divisions into tens of hostile governments, with its emperors, kings, troops, diplomats, with its robbing the peoples of the produce of their labour for armaments and the maintenance of troops, when the peoples still thought naively each on its own account that it alone was the true people, and that all other peoples were enemies, barbarians, and that it was not only praiseworthy to give up one's labour and life in defence of one's people and government, but that it could not even be otherwise, that this was as natural as eating, marrying, breathing. Such a life was possible for men, when men believed that poverty and riches were essential conditions of life, predestined by God; when the rulers and the rich not only had no doubt of the lawfulness of their position, but took pride in them in their souls before God, considering themselves the elect, a special breed of men, and men of the people "mean," occupied in manual labour or even trade, considered an inferior race of men, while the subjects and the poor believed that the rulers and the rich were special breeds of men, predestined to power by God himself, so that their life as subjects and as poor men was itself predestined by God.

Such a life was possible in the Christian world when it had

not entered the heads of people, whether rulers or subjects, to doubt that religion, Catholic, Orthodox or Lutheran, which allowed not only the complete inequality of men but their direct enslavement, considered possible and even praiseworthy the killing of men; when men believed in this artificial religion to a degree that it was not necessary to defend it either by conscious deceit or by violence.

It continued thus for centuries, but there came a time when all that made such a life possible began little by little to be destroyed, and finally the people of the whole world and especially of the Christian world have come to recognise more or less clearly that they are not the only ones, German, French, Japanese, Russians, living in the world, that they are not the only ones who want to uphold the advantages of their people, but that all peoples are in that same situation, and that therefore all wars are not only ruinous for the mass of the peoples who do not get from war advantages of any kind but only privations, but also absolutely meaningless. In addition men in our time have come to recognise more or less clearly that all the taxes collected from them do not serve their welfare, but are squandered largely to their injury in war and in the luxury of the rulers, that wealth is nowhere preordained from on high, as was represented to them previously, but is the fruit of a whole series of deceits, extortions, acts of violence upon the labouring peoples. Everyone in our time knows this in the depth of their souls, both rulers and rich, but they do not have the strength to give up their position, and by rude violence or deceptions or compromises they struggle to hold on to their position. Therefore now, when all men, all apart from those divided from one another by different nationalities, crushed and wishing to free themselves, or wishing to retain their hold over those who are subjugated, are still everywhere divided into two embittered, mutually hostile camps; the ones workers, deprived of their fair share, abased, and conscious of the injustice of their position, and the others powerful and wealthy, also conscious of the injustice of their position, but for all that, hanging on to that position at all costs, and these and the others in order to attain their ends ready to perpetrate and, to perpetrate against each other, the greatest crimes—deceptions, thefts, spying, killings, dynamitings, executions—the position of men being such, it evidently cannot continue.

The truth is that there are still some who want to persuade themselves and the workers, that we are on the point of yet one more convincing explanation of existing injustices, one more, the most wonderful theory of the future arrangement of life, one more small effort to overcome the enemy—and at last there will be established that new order in which evil will be no more and all men will prosper. There are assuredly such men, and among the rulers too. These men try to persuade themselves and others that mankind cannot live otherwise because it has lived thus for centuries, for millenia; that it is not necessary to change anything, that it is necessary only, since this is not disagreeable, to suppress strictly with force all attempts to change the existing order, and not refusing the "reasonable" demands of the people, lead it firmly along the path of moderate progress and all will be well. There are men who believe this in the one camp and the other, but already people do not believe them, and the two hostile camps are ever more and more sharply divided: greater and greater grow the envy, hatred, anger of the workers toward the powerful and wealthy, and greater and greater the fear and hatred of the powerful and wealthy towards the workers and those deprived of their fair share, and ever more and more do both sides infect one another with their mutual hatred.

VI

The situation of men in our time is terrible. The reason
for this terrible situation is that we, the men of our time, live
not in accord with that world view, which is characteristic of
our consciousness, but in accord with that world view, which
for thousands of years down to our era was characteristic of
our predecessors, but now no longer satisfies our spiritual
demands. The reason for this is that while we more or less
clearly recognise already that basis of love, which, replacing
violence, can and must unite people, everyone still lives by
that violence which in earlier times united men, but is now
already out of character, repugnant to our consciousness and
therefore not only does not unite but now only disunites
men.

Can an old man be happy or more precisely not be unhappy
if he wanted to live the life of a young man, or an adult wanting
to live the life of a child? In the same way a man would not
attempt to continue to live the life of a previous age no longer
in keeping with his character, and if he were to be
unreasonable, he would be brought by his sufferings whether
he liked it or not to the inevitability of living in conformity
with his age. It is exactly the same with human societies and
with the whole of mankind, if it is guided in its life by a
consciousness not in character with its age, but by that which
it has already long outlived. And this very thing is now being
accomplished by the mankind of our time.

We do not know and cannot know the conditions of birth,
or origin or disappearance of individual men nor of mankind,
but within the limits of time accessible to us we know and
know indubitably that the life of mankind has always been
subject to and is subject to that self-same law of gradual

growth and development to which the life of the separate individual is also subject. As in the life of each separate individual we see that a man is guided in the main direction of his activities by his understanding of the purpose of his life, that is, by his conscious or unconscious religious world view, so we see the same thing in the life of the whole of mankind also.

And as the life of the separate individual does not cease to change parallel with its growth, that is, in accordance with the change of the general understanding of the purpose of his life, precisely in the same way does life also, not ceasing to grow, not ceasing to change and unable not to change, move forward to a more reasonable life for the whole of mankind. And just as the forward movement of the separate individual is always naturally, almost inevitably delayed by his having mastered the habits of the previous age that he has lived through, he does not willingly nor quickly grow with them, often deliberately trying, as he abandons the activities of the previous age, to justify by various rationalisations thought up from his previous life which though continuing is already out of character, so in just the same way does mankind also naturally kept back through inertia in the previous already outlived mode of life, justify to itself these delays by artificial religious beliefs and equally false scientific constructions.

There are many superstitions from which men suffer, but there is none more general, more ruinous in its consequences than that superstition according to which men persuade themselves that the consciousness of mankind (that which is expressed in the teachings of the purpose of life and of the guidance for behaviour flowing from it, called religious) that this consciousness can be brought to a halt and be one and the same for all the epochs of the life of men.

Thus it is with that superstition, impelling human society to live according to religious and scientific teachings which always lag behind the current developing consciousness of humanity, and this has always been one of the principal sources of those ills that have befallen human societies. And the more these ills have continued to occur, the more the bulk of mankind has been subjected to these delays in movement and the longer they have lasted.

It happens sometimes that these delays take hold and are expressed especially clearly and are resolved in a single small part of mankind, but it also happens that these delays take hold of the life of the whole of mankind, as is now happening.

So, for example, delays in the movement towards a more reasonable life for a single part of mankind, produced by abuses in the church of Rome, extending to the extreme corruption of the essential teaching of Christ, held sway over only a small part of mankind, falling under papist superstition incongruous with the consciousness of men, and the ills, arising out of the Reformation and the wars consequent upon, continued for a relatively short time.

But it also happens that the whole of mankind and not just certain peoples, and as regards the principles of life common to all peoples, and not as regards private questions or any parochial question whatever, religious or social, lives for centuries incompatibly with its consciousness. And then ills, flowing from such brakes on life, brought about by the fact that men's consciousness is already incompatible with their religious principles, continue for a particularly long time and are particularly great. And such is the position in which now lives not a part but the whole of mankind, in consequence of which, while under universal inertia still continuing to be guided for unity one with another by the violence which was formerly inevitable and common to all peoples, men ever more and more clearly already recognise another higher principle of love, obliging them to change the previous way of violence.

VII

Three, two centuries ago men, called to the colours at the command of the head of the government, did not for a moment doubt that however difficult that which was demanded of them might be, they in going to war, were doing not only a good but an inevitable, necessary thing, sacrificing their freedom, labour, life itself in a sacred business: the defence of the fatherland against its enemies, above all the fulfillment of the will of the sovereign provided by God. But nowadays, every man who is driven to war (universal military conscription has particularly helped to destroy the fraud of patriotism), everybody knows that those against whom they are driven are men such as themselves, who are also deceived by their governments, and knowing this, already they cannot fail to see particularly in the Christian world the whole senselessness and immorality of the business into which they are forced. And understanding the senselessness and immorality of the business to which they are summoned, they cannot fail to despise and hate those men who force them.

In exactly the same way formerly men, handing over their taxes, that is, their labour to the governments, were convinced that this handing over to the government was inevitable for important and necessary activities; but, that apart, they considered those men who disposed of these products of their labour scarcely as holy, sinless men.

Nowadays almost every worker considers the government if not a gang of thieves, as men who in all circumstances are concerned with their own interests and in no wise with the interests of the people, and the unavoidability of placing his labour at their disposal only as a temporary calamity, from which he desires with all the strength of his soul and hopes by one means or another soon to be delivered.

Two hundred, even one hundred years ago people looked at wealth as worthy of respect and at the amassing of wealth as a virtue and respected the rich and tried to imitate them, whereas now people, and especially the poor despise and hate the rich in as much as they are rich, and all attempts by the rich by one means or another to ingratiate themselves with the poor evoke in the poor themselves only a still greater hatred towards the rich.

In previous times the rulers and the wealthy believed in their position, and knew that the working people believed in its lawfulness and the people actually did believe that their own position and that of their rulers were predestined. Now, however, they and the others know that there is no justification of any kind for the rule of the government nor for the wealth of the rich, nor for the crushing of the workers in order to maintain the rulers and the rich in their position, but that in order that the workers might free themselves from being crushed, it is necessary both for them and for the others to spurn the use to this end of every means possible: deceits, bribery, killing. Both the ones and the others do this, and what is worst of all, doing these things, in the depth of their souls the majority know that nothing is achieved by this, and that the continuation of such a life becomes ever more and more impossible, and they seek and do not find a way out of their situation. But that the way out is unavoidable and one and the same for all grows ever clearer and clearer to people. There is only one way out: to free oneself from that formerly characteristic human belief in the inevitability and lawfulness of violence and to master the belief that answers to the present stage of mankind's growth, the only one professed in all the religions of the world, the belief in the inevitability and lawfulness of love, excluding, come what may, the violence of man over man.

Before this decisive step which is impending in our time for all mankind, the men of our world and time now stand in indecision.

But whether men want to or whether they do not want to, they cannot not undertake this step. They cannot not undertake it, because the religious belief which was the basis of the power of one set of people over the others, has outlived its time, and the new belief in conformity to the time, in the supreme law of love ever more and more enters into the consciousness of men.

VIII

It would seem that the ills, flowing from the violence inflicted by people on one another ought to arouse in them the thought that they themselves might be guilty of these ills. And if men are themselves guilty, and I am a man, might it be that I too am guilty, it would appear that each might say to himself, and then ask himself, in what is my guilt in the ills suffered by myself and by all men?

So it would appear ought to be the case, but the superstition that some people not only have the right, but are also called to and are able to arrange the life of other people, on account of a duty to a life based on violence, is to such an extent rooted in the customs of men, that the idea of their own participation in the wretched arrangement of the life of the people does not enter anyone's head. Everybody accuses each other. The ones accuse those who, in their opinion, are responsible for arranging their life and arrange it not in the way that they consider necessary. Others again, arranging the lives of people strangers to them are dissatisfied with those whose lives they arrange. And both the ones and the others think of most complicated and difficult questions, but one question alone they do not set themselves, and that one, it would appear, the most natural question: what must I do in order to change that arrangement of life which I consider bad and in which in one way or another I cannot not participate.

"Love ought to take the place of violence. We admit that this is so, men say, but how, by what road ought and can this revolution take place? *What is to be done* so that this revolution shall be realised in order that a life of violence shall be replaced by a life of peace, of love?"

What is to be done? ask alike both rulers and subjects, revolutionaries and people in public life, implicated in the question: *What is to be done?*—always a question concerning how the life of men ought to be arranged.

Everyone asks how the life of men ought to be arranged, that is, what to do with other people? Everyone asks what is to be done with others, but nobody asks what is to be done with me myself?

The superstition of the immutability of religion, engendering the recognition of the lawfulness of the rule of some men over others, has given rise to yet another superstition, flowing from the first, which most of all prevents people from going over from the life of violence to the life of peace, of love, the superstition that some men ought and are able to arrange the life of other men.

So that the principal reason for the stagnation of men in the arrangement of life, already acknowledged by them as false, consists in the astonishing superstition (proceeding from the superstition of the immutability of religion) that some people not only are able but also have the right to determine in advance and arrange by violence the life of other people.

Once people have freed themselves from this customary superstition, it would immediately become clear to all that the life of every combination of men is arranged only in so far as each person arranges his own life for himself. And men would understand this, both those who arrange the life of others and also those who are subjected to this arrangement, so evident would it become to all that all violence of man over man cannot in any way be justified, but is not simply a violation of love nor even of justice, but also of common sense.

So the deliverance of men from those ills which they are living through in our time, lies first of all in freeing themselves from the superstition of the immutability of religion and then also from the false religious teaching, already outlived by the men of our time, of the divinity of power and flowing from it the recognition of the lawfulness and usefulness of violence.

IX

"Fine, love instead of laws, made effective by violence. Let us admit that the recognition by all men of love as a means of uniting with each other instead of violence would increase men's welfare, but it would increase it only when all men would have acknowledged for themselves the obligation of the law of love," is usually said. "But what will be the fate of all those who, themselves renouncing violence, are living among people who have not renounced it? These men will be robbed of everything, will be tormented, these be the slaves of men living by violence."

Thus always and everywhere the defenders of violence say one and the same thing and they do not try to understand that which is embraced within the law of love itself.

I will not speak of the fact that, whether violence has at any time whatever defended the life and tranquillity of men, it has on the other hand been on a countless number of occasions the cause of the greatest ills which could have occurred if the people had not permitted the violence. I will not speak of all those horrors which from the most ancient times have been perpetrated in the name of acknowledging the inevitability of violence nor of the horrors of the wars of the ancient world and of the Middle Ages, nor of the horrors of the great French Revolution, of the 30,000 communards of the year of '70, of the horrors of the Napoleonic, the Franco-Prussian, the Turkish, the Japanese wars, of the suppression of the Indians, now the affair with the Persians, now the perpetration of the butchery of the Armenians, the killings and executions in Russia, nor of the milliards of the unending death roll of the workers from want and hunger. We are not in any way able to weigh and decide the question as to whether there would have been or will be greater or less material ashes from the application in social life of violence or of the law of love, because we do not know—and cannot know—what would have been if at least a small number of men had followed the law of love, and the majority [had lived by violence]. This question cannot be decided either way by experiment or by reason. This question is a religious-moral question and therefore is decided not by experiment, but by the inner consciousness, as all religious-moral questions are decided not by consideration of what is more advantageous, but by that which a man recognises good and what is evil, what is a duty and what is not.

In nothing so much as in the attitude of people of our world to the question of the application to life of the law of love and the understanding of non-resistance to evil by violence indissolubly connected with it, is so evident the complete absence in men of our time not only of Christian belief, but even of any religious belief whatever, and not only of any religious belief whatever, but even an understanding of what religious belief consists.

"The law of love, excluding violence, is not observed, because it could come about that a scoundrel might under our eyes kill a defenceless child," people say.

These people do not ask what is to be done by them when they see a man being led to execution or when they see men training people to kill, or when they see the starving to death of people in the factories from the unhealthy labour of workers, women and children. All this they see and not only do not ask what they are to do in the presence of these things, but themselves participate in these affairs, in executions, soldiers training others to kill, in wars, in the starving of workers and in many other matters as well. But then, you see, they are all very occupied and worried by the question of what they are to do with the imaginary child that is being killed before their very eyes. The fate of this imaginary child moves them to such an extent that they cannot in any way admit that the non-employment of violence would have been one of the inevitable conditions of love. Essentially what occupies these people, wishing to justify violence is not in any way the fate of the imaginary child, but their own fate, their whole life based on violence, which in the presence of the negation of violence cannot continue.

To protect a child from being killed it is always possible to put one's own breast beneath the blow of the killer, but this thought, natural for a man, guided by love, cannot enter the heads of people living by violence, because for these men there are not and cannot be others besides brutes—impelled to activity.

In reality the question of the application to life of the demands of love leads to the simplest of conclusions, a conclusion always acknowledged and impossible not to be acknowledged by men's reason, the conclusion, to be sure, that love is incompatible with doing to another what you would not yourself wish, and therefore incompatible with injuries, deprivation of freedom, the killing of other men, which is always inevitably included in the concept of violence. That is why it is possible to live by violence, not recognising the law of love as a religious law of love; and it is also possible to live in accordance with the law of love, not recognising the inevitability of violence. But to acknowledge the divinity of the law of power, that is, of violence, at the same time as the divinity of the law of love, that, it would seem, is impossible. Yet it is in this contradiction which cries to heaven that all the people of our time and particularly the people of the Christian world live.

X

"But this is still the general mode of reasoning. Let us admit that I do believe in the law of love," they say about this, "what am I, what is Ivan, Petya, Marya, every man to do, if he acknowledges the justice of the fact that mankind has lived so long that it is inevitable that he enters on a new way of life? What am I, Ivan, Petya, Marya to do in order that that evil life of violence be destroyed and the good life in accord with love be established? What indeed must I, Ivan, Petya, Marya do in order to promote this revolution?"

This question, despite the fact that it appears to us so natural, is strange, as strange as the question a man, ruining his life by drunkenness, gaming, profligacy, quarrelling might ask: what am I to do in order to improve my life?

However much one may regret the fact of replying to such a naive question, I will all the same reply for those to whom such a question can be necessary.

The reply to the question of what needs to be done by a man, condemning the existing arrangement of life and wishing to replace and improve it, is a simple reply, natural and one and the same for each man, over whom the superstition of man's violence has not gained the upper hand, it is as follows: First: *oneself to stop doing direct violence, but also to prepare oneself for this*. This first, secondly, *not to take part in any violence whatever done by other people, and also in preparations for violence*, thirdly, *not to approve of any violence whatever*.

1. Not oneself to do direct violence means not to seize hold of anyone with one's hands, not to beat, not to kill, not to do those things for one's own personal ends, but also under the pretext of public activities.

2. Not to take part in any violence whatever means not only not to be a chief constable, a governor, a judge, a guard, a tax collector, a Tsar, a minister, a soldier, but also not to take part in the courts as a petitioner, defending counsel, warder, barrister.

3. Not to approve of any sort of violence means beside not using any kind of violence for one's own advantage, neither

in speech nor in writing, nor in deeds: not to express praise or agreement with violence itself or with affairs maintained by violence or based on violence.

It can well be that if a man shall so behave, repudiating the soldiery, courts, passports, payment of taxes, the recognition of power and will expose the oppressors and their adherents, he will be subjected to persecution. It is highly probable that such a man in times like the present will be tormented: they will confiscate his property, banish him, shut him in prison and perhaps kill him. But it can also be that that man who does not do any of this and on the contrary fulfils the demands of power, may suffer from other causes in precisely the same way and perhaps still greater than he who refuses obedience. And it can also happen that the refusal of a man to participate in violence, based on the demands of love, may open the eyes of other men and influence many to make such refusals too, so that the rulers will already not be in any condition to apply violence to all those refusing.

All this can be, but it can also not be. And it is for this reason that the reply to the question of what is a man to do, who acknowledges the truth and the application of life of the law of love, cannot be based on conjectured consequences.

The consequences of our actions are not within our power. In our power are only our actions themselves. The actions which characterise what a man does, and above all which characterise what he does not do, are based always on the man's beliefs alone. Let a man believe in the inevitability of violence, believe it religiously, and such a man will carry out violence not in the name of the happy consequences which he expects from the violence, but only because he believes. If then a man believes in the law of love, in precisely the same way he will fulfil the demands of love and will refrain from acts, contrary to the law of love, independently of any considerations whatever of consequences, but only because he believes and on that account he cannot act otherwise.

And that is why for the realisation in life of the law of love and the replacement of the law of violence, only one thing is necessary: that men should believe in the law of love in the same way that they now believe in the inevitability of violence. Only when people believe in the law of love at least approximately the same as they now believe in the inevitability of violence, will the question of how people, renouncing violence, are to behave with people perpetrating violence cease to be a question, and the life of men will be without any violence and the upheaval will assume a form of life unknown to us towards which mankind is heading and which will deliver it from those evils from which it now suffers.

Is this possible?

XI

The solution not of the single question of the social arrangements, but of *all*, all the questions troubling mankind, lies in one thing, in transferring the question from the sphere which appears to be one of breadth and significance but is in reality most narrow, insignificant and always dubious: from the sphere of external activities (having, allegedly, in view of the welfare of all mankind, scientific, public activities), to the sphere, apparently narrow, but in reality most broad and deep, and above all, indubitable: to the sphere of the most personal, not physical, but spiritual life, to the religious sphere.

Only when each man does this for himself, asking himself, his real self, his soul what is necessary for you before God or before conscience (if you do not want to acknowledge God), and immediately there will be received the most simple, clear, indubitable replies to the most apparently complicated and insoluble questions, and in large part the questions themselves will be abolished, and all that was complicated, involved, insoluble, agonising, all will immediately become simple, clear, joyful and indubitable.

Whoever you may be: emperor, king, executioner, millionaire, gaoler, beggar, minister, thief, writer, monk, stop for a minute in your activities, and glance into that most sacred place, into your heart and ask yourself what is necessary for you, your real self in order to live through in the best manner those hours or decades which may still lie before you. And whoever you may be, if only you **will** sincerely and seriously ask yourself about this, you cannot not give to yourself that self-same answer which all men have given and do give to themselves as they have and do seriously and sincerely put to themselves this question: one thing is necessary to you, probably one thing only, that very thing which was always and is now necessary for everyone: wellbeing, true wellbeing, not such wellbeing as today can be wellbeing, but tomorrow can become harmful, and not such as would be harmful for yourself alone, but harmful for others, but that true indubitable wellbeing alone, such wellbeing as is wellbeing both for you and for all men both today and tomorrow and everywhere. But such true wellbeing is given only to him who fulfils the law of his life. This is the law that you know both by reason and by the teachings of all the wise men of the world and by the inclination of your own heart. This law is love: love for the highest perfection, for God and for all living things and in particular for those beings akin to oneself—men.

If only each of us would grasp this he would immediately grasp the fact that the cause of the suffering of ourselves and of all the world lies not in whatever evils are committed by men, guilty of wrong-doing, but in one thing alone: in the fact that men live in conditions of life, made up of violence, conditions contrary to love, incompatible with it, and that is the reason for that evil from which we all suffer, not in men, but in that false arrangement of life on violence, which men consider inevitable.

But if each man would grasp this—he would also grasp that the thief who steals and the rich man, amassing and maintaining wealth, and the ruler, signing the death sentence, and the executioner carrying it out, and the revolutionary throwing a bomb, and the diplomat, preparing for war, and the prostitute, profaning her soul and body, and the soldier shooting at whomever he is ordered to, all equally are not guilty, but do what they do only because they live according to a false belief in the [inevitability] of violence, without which they cannot themselves imagine life.

But let a man grasp this, and he will clearly see the entire injustice, the cruelty, the irrationality of blaming people, with their outlived belief in violence, and flowing from it the complicated conditions of life, leading to their actions contrary to love, he will grasp that men do ill not because they are guilty but because there exists the superstition of violence, which can in no wise be destructive of violence, and which can be destroyed only by each man freeing himself from this baneful superstition.

Emancipation from the superstition of violence lies in one thing: in freeing oneself from the general questions of imaginary importance of social life, by transferring all the efforts of the soul from the social sphere, of external activities, to the fulfilment of the demands of one's inner spiritual life. These very demands clearly expressed in the teachings of all the religious teachers of mankind, and also in the inner consciousness of every man; those demands consist in the increase in each man himself of the capacity of love.

XII

In our time the continuation of life on bases which are outlived and already sharply opposed to all men's consciousness of truth has become impossible, and that is why, whether we wish it or not, we must in the arrangement of our life establish the law of love in the place of violence. But how in effect is the life of men to be established on a basis of love, excluding violence? No one can answer this question, and moreover, such an answer is not necessary for anyone either. The law of love is not the law of the social arrangements of this or that people or government which can be furthered when you foresee or rather imagine that you foresee those conditions, under which the wished for change may be accomplished. The law of love, that will be the law of life of each separate individual, is in place of that law of life of the whole of mankind and that is why it would be senseless to imagine that it is possible to know and to wish to know the ultimate end of one's own life and still more of the life of all mankind.

The fact that we do not know and cannot even represent to ourselves how will be the life of men, believing in the law of love just as people now believe in the inevitability of violence, shows only that when we follow the law of love, we truly live, doing that which each ought to do for himself what as well he ought to do for the life of all mankind. We know that following the law of love we do that which we ought for ourselves, because only when we follow this law do we receive the greatest wellbeing. We know also that, following this law, we do that too which we ought [and] for the whole of mankind, because the wellbeing of mankind is in unity, and nothing can of its own nature so closely and joyfully unite men as that very law of love which gives the highest wellbeing to each separate man.

That is all that I wished to say.

Believing with my whole soul that we are living on the eve of a world-wide great revolution in the life of men and that every effort for the swiftest destruction of that which cannot be destroyed and the swiftest realisation of that which cannot not be realised, every effort, however weak, assists the coming of this revolution, I could not, living in all probability the last days of my life, not attempt to convey to other men this, my belief.

Yes, we stand on the threshold of a quite new joyful life and entry into this life depends only on our freeing ourselves from the superstition, tormenting us ever more and more, of the inevitability of violence for the common life of men and on acknowledging that eternal principle of love, which has already lived a long time in the consciousness of men and must inevitably replace the principle of violence, outlived and already long unnecessary and only ruinous for men.

BIBLIOGRAPHY

TOLSTOY'S WORKS

Source: Spence, Gordon W. *Tolstoy the Ascetic.*
New York: Barnes & Noble, Inc., 1968.

Sketches, Stories, and Novels

Childhood, 1852.
The Raid, 1853.
Boyhood, 1854.
Recollections of a Billiard-Marker, 1855.
Sevastopol in December, 1855.
Sevastopol in May, 1855.
The Wood-Felling, 1855.
Sevastopol in August, 1856.
The Snow Storm, 1856.
Two Hussars, 1856.
Meeting a Moscow Acquaintance in the Detachment (Reduced to the Ranks), 1856.
A Landlord's Morning, 1856.
Youth, 1857.
Lucerne, 1857.
Albert, 1858.
Three Deaths, 1859.

Family Happiness, 1859.
The Cossacks, 1863.
Polikushka, 1863.
1805 (Parts I and II of *War and Peace*), 1865–6.
War and Peace, 1868–9.
A Prisoner in the Caucasus, 1872.
God Sees the Truth, 1872.
Anna Karenina, 1875–7.
What Men Live By, 1881.
The Decembrists, 1884.
Where Love Is, God Is, 1886.
A Spark Neglected Burns the House, 1886.
Two Old Men, 1886.
The Story of Ivan the Fool, 1886.
How Much Land Does a Man Need?, 1886.
The Three Hermits, 1886.
The Candle, 1886.
The Godson, 1886.
Kholstomer, 1886.
The Death of Ivan Illich, 1886.
The Kreutzer Sonata, 1890.
Emelyan and the Empty Drum, 1891.
Walk in the Light While There Is Light, 1892.
Master and Man, 1895.
Resurrection, 1899.
The Restoration of Hell, 1903.
Three Days in the Country, 1910.

Posthumous

The Devil, 1911.
Father Sergius, 1911.

After the Ball, 1911.
The Forged Coupon, 1911.
Alësha Gorshok, 1911.
What I Dreamt, 1911.
The Wisdom of Children, 1911.
No One in the World Is Guilty, 1911.
The Memoirs of a Madman, 1912.
Hadji Murad, 1912.
Posthumous Memoirs of the Hermit, Fëdor Kuzmich, 1912.

Plays

The First Distiller, 1886.
The Power of Darkness, 1886.
The Fruits of Enlightenment, 1890.

Posthumous

The Light Shines in Darkness, 1911.
The Cause of it All, 1911.
The Live Corpse, 1912.

Miscellanies, etc.

ABC Book, 1872.
New ABC Book, 1875.
Russian Readers, 1875.
A Circle of Reading, 1906.
For Every Day, 1909–10.

Posthumous
The Path of Life, 1911.

Articles and Treatises

Yasnaya Polyana, 1862.
On Popular Education, 1874.
Confession, 1884.
What I Believe, 1884.
What Then Must We Do?, 1886.
On Life, 1888.
The Gospel in Brief, 1890.
A Criticism of Dogmatic Theology, 1891.
Why Do Men Stupefy Themselves?, 1891.
The First Step, 1892.
On Hunger, 1892.
Harmony and Translation of the Four Gospels, 1892–4.
Non-Acting, 1893.
The Kingdom of God Is Within You, 1893–4.
Religion and Morality, 1894.
"Preface," to Guy de Maupassant's *Mont-Oriol*, 1894.
Christianity and Patriotism, 1895.
What Is Art?, 1897–8.
"Preface," to a translation of Edward Carpenter's
    Modern Science, 1898.
The Christian Teaching, 1898.
The Slavery of Our Times, 1900.
Patriotism and Government, 1900.
A Reply to the Synod's Edict, 1901.
What Is Religion?, 1902.
"Preface," to W. von Polenz's *Der Büttnerbauer*, 1902.
An Appeal to the Clergy, 1903.
Bethink Yourselves!, 1904.

The End of the Century, 1905.
A Great Iniquity, 1905.
On the Meaning of the Russian Revolution, 1906.
Shakespeare and the Drama, 1906.
Believe Yourselves, 1907.
I Cannot Be Silent, 1908.
The Teaching of Christ, 1908.
The Law of Violence and the Law of Love, 1909.
On Science, 1909.

Posthumous

An Inevitable Revolution, 1911.

SOURCES ABOUT TOLSTOY

Bayley, John. *Tolstoy and the Novel*. New York: Viking Press, 1966.

> A well-respected literary interpretation of Tolstoy's major works, especially *War and Peace*, *Anna Karenina*, and *Resurrection*.

Berlin, Isaiah. *The Hedgehog and the Fox: An Essay on Tolstoy's View of History*. London: Weidenfeld and Nicholson, 1954.

Fausset, Hugh l'Anson. *Tolstoy, the Inner Drama*. New York: Russell and Russell, 1927.

> This study examines forces in Tolstoy's personality, issues that his writing raised, and criticism of Tolstoy's philosophical positions.

Gorky, Maxim. *Reminiscences of Tolstoy*. London: Hogarth Press, 1934.
A moving and splendid description of Tolstoy in brief glimpses.

Green, Martin. *Tolstoy and Gandhi: Men of Peace*. New York: Basic Books, Harper and Row, 1983.

Lavrin, Janko. *Tolstoy*. New York: Russell and Russell, 1968.
An interpretation of Tolstoy as a thinker in light of modern issues.

Mann, Thomas. *Essays of Three Decades*. New York: Alfred A. Knopf, 1947.
Mann's essay "Goethe and Tolstoy" is included—about the literary giants and the nature of art.

Matlaw, Ralph E. (ed.) *Tolstoy, Twentieth Century Views*. Englewood Cliffs, NJ: Prentice-Hall, Inc., 1967.
This anthology of short critical and interpretative essays deals mainly with Tolstoy's literary concepts, but philosophical issues are also discussed. Chronology.

Noyes, George Rapall. *Tolstoy*. New York: Dover Publications, Inc., 1968.
Standard chronological account and interpretation of Tolstoy and his works. Often referred to.

Rollans, Romain. *The Life of Tolstoy* (Bernard Miall, trans.). New York: Dutton, 1911. (First published in Paris by Hachette in 1911 as *Vie de Tolstoi*.)

Sympathetic, penetrating and many-sided appreciation of Tolstoy as an artist and thinker.

Simmons, Ernest J. *Introduction to Tolstoy's Writings.* Chicago: University of Chicago Press, 1968.
The author describes this book as a "biography of [Tolstoy's] literary career...." This book is a useful introduction for the non-specialist.

————. *Leo Tolstoy.* Boston: Little Brown and Co., 1946.
This is the standard biography of Tolstoy in English.

————. *Tolstoy.* (Routledge Author Guides.) Boston: Routledge and Kegan Paul, 1973.
This book combines biography with historical background and has chapters interpreting major works of Tolstoy. Designed for non-specialist readers.

Spence, Gordon W. *Tolstoy the Ascetic.* New York: Barnes and Noble, Inc., 1968.
This book examines important themes in Tolstoy's works: dualism, death and illumination, god, suicide and sacrifice, the kingdom of god, and resurrection.

Steiner, George. *Tolstoy or Dostoevsky: An Essay in the Old Criticism.* New York: Knopf, 1959.

Stuve, Gleb. "Tolstoy in Soviet Criticism." *The Russian Review*, April, 1960.
A concise review of the issues and achievements of Tolstoy criticism, 1910–1960. The entire issue of the *Review* is devoted to Tolstoy.

Tolstoy, Alexandra. *Tolstoy: A Life of My Father* (E. R. Hapgood, trans.). New York: Harper, 1953.

Troyat, Henri. *Tolstoy*. New York: Harmony Books, 1980.

Zweig, Stefan. *Master Builders: A Typology of the Spirit*. New York: Viking Press, 1939.

A stimulating biography of Tolstoy based on Tolstoy's artistic works.

SOURCES DEALING WITH
ISSUES IMPORTANT TO TOLSTOY

Ansbro, John J. *Martin Luther King, Jr., The Making of a Mind*. Maryknoll, NY: Orbis Books, 1984.

Bacon, Margaret. *The Quiet Rebels: The Story of the Quakers in America*. Philadelphia: New Society Publishers, 1985.

Bedau, Hugh Adam (ed.). *Civil Disobedience: Theory and Practice*. New York: Pegasus, 1969.

Bodner, Joan (ed.). *Taking Charge of Our Lives, Living Responsibly in the World*. San Francisco: American Friends Service Committee, 1984.

Bondurant, Joan. *Conquest of Violence* (rev. ed.). Los Angeles: University of California Press, 1965.

This book provides a discussion of political theory of Gandhian nonviolent action with good case studies. This is one of the best sources on nonviolence.

Cooney, Robert, and Helen Michalowski (eds.). *The Power of the People: Active Nonviolence in the United States* (rev. ed.). Philadelphia: New Society Publishers, 1986.

Coover, Deacon, Esser, and Moore. *Resource Manual for a Living Revolution* (rev. ed.). Philadelphia: New Society Publishers, 1985.

This is the primary source of training tools that Movement for a New Society members have used since 1971.

Dellinger, Dave. *Revolutionary Nonviolence*. New York: Bobbs-Merrill Co., 1970.

Analysis and practice of militant nonviolent action against war in the U.S. in the 1960s, by one of the most respected activists.

Esquival, Adolfo Perez. *Christ in a Poncho*. Maryknoll, NY: Orbis Books, 1984.

Gandhi, M. K. *Nonviolent Resistance (Satyagraha)*. New York: Schocken Books, 1961.

Readable and interesting vintage Gandhi.

Hentoff, Nat (ed.). *The Essays of A. J. Muste*. New York: Bobbs-Merrill Co., 1967.

———. *Peace Agitator, The Story of A. J. Muste*. New York: Macmillan Co., 1963.

Huxley, Aldous. *Ends and Means*. New York: Harper and Brothers, 1937.

King, Martin Luther, Jr. *The Trumpet of Conscience*. New York: Harper and Row, 1967.

————. *Why We Can't Wait*. New York: Signet, 1964.

Lakey, George. *Powerful Peacemaking: Strategy for a Living Revolution*. Philadelphia: New Society Publishers, 1987.
    The only book to examine in detail what a revolutionary nonviolent strategy would look like.

Lappé, Frances Moore. *Diet for a Small Planet*. Tenth Anniversary Edition. New York: Ballantine, 1982.
    This book explains how the developed world can de-develop its lifestyle to stop, at least partly, economic oppression of the underdeveloped world.

Mabee, Carleton. *Black Freedom, the Nonviolent Abolitionists from 1830 through the Civil War*. London: Collier-Macmillan Ltd., 1970.
    In *The Kingdom of God Is Within You*, Tolstoy wrote that the American abolition movement was the best example of nonviolent resistance he knew about. This book explains why.

Macgregor, G. H. C. *The New Testament Basis of Pacifism* (rev. ed.) and *The Relevance of an Impossible Ideal*. Nyack, NY: Fellowship Publications, 1954.

Sharp, Gene. *The Politics of Nonviolent Action*. Boston: Porter Sargent, 1973.

This monumental work provides a nonviolent perspective on the process and analysis of social change, as well as an examination of almost two hundred tactics of nonviolent action with case studies.

Taylor, Richard. *Blockade, A Guide to Non-violent Intervention*. Maryknoll, NY: Orbis Books, 1977.

Thoreau, Henry David. "An Essay on Civil Disobedience." *The Portable Thoreau*, edited by Carl Bode. New York: The Viking Press, Inc., 1980.

Compiled by
Lynn Shivers